D0154133

UTSA DT L̶I̶B̶ ̶ ̶ ̶ ̶ ̶ ̶ ̶ 458-244̶

Understanding Research Methods

A Guide for the Public and Nonprofit Manager

Library
University of Texas
at San Antonio

WITHDRAWN
UTSA LIBRARIES

PUBLIC ADMINISTRATION AND PUBLIC POLICY

A Comprehensive Publication Program

Library
University of Texas
at San Antonio

EDITOR-IN-CHIEF

EVAN M. BERMAN

Huey McElveen Distinguished Professor
Louisiana State University
Public Administration Institute
Baton Rouge, Louisiana

Founding Editor

JACK RABIN

Professor of Public Administration and Public Policy
The Pennsylvania State University—Harrisburg
School of Public Affairs
Middletown, Pennsylvania

1. *Public Administration as a Developing Discipline,*
   Robert T. Golembiewski
2. *Comparative National Policies on Health Care,* Milton I. Roemer, M.D.
3. *Exclusionary Injustice: The Problem of Illegally Obtained Evidence,*
   Steven R. Schlesinger
5. *Organization Development in Public Administration,* edited by
   Robert T. Golembiewski and William B. Eddy
7. *Approaches to Planned Change,* Robert T. Golembiewski
8. *Program Evaluation at HEW,* edited by James G. Abert
9. *The States and the Metropolis,* Patricia S. Florestano
   and Vincent L. Marando
11. *Changing Bureaucracies: Understanding the Organization before
    Selecting the Approach,* William A. Medina
12. *Handbook on Public Budgeting and Financial Management,* edited by
    Jack Rabin and Thomas D. Lynch
15. *Handbook on Public Personnel Administration and Labor Relations,*
    edited by Jack Rabin, Thomas Vocino, W. Bartley Hildreth,
    and Gerald J. Miller
19. *Handbook of Organization Management,* edited by William B. Eddy
22. *Politics and Administration: Woodrow Wilson and American Public
    Administration,* edited by Jack Rabin and James S. Bowman
23. *Making and Managing Policy: Formulation, Analysis, Evaluation,*
    edited by G. Ronald Gilbert
25. *Decision Making in the Public Sector,* edited by Lloyd G. Nigro
26. *Managing Administration,* edited by Jack Rabin, Samuel Humes,
    and Brian S. Morgan
27. *Public Personnel Update,* edited by Michael Cohen
    and Robert T. Golembiewski

Available Electronically

Principles and Practices of Public Administration, edited by Jack Rabin, Robert F. Munzenrider, and Sherrie M. Bartell

PublicADMINISTRATION*netBASE*

Understanding Research Methods

A Guide for the Public and Nonprofit Manager

Donijo Robbins
Grand Valley State University
Grand Rapids, Michigan, U.S.A.

CRC Press
Taylor & Francis Group
Boca Raton   London   New York

CRC Press is an imprint of the
Taylor & Francis Group, an **informa** business

CRC Press
Taylor & Francis Group
6000 Broken Sound Parkway NW, Suite 300
Boca Raton, FL 33487-2742

© 2009 by Taylor & Francis Group, LLC
CRC Press is an imprint of Taylor & Francis Group, an Informa business

No claim to original U.S. Government works
Printed in the United States of America on acid-free paper
10 9 8 7 6 5 4 3 2 1

International Standard Book Number-13: 978-1-57444-585-5 (Hardcover)

This book contains information obtained from authentic and highly regarded sources. Reasonable efforts have been made to publish reliable data and information, but the author and publisher cannot assume responsibility for the validity of all materials or the consequences of their use. The authors and publishers have attempted to trace the copyright holders of all material reproduced in this publication and apologize to copyright holders if permission to publish in this form has not been obtained. If any copyright material has not been acknowledged please write and let us know so we may rectify in any future reprint.

Except as permitted under U.S. Copyright Law, no part of this book may be reprinted, reproduced, transmitted, or utilized in any form by any electronic, mechanical, or other means, now known or hereafter invented, including photocopying, microfilming, and recording, or in any information storage or retrieval system, without written permission from the publishers.

For permission to photocopy or use material electronically from this work, please access www.copy-right.com (http://www.copyright.com/) or contact the Copyright Clearance Center, Inc. (CCC), 222 Rosewood Drive, Danvers, MA 01923, 978-750-8400. CCC is a not-for-profit organization that provides licenses and registration for a variety of users. For organizations that have been granted a photocopy license by the CCC, a separate system of payment has been arranged.

Trademark Notice: Product or corporate names may be trademarks or registered trademarks, and are used only for identification and explanation without intent to infringe.

Visit the Taylor & Francis Web site at
http://www.taylorandfrancis.com

and the CRC Press Web site at
http://www.crcpress.com

Contents

Preface

Understanding research methods enables public and nonprofit managers to better answer questions and analyze information, which improves their decision-making capabilities. By understanding research methods, administrators become better consumers and producers of research. This book equips managers, administrators, and the like to understand research and development, and produce valid and reliable information.

The completion of this book would have never been possible without so many people, and for them, I am truly grateful. Thank you to my students; to the late Jack Rabin for his encouragement and defense of the initial proposal; to RaJade Berry-James, Jerry Miller, and Ken Nichols for their most valuable assistance and helpful insight; to my family, especially my husband, for reading many drafts, for his love of semicolons, and for putting up with me throughout the writing process; to the production staff at Taylor and Francis; and to Drs. Whicker and Westen, to whom I dedicate this book. They inspired my passion in a topic generally reviled and rejected by so many students. I hope I can have the same impact on others as they had on me. I welcome comments and feedback to improve future editions of this text.

Donijo Robbins

The Author

Donijo Robbins is an associate professor in the School of Public and Nonprofit Administration at Grand Valley State University in Grand Rapids, Michigan. She teaches graduate and undergraduate courses in public budgeting, financial management, and research methods. Professor Robbins received a B.S. degree in economics and political science from Central Michigan University, an M.A. degree in economics, and her Ph.D. degree in public administration from Rutgers University, Newark, New Jersey.

Chapter 1

Introduction to Research

1.1 Introduction

Becoming a master of administration and management rests on the ability of the manager, director, administrator, or practitioner to think analytically. As such, administrators ask and answer questions that will improve the organization's performance, customer service, financial position, and overall decision-making capabilities. Research provides managers with the diagnostic capacity to accomplish these mighty tasks. The veracity and pervasiveness of the information, facts, and figures collected in the research process are the elements that ultimately influence the decision-making process. As a result, the public and nonprofit administrators and decision makers must understand research, its definition, process, importance, and capabilities, and do so from the views of both the consumer and producer of research. This book provides that understanding. More specifically, this book journeys through the development of research such that the novice research begins to appreciate research and understand its usefulness in the decision-making process.

1.2 Research

Research is information gathering through a variety of methods to describe a concept and then explore or explain relationships between the concepts. This definition encompasses two guiding questions of the research process: what does the researcher want to know, and how will the researcher measure it?

To answer these questions, all researchers follow a similar process. They begin with a question, develop a research plan, collect and analyze the data, and communicate their findings. Consider the following examples of research.

1. The U.S. Food and Drug Administration's (FDA) Center for Veterinary Medicine conducted a 4-year risk assessment of cloned animals to determine if animals or humans are at risk. Using data from cloned animals provided by two cloning companies and literature written by experts in the field, the FDA concluded that cloning poses no risk to the cloned animals and that the food from cloned animals is safe for human consumption.[1]

2. The San Joaquin Valley in Kern County, California, is home to a thriving dairy industry as well as extreme ozone pollution. The pollution is thought to come from bovines and the farms in which they live, but the amount and source of pollution is debated. Some scientists blame fermented manure and lagoons for the pollution, whereas others blame cow belching.[2] In addition, the science supporting the belching theory estimates the emissions to be half of what the other scientists believe. Moreover, citizens of the Valley perceive the quality of air to be worse than it was 10 years ago; however, pollution has decreased 80% in the past 10 years.[3]

3. Twenty-seven different groups made 27 different recommendations regarding children and exercise. To put an end to the conflicting information, a panel funded by the Centers for Disease Control concluded that children should get one hour of exercise over the course of each day.[4]

4. The federal government invested $150 million and established a task force to combat human trafficking in the United States because expert testimony suggested that an estimated 50,000 people were trafficked into the country every year.[5]

The research and conclusions just described vary by researcher, but in all cases, the researchers follow a similar path: he or she asks questions and seeks out information to answer these questions, and in all instances, the findings could potentially influence the decision-making process, particularly policy changes. Therefore, even when the research might be incorrect, the decision maker must understand the validity and reliability of all research.

1.3 Overview of Book

This book is short and to the point, and is the result of 10 years of classroom and service learning experiences from teaching graduate and undergraduate students who have little to no statistical or mathematical background and who work in hospitals, nonprofits, and small government organizations. It supplies practical knowledge of the most common research techniques used by practitioners. Therefore, this book is more basic than advanced, and relies more on the administrator's conceptual and analytical skills rather than mathematical skills.

This book is divided into three sections, each organized according to the research process that is most useful for public and nonprofit administrators. The first section provides an overview of the research process, the construction of measures, and research ethics. The second section, the research plan, presents the common research designs practitioners use and the most popular ways to collect data. The third section focuses on the tools available to practitioners to analyze and communicate the data collected. Specifically, univariate and bivariate analyses are discussed. In addition, directions to compute these analyses in Microsoft Excel 2003 and 2007 are included. Excel is used because it is available to almost everyone, whereas other statistical programs require an expensive site license.

Research conducted by academicians is different from that produced by practitioners. Both groups, however, follow the research process mentioned earlier. In general, practitioner research is directly relevant to the practitioners' field, whereas academic research tends to be more theoretical, perhaps abstract, and less relevant to what practitioners do on a daily basis. Practitioners argue that academic research places too much emphasis on rigorous methodological approaches and focuses too little on application and relevance.[6] What practitioners need to understand and use in their decision-making processes is much different from what academics think practitioners need.

Consequently, this book serves two different but equally important, and perhaps overlapping, groups: students studying to become administrators, and those desiring to be practitioners. This text equips current and future decision makers with the necessary tools to design, carry out, and communicate valid and reliable research projects. Moreover, these tools allow decision makers to evaluate the research reports, studies, and projects produced by other researchers. However, this book alone is not sufficient to train those students wishing to pursue advanced graduate studies or write academic-type papers; these are not of practical significance to the average administrator, and are therefore omitted.

1.4   Summary

If I have learned anything from the years of teaching research methods, it is that a course in it, which is generally not taken by choice, is one of the more difficult courses in the graduate program or undergraduate major. At least this is the belief most students have upon entering the class, which results in their asking many questions, including "Why is this class required?" "Why do I have to take this course when my job duties do not include analyzing data or writing reports?"

This attitude produces poorer work habits in the course—doing just enough to get by—and less understanding of the subject. All of these actions lead to bitterness on the part of the students and the professor. So, lose this attitude right now. Take a deep breath, sit back, and relax. There is no binary code to memorize, no imaginary numbers or derivatives to calculate; just basic math skills. Although the formulas look intimidating, they are quite harmless; in fact, the book provides only a few. Mathematical notations, plain English, and examples are used to illustrate the statistical procedures most useful to practitioners. In the end, you will see that research rests more on your ability to think and ask questions than solving formulas.

Exercises

1. Think of the most recent decision you have made on the job. Did you look for support or evidence for various alternative explanations? If so, how did you go about it, what information did you use, how did you collect it, and how did you apply it to what you wanted to know? What convinced you that one alternative bested the others? Thinking back, do you believe you used the information you gathered properly, that you should have searched for more facts and figures? Explain.

Recommended Reading

Best, J. (2001). *Damned Lies and Statistics: Untangling Numbers From the Media, Politicians, and Activists*. Berkeley, CA: University of California Press.

Bolton, M. J. and Stolcis, G. B. (2003). Ties that do not bind: Musings on the specious relevance of academic research. *Public Administration Review, 63*, 626–630.

Kraemer, K. L. and Perry, J. L. (1989). Institutional requirements for academic research in public administration. *Public Administration Review, 49*, 9–16.

McCurdy, H. E. and Clearly, R. E. (1984). Why can't we resolve the research issue in public administration? *Public Administration Review, 44*, 49–55.

Meier, K. J. and Keiser, L. R. (1996). Public administration as a science of the artificial: A methodology for prescription. *Public Administration Review, 56*, 459–466.

Penner, R. (2003). *Congress and Statistics*. Washington, DC: Urban Institute. Available at http://www.urban.org/publications/1000584.html.

Rodgers, R. and Rodgers, N. (1999). The scared spark of academic research. *Journal of Public Administration Research and Theory, 9*, 473–492.

Waugh, W. L., Hy, R. J., and Brudney, J. L. (1994). Quantitative analysis and skill building in public administration graduate education. *Public Administration Quarterly, 18*, 204–222.

Wright, B. E., Manigault, L. J., and Black, T. R. (2004). Quantitative research measurement in public administration: An assessment of journal publications. *Administration and Society, 35*, 747–764.

Endnotes

1. U.S. Food and Drug Administration Center for Veterinary Medicine (2006). Animal cloning: A draft risk assessment. Rockville, MD: Department of Health and Human Services. Available at http://www.fda.gov/cvm/Documents/Cloning_Risk_Assessment.pdf.

2. Ruby, S. (2005, January 27). Holy cow! Study cuts emissions in half. *Bakersfield Californian*.

3. Sadredin, S. (n.d.). New poll reveals strong feelings, commitments. San Joaquin Valley Air Pollution Control District Commentary on the air quality. Posted on www.valleyair.org. Accessed November 4, 2007.

4. Yee, D. (2005). Panel says children need an hour of exercise over the course of a day. NCTimes.com. Accessed June 22, 2005, from: http://www.nctimes.com/articles/2005/06/22/special_reports/science_technology/17_40_416_21_05.txt.

5. Markon, J. (2007, September 23). Human trafficking evokes outrage, little evidence. *Washington Post*, p. A01. Accessed from Washington Post.com http://www.washingtonpost.com/wp-dyn/content/article/2007/09/22/AR2007092201401.html?referrer=emailarticle.

6. Bolton, M. J. and Stolcis, G. B. (2003). Ties that do not bind: Musings on the specious relevance of academic research. *Public Administration Review, 63*, 626–630.

Chapter 2

The Research Process

2.1 Introduction

The process of developing any research project entails asking and answering two very simple questions: What do we want to know? And how are we going to measure it? The questions decision makers ask come from experience, curiosity, the drive for more information or knowledge, as well as the ability to ask questions about existing theories or presumptions. The questions develop from a defined way of thinking that evolves from the individual's approach to inquiry (i.e., logic). Finally, the act of asking questions falls within the confines of the first step of the research process.

For example, a city planner might want to know how many of the city's households recycle, how much is recycled, or why some residents recycle and others do not. A hospital administrator may wonder what makes the hospital's emergency department efficient. A nonprofit development officer could be interested in the characteristics of the organization's donors. To research these and all questions asked, a "how to" plan is developed first and then implemented by collecting and analyzing data and drawing conclusions. Finally, the answers to the questions provide insight, assisting decision makers in improving the management of an organization or changing policy.

The research process is inherent in the definition of research discussed in the first chapter. Researchers begin with an interest, an idea, or a question that they want to answer, and this leads to the creation of the study's focus. They develop the plan of action (i.e., the research methods) to measure the idea, concept, or question. Subsequently, researchers carry out the plan by collecting and analyzing the information. From the analysis, they state their findings (i.e., describes information) and draw conclusions. That is, the researchers explain what is happening or why it is happening by linking the information gathered and analyzed to the purpose of the research—they answer the questions that were asked. In general, the research process entails the following steps, and this chapter focuses on the first two steps:

1. Determine the purpose of research
   a. Decide to explore, describe, or explain the phenomenon
2. Develop the focus of the research
   a. Decide whom or what to study
   b. Establish dimension of time
   c. Develop concepts and variables
   d. State hypotheses or research questions
3. Create a research plan
   a. Select type of design
   b. Determine and develop method to collect data
   c. Determine data analysis
4. Collect, analyze, and interpret data
5. Draw and report conclusions
   a. Tie focus and purpose of the research to the findings

All research projects begin with a plan of attack—a plan that asks and answers the two guiding questions: "What do I want to know? How am I going to measure what I want to know?" Collectively, the first two steps of the research process establish the purpose of the research and create the research questions or hypotheses. At this stage, the researcher relies on his or her own approach to inquiry as well as what the experts say. The establishment of the research purpose guides the researcher through the remaining steps of the research process.

The purpose of the research dictates what researchers do in Steps 3 and 4 of the research process. The research plan is a blueprint for the project; it lays the foundation where, with the focus and purpose established, the researcher decides how to pursue the research. The plan links the focus and the purpose—what is to be known—from steps 1 and 2 to steps 4 and 5, analyzing the data and drawing conclusions. Given this overlapping nature of the steps in the research process, researchers edit, modify, and rework the plan of attack, as they are able to better define and develop variables and locate or collect the necessary data. Consequently, research is ever evolving, changing, and manifesting itself to reveal the answers to our questions.

This chapter, as well as the chapters to come, discusses the research process from beginning to end. In doing so, this chapter devotes particular attention to the first question—what do we want to know—by presenting the development of the purpose and focus of the research. The remaining chapters provide in-depth discussions on how to measure what we want to know.

2.2 The Purpose of Research

Three theoretical purposes of research exist—exploratory, descriptive, and explanatory—and each shapes the research process in what the researcher can and cannot do. For example, if researchers want to infer their findings of the research to a larger population (i.e., generalize the results), then certain protocols apply, and researchers use descriptive designs and analyses. However, if researchers want to examine a relationship to show cause and effect, then they follow a different set of criteria that relies on explanatory designs and analyses. If analysts wish to understand what is happening without generalizing or showing cause and effect, then they draw on the advantages of exploratory research.

Exploratory research starts at the beginning; researchers are exploring what is happening because not much, if any, is known. Examples of exploratory research include case studies and needs assessments where the researcher studies one organization, one city, or one group of people. For instance, researchers start at the beginning, exploring the actions, strengths, and weaknesses of an organization, or perhaps researchers explore the needs of the organization's clients and staff. Researchers typically collect data for exploratory studies by way of small groups, such as town hall meetings, neighborhood gatherings, or focus group discussions. Overall, exploratory research acts as a good starting point to guide us to the next type of research: descriptive research.

Descriptive research describes what is happening. Most of the statistics reported in the news, academic journal articles, and government and nonprofit reports are descriptive in nature. A few examples of descriptive research include the number of new local jobs, the percentage of people who get fewer than seven hours of sleep each night, the percentage of households in poverty, the number of people who rate the quality of the local park as very good, survival rates, and approval ratings of the president and Congress. These statistics describe what is happening. The data used to aggregate the descriptors come from a small subset of the population, called a sample. When researchers use proper sampling techniques, the descriptors can be generalized to the population at different times and places.

Explanatory research examines why something is happening; that is, it attempts to explain why one variable causes change in another variable, or why one variable predicts changes in the other. The presence of causality intensifies when a statistical association exists between two variables, time order is present, alternative explanations are eliminated, spurious relationships are removed, and random assignment is present. Although causality is impossible to prove, the use of an experiment provides evidence for the researcher to suggest cause and effect.

Chapter 5 discusses experiments and other designs, but briefly, an experiment occurs when research objects or subjects are randomly assigned to two different groups—a control group and a treatment group. The treatment group receives the treatment or element being studied, and the control group does not receive the treatment. To understand the effects of the treatment on the research objects or

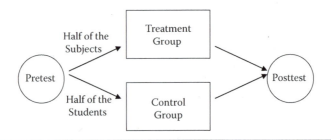

Figure 2.1   Illustration of an experiment.

subjects, the researchers gather information from both groups prior to the administration of the treatment. This is called the pretest. The same information is gathered at the conclusion of the treatment, and this is called the posttest. Figure 2.1 illustrates experimental design.

For example, pharmaceutical companies test their drugs using experimental designs. Researchers randomly assign subjects to the two different groups, and each subject's health information; for example, age, gender, weight, height, blood pressure, and cholesterol level, are noted. After the collection of information, one group receives the drug (the treatment group) and the other group receives a placebo (the control group). Neither the research subject nor the individual administering the medication is aware of the group assignments—participants and administrators do not know who is in the treatment group and who is in the control group. Researchers called this design a double-blind study. At the conclusion of the treatment, researchers collect the same information that was collected prior to the administration of the treatment.

Experiments allow researchers to compare the two groups to each other as well as analyze the changes within each group; that is, the change from the pretest to the posttest. The presence of a pretest, posttest, treatment group, control group, and randomization allow researchers to study cause and effect. When the design lacks one or more of these elements, the researcher's ability to explain cause and effect diminishes.

For example, researchers using exploratory research designs cannot generalize the findings to a larger population because the designs lack randomization, that is, the objects studied are not randomly selected from the target population. In addition, when researchers explore relationships between two or more variables, conclusions about the cause and effect of these relationships are sweeping at best. Analysts cannot say, with confidence, that one variable caused another to change because most of the necessary elements for causality—a control group and random assignment—are absent from exploratory studies.

Descriptive research adds the element of random selection but also lacks one or more elements of an experiment. Therefore, the findings from descriptive research designs can be generalized to a larger population, but the findings cannot suggest cause and effect with as much confidence as an experiment can. Statistical associations are possible, but they only describe the association between two variables; they do not fully explain the relationship.

Finally, as demonstrated earlier, explanatory research is best able to explain causality within reason. However, given the presence of a controlled environment, which is often the most conducive environment for experiments, and the general absence of random selection,[1] generalizing results to different populations is difficult. That is, the findings from research conducted in a controlled environment may not be similar to the results of research performed in an uncontrolled setting.

In the practical world, these purposes and the rigor they employ provide researchers with a theoretical understanding of what administrators should aspire to, but practically, three different purposes guide practitioners—descriptive, predictive, and prescriptive. Research helps managers learn what is happening (descriptive), what to anticipate (predictive), and what to do or how to react (prescriptive). For example, the city manager investigates neighborhood recycling efforts to describe who recycles and what they recycle; the nonprofit director analyzes donor demographics to predict what next year's donations will be; and the hospital administrator studies emergency department efficiency to create a plan to improve it.

The practical world is drastically different from the theoretical world. Often, managers cannot conduct experiments because of their inability to randomize or control the environments. For example, the hospital administrator cannot randomly assign patients with different ailments to different doctors to see which doctor is faster at treating the patient when the situation calls for an immediate and effective response. Nor can the hospital administrator control who can come into the hospital to determine the types of patients the doctors are best at repairing and healing.

When conducting research, the manager often sacrifices the scientific rigor demanded by academics for expediency because the controlled atmosphere is frequently unattainable. How would the public react if government officials decided to purposefully deny people access to already existing services just so they could compare two groups? Those who benefit from the service and the community at large might be outraged. Although randomization and/or controlled settings are what managers should seek to employ when possible, the lack of resources and time, and the demand for immediate results by decision makers and stakeholders, force practitioners to rely on research that is more focused and practical.

2.3   Development of Research Focus

The development of what a researcher wants to know stems from experience, general curiosity, the desire for more information, or to the need to challenge what others say, all of which evolve from the researcher's purpose. For example, the focus of a research project may evolve from very broad-based questions asked by the researcher, such as asking why something happens. For instance, some people might ask, why do people drop out of high school, why do some people abuse others, or why do some people spend too much money. On the other hand, the focus of the research might develop from very specific questions; for instance, who recycles and what do they recycle, what are the most common diagnoses in the emergency department, or who are the major donors for a nonprofit organization. To investigate these questions, researchers develop measurable concepts, decide whom or what to study, and how long to study it. They consult the existing literature and rely on their logic to guide them through this process.

2.3.1   Concepts and Variables

The phenomenon of interest, such as events, characteristics, behaviors, opinions, and so forth in the social world are all typically referred to as concepts. From the illustrations discussed in the introduction, the city planner is interested in recycling efforts, the hospital administrator is concerned with efficiency, and the director of the nonprofit wants to know the characteristics of donors. These concepts—efforts, efficiency, characteristics—have to be better defined.

Measurable variables emerge from the concepts of interest. A variable is a concept or quantity that varies and has a definition and attributes. Attributes are the elements that make up the variable and are defined prior to collecting data. Every variable has at least two attributes. For example, male and female are the attributes for the variable gender; married and not married are the attributes for marital status. Education level, income, distance, race/ethnicity, height, occupation, and weight are also variables; however, professor, student, 40 years old, $50,000, Republican, or urban dweller are attributes, not variables, because they do not vary. Overall, the questions researchers ask are measured by the variables and their attributes, which are constructed to encompass the concept and hence the focus of the research.

When researchers explore or describe a concept of interest, typically they use one variable at a time. For example, the city planner measures the tonnage of recycled materials produced monthly by the residents of the city. Tonnage of material is the variable, and its attributes range from zero tons of material to 1000 tons or more. Researchers can further explore or describe the concept by crossing variables analyzing one against the other. For example, the manager can analyze the tonnage of recycled material produced by businesses and residents. Here, the two variables are tonnage of recycled materials and the producer of the material. The producer has two attributes—business or resident. In this instance, the manager can describe which group produces more recycled material.

When researchers study cause and effect or simple relationships between variables, the variables are classified as either independent variables or dependent variables. The independent variable, denoted as x, causes an effect on the dependent variable, labeled y. Researchers might say that a change in x causes a change in y ($x \rightarrow y$), or mathematically, y is a function of x: $y = f(x)$. For example, researchers might say political party affiliation depends on the gender of the voter, or the quantity demanded of goods is a function of price. To investigate these relationships, researchers define the variables. Political party affiliation and quantity demanded are the dependent variables, whereas gender and price are the independent variables.

The independent variable must not be affected by other variables in order to be truly independent. Other variables can affect seemingly independent variables. Consider the following statement: Voters with high incomes are more likely to vote for a Republican. The political party vote is the dependent variable, and income level is the independent variable. A number of different variables, such as education level, region of the country, type of job, or gender may influence an individual's income. As a result, intervening variables emerge. These result when the independent variable is not truly independent. For example, if *A* causes *B* to change, and *B* causes *C* to change, then *B* is the intervening variable. This can also be written as: If *A* predicts changes in *B*, and *B* predicts changes in *C*, then *B* is the intervening variable. Both sequences of events do not mean that *A* causes changes or predicts changes in *C*; the intervening variable, *B*, has to be present for the changes to occur.

However, if *A* causes a change or explains a change in *C*, and *A* also causes a change to or explains a change in *B*, then *B* is no longer an intervening variable; *B* becomes a dependent variable. Relationships that include dependent variables as intervening variables are called spurious relationships, and these relationships threaten the strength (i.e., validity) of the research.

Some concepts are easily translated into variables, whereas others are not, but the variables embody the concepts researchers want to measure; they are what researchers use to capture the phenomenon of interest. Nevertheless, researchers do not always agree with one another on how to measure concepts. In fact, some variables and even attributes are often disputed. The next chapter discusses measurement development as well as the validity and reliability of the measures, but the case in Box 2.1 illustrates different ways to measure the concept of pollution.

2.3.2   Unit of Analysis and Dimension of Time

As part of the development of the research focus, researchers determine whom or what to study (called the unit of analysis) and select a dimension of time. The unit of analysis is where the researcher goes to get the information, and it can be anything—individuals, groups, documents, organizations, and so forth—but in any case it is the level at which the data are collected or research is being studied. For example, the unit of analysis for the city planner's research—who recycles and how much they recycle—is the citizens. Donors and emergency departments are the unit of analysis for the nonprofit director and hospital administrator, respectively. The unit of analysis is not recycled material, dollars donated, or efficiency; these are variables, and the data for these variables come from individuals (e.g., residents or donors) or groups (e.g., emergency departments).

BOX 2.1   COW EMISSIONS[3]

The 180,000 dairy cows poised to move into Kern County produce half as much ozone-causing gas as previously thought, according to researchers at the University of California, Davis. "That was just stunning for us," said the study's lead scientist Frank Mitloehner at a livestock emissions conference in Fresno Wednesday.

Mitloehner said his study shows that most ozone-causing pollutants come from belching cows rather than the traditional culprit, manure. Based on his calculations, individual cows and their waste produce 6.4 lb of ozone-causing gas every year—half the current estimate of 12.8 lb per year, which is based on research from 1938.

Although dairy industry representatives said they felt vindicated by the new data, air quality regulators and environmentalists said Mitloehner was reckless to draw such dramatic conclusions from an unfinished study that hasn't been peer-reviewed. "(Mitloehner) is a bit premature," said Seyed Sadredin, second in command at the San Joaquin Valley Air Pollution Control District. "There is a lot of information we need to understand better. We've just begun scratching the surface."

Dairy skeptic Bill Descary said it doesn't matter if dairy cows emit relatively less gas, they would still harm the valley's air quality, which is already among the worst in the nation. "What we have are dairies essentially coming into a metropolitan area," said Descary, former treasurer of the city of Bakersfield. "There's only so much room in the valley if there's going to be any quality of life at all."

In the next 18 months, the county will put dairies through $783,100 in environmental studies to figure out what a wave of eight new dairies would do to Kern's traffic, air quality, water quality, odor, floodplain, and other environmental considerations.

All research has a dimension of time; research is either conducted at one point in time or over a period of time. Cross-sectional studies collect and analyze information at one point in time; for example, the 2000 United States Census. In addition, cross-sectional studies are conducive to the collection and analysis of desired information for the city manager, nonprofit director, and hospital administrator. Although information gathering takes researchers days and sometimes months, the dimension of time remains cross-sectional. Research participants (e.g., those who completed the 2000 Census form) answer a series of questions at one point in time.

Longitudinal studies collect and analyze the same information over a period of time, such as over days, months, or years, for example, studying the past 20 years of the city's revenue. Three types of longitudinal studies exist: panel, cohort, and

A total of about 20 dairies have applied to locate in Kern County from Chino, where they've been crowded out by suburban homes. By federal standards, the San Joaquin Valley's ozone pollution is "extreme." California's Office of Environmental Health Hazard Assessment calls ozone "a powerful respiratory irritant" that can lead to chronic illness.

Dairy cows also produce ammonia and other asthma-inducing particles, which scientists are trying to quantify.

Whether Mitloehner's study of dairy cows is the final word on their air quality impact, it's contributed much to the debate. In what is known as the "bovine bubble" study, Mitloehner tented a herd of dairy cows and measured their emissions in a temperature-controlled [experiment]. He measured emissions from cow pies and flatulence, and found that flatulence, not fresh pies, pollute the air. What his study didn't address is how much pollution comes from fermented manure in pens and lagoons.

Another scientist at Wednesday's conference, C. E. Schmidt, studied standing manure and calculated that emissions per cow ranged from 3.6 lb per year to 19 lb per year.

The dairy lobby is optimistic that scientists will continue to lower their estimates of air pollution from dairies. "This (new data) confirms some suspicions we have had," said John Dunlap, spokesman for the Dairy Action Network and former chair of the California Air Resources Board. County Supervisor Ray Watson said it's great news if dairy cows pollute less than previous estimates, but he'd still insist that new dairies employ the latest technology—such as capturing gases before they leave the farm and use them as electricity for the dairy." I am happy to see progress being made," he said. "We (still) need to track down where every particle of pollution is coming from and what we can do about it."

---

time-series. A panel study uses the exact same units—the same people, the same organizations, and so forth—in every period. For example, the hospital administrator interested in the success of a new efficiency program for emergency departments would follow the same department over time, say, every month for two years. A cohort study examines individuals with shared characteristics. For instance, the city manager might study the effectiveness of the recycling program by interviewing a sample of the city's population who recycle. A time-series study analyzes data over time about the same concept, but the people, organizations, or groups do not have to be the same or share similar characteristics; for example, the nonprofit director may study individual donations regardless of donor and amount of monetary gift each month for three years.

2.3.3   Research Questions and Hypotheses

Recall the three researchers we have been following throughout this chapter. Each wants to know something about a phenomenon of interest. The planner wants to understand recycling efforts, the hospital administrator wants to know about efficiencies in the emergency department, and the nonprofit director wants to discern more about those who donate money to the organization. They want to explore, describe, or explain. Overall, the purpose of any research project is to explore what is out there, describe what is happening, or explain why it is happening. Researchers link the purpose of the research to the development of the measure. Each researcher is asking and wants to answer certain questions regarding recycling, efficiency, and donations. By the end of the first two steps of the research process, researchers have defined the focus of their research through specific research questions or, in special cases, through a supposition (i.e., hypothesis) statement.

Research questions are more general. They ask descriptive questions and appear in exploratory and descriptive type research projects. For example, the city planner might ask:

a. On average, how much do the city's residents recycle?
b. How often do the residents recycle?
c. Do different household sizes recycle different amounts of trash?

A hypothesis is a testable statement that proposes an association between two or more variables and is popular in descriptive research, and especially in explanatory research. For example, the city planner tests the relationship between the recycling frequency and household size. He could state the hypothesis in a number of ways:

a. Larger households (those with four or more people) recycle more than smaller households (those with three or fewer people).
b. There is a positive association between household size and the amount recycled.
c. There is no association between household size and amount recycled.

Regardless of the question or statement, the purpose of the research and the development of the variables relate directly to the research question or supposition statement.

2.3.4   The Literature

Researchers rely on what others have done (or not done) as a good starting point for narrowing the research focus, concepts, and variables. Thus, they consult the literature and experts to develop concepts and variables that will lead to a more focused research idea. The literature assists with the building of the research model and development of the research plan. The literature might reveal that a variable or set of variables is better suited to measure a particular concept, or the literature may generate new questions about the appropriateness of a particular variable, data collection tool, or data analysis technique.

In any event, plenty of literature is readily available; for example, information is found in academic research journals, government-sponsored studies, think-tank policy reports, and journalistic news articles. Researchers generally accept published research projects from these sources at face value because they endured a review process. However, a review conducted by one or more experts in the field does not imply automatic acceptance in the research community. Therefore, researchers evaluate the methods of all the research used to develop their research plan. In doing so, researchers can ask the following questions about the research conducted by others:

1. What is the focus and purpose of the research?
2. What concepts are used, how are they defined and measured, and do they really capture the purpose of the study?
3. Who or what is the focus of the research?
4. What type of data is collected, and how are they collected?
5. Do the data really measure the concepts?
6. How are the data analyzed? Is the analysis appropriate for the purpose and type of data?
7. Do the conclusions fit the focus and purpose of the research?

In addition, the evaluation of research is even more important when using it to assist in the decision-making process. Consider the example on pollution presented in Box 2.1. In this example, different researchers reached different conclusions. In fact, the results from the bovine emissions study suggest that cows do not emit as much pollution as once thought.

Finally, the Internet and library databases provide access to the literature researchers use to develop and carry out their research projects. Using the Internet to find research is an acceptable practice, but it does not provide free access to everything. For example, books, academic journal articles, some government documents, and law cases are available for a fee. However, these are available through university libraries. Because anyone, even so-called legitimate organizations, can write, post, or publish anything, claiming whatever they want no matter how erroneous or unfounded the claims, researchers must investigate the authors and their credentials prior to accepting the research as valid and reliable. The following is a list of questions researchers ask when evaluating those responsible for conducting the research:

1. Who conducted the research?
2. What is the researcher's area of expertise, and is the research focused on that area or something else?
3. With whom or what are they affiliated—a political party or organization?
4. Who sponsored the research, if anyone? What type of organization is it, that is, a think tank, government organization, political organization, university, corporation?

5. Who is on the board of the organization sponsoring the research? Is there any affiliation among the board members and the researchers? Is the focus of the research on a competitor of someone on the board?
6. Why is the study getting so much attention? Is there an agenda behind the research? Is there a particular organization acting as the driving force? Are advocates pushing the research and the findings?
7. What media sources, if any, picked up the information about the study?

2.3.5   Logic

Logic is how researchers think and reason, and it guides them through the research process—from the development of the research focus and purpose to the methods used to answer the questions. Two different types of logic exist: inductive and deductive logic. Deductive logic makes inferences from information, facts, and theories that are considered true about general ideas and concepts to specific cases. Inductive logic is the opposite; it relies on specific information and infers them to other people, places, or times.

For example, the judicial system uses both types of logic. Lawyers, judges, and juries use a deductive approach to determine the constitutionality of a specific case; they use the Constitution (broad-based rights such as speech, assembly, bearing of arms, religion, and so forth) and apply it to something specific. On the other hand, induction exists when a previously decided case is used as precedence to support or oppose the current case.

Therefore, logic is simply one's approach to thinking with no real distinction between inductive and deductive because the two approaches overlap and most likely are used concurrently. However, logic is subjective and relative; what seems logical to one person may very well be illogical to another and might change in an instant. Moreover, logic forms paradigms.

The subjective nature of logic stems from the paradigms that influence or dominate subjectivity. A paradigm is a belief system that shapes the way an individual views the world. Different paradigms, or schools of thought, exist for just about any subject, from religion to research, economics to strategic planning. Therefore, logic is how we think, but paradigms influence our ability to think and tell us what is or is not logical.

Social science research (which includes public and nonprofit administration and policy) is similar to religion in some ways. There are many different types of belief systems or religions, for example, Hindu, Jewish, Christian, Buddhist, and Muslim, to name a few. Most of the religions believe in some form of a higher power, but their approaches to believing are all very different. Even within a different broad-based religion, there are different groups. For example, Catholics and Protestants are two different groups among many labeled as Christians. Among the Protestants, there are Lutherans, Methodists, Baptists, and Presbyterians, to name a few, and each of these have a number of different factions. Then there are those within a general classification who disagree with the categorization of certain other religious groups under the same umbrella. Finally, there are those who question the idea of religion and higher powers altogether. In a nutshell, these are all paradigms.

Similarly, many different types of social science research paradigms exist, all of which are trying to explore, describe, or explain relationships. There are researchers who argue that numerical explanations can explain social constructs while dismissing qualitative research altogether. Others claim that few, if any, social constructs can be reduced to a number, thus limiting the certainty (i.e., validity and reliability) of quantitative research. Finally, there are camps of doubters, including the natural scientists, who question the ability of social science research to measure, describe, or explore anything at all. The purpose here is not to discuss all the different paradigms in social science research or to defend some and oppose others. Rather, the point is that logic and paradigms convince us to accept or reject what others accept as valid and logical.

Overall, a belief system influences reasoning skills, as well as the validity and reliability of all social science research. Regardless of these different opinions, the research community is best served when researchers recognize that nothing can be proved for certain because research is not perfect. But research helps us understand the world around us and helps us make decisions.

2.4   Summary

The chapter began asking the two questions that encompass the idea of research: what do we want to measure, and how are we going to measure it. The process of asking and answering these questions depends on what experts have said, the researcher's approach in inquiry, and the overall purpose of the research—explore, describe, or explain. In addition, the development of specific research questions or hypotheses builds from the definition of the concepts, the unit of analysis, and the dimension of time. Answering the second question rests on the remaining steps of the research process, which subsequent chapters discuss.

Key Terms

Attributes	Hypothesis	Posttest
Cohort study	Independent variable	Random assignment
Cross-sectional	Intervening variable	Random selection
Dependent variable	Longitudinal	Time order
Descriptive research	Logic	Time series
Experiment	Paradigms	Treatment group
Explanatory research	Panel study	Selection bias
Exploratory research	Pretest	Unit of analysis

Exercises

1. Explain the role that the research purpose has in the entire research process.
2. If the dairy lobby's optimism prevails and the studies from Box 2.1 that suggest cows pollute less than once thought are true, should the policy makers in San Joaquin Valley accept the new study's findings at face value and use it to make decisions? Explain what else they might do before making decisions of setting new policies.
3. Find a research report from a government, nonprofit, or political organization. What is its research purpose and focus? Do they ask research questions or test hypotheses? What are the variables and their respective attributes? What is the unit of analysis and dimension of time?
4. Using the report from question three, ask and answer the questions research uses to evaluate the methods of the research and credentials of the author.
5. Consider the most recent research you have conducted for your organization. What purpose and dimension of time best describes this research? What were the research questions you posed? What variables did you measure to answer these questions?

Recommended Reading

Abbott, A. (2004). *Methods of Discovery: Heuristics for the Social Sciences*. New York: W. W. Norton.

Brady, H. E. and Collier, D. (2004). *Rethinking Social Inquiry: Diverse Tools, Shared Standards*. Lanham, MD: Rowman & Littlefield.

Dodge, J., Ospina, S. M., and Foldy, E. G. (2005). Integrating rigor and relevance in public administration scholarship: The contribution of narrative inquiry. *Public Administration Review, 65*, 286–300.

King, G., Koehane, R. O., and Verba, S. (1994). *Designing Social Inquiry: Scientific Inference in Qualitative Research*. Princeton, NJ: Princeton University Press.

Kuhn, T. S. (1962). *Structure of Scientific Revolutions*. Chicago, IL: University of Chicago Press.

Ospina, S. M. and Dodge, J. (2005). It's about time: Catching method up to meaning, the usefulness of narrative inquiry in public administration research. *Public Administration Review, 65*, 143–157.

Ospina, S. M. and Dodge, J. (2005). Narrative inquiry and the search for connectedness: Practitioners and academics developing public administration scholarship. *Public Administration Review, 65*, 409–423.

Endnotes

1. Random selection and random assignment are different. Most participants in experiments are volunteers who are not randomly selected by the researcher but are randomly assigned to a group. The research subjects used in a descriptive study—for instance, those who receive a phone call or questionnaire in the mail—generally are randomly selected. Sampling is discussed in Chapter 7.
2. Accessed on November 11, 2007 from http://www.valleyair.org/Recent_news/News_Clippings/2005/In%20the%20News%20--%20Jan.%2027%202005.pdf.
3. Ruby, S. (2005, January 27). Holy cow! Study cuts emissions in half, dairy livestock create less pollutants than previously thought, researchers say. *Bakersfield Californian.* Used with permission.

Chapter 3

Variable Construction

3.1 Introduction

Crime rate, commute time, annual income, performance, safety, and efficiency are all examples of variables measured by researchers. Recall that a variable is a concept or quantity that varies and has a definition and attributes. For example, the American Community Survey created and administered by the U.S. Census Bureau collects information on individual demographics, employment situation, housing characteristics, and so forth. In one document, the Census Bureau provides definitions for all of the variables for which information is collected, one of which is the number of rooms in a housing unit (HU). The Census questionnaire defines the variable "rooms" in the following manner:

> **Rooms.** The intent of this question is to determine the number of whole rooms in each HU that are used for living purposes. Living rooms, dining rooms, kitchens, bedrooms, finished recreation rooms, enclosed porches suitable for year-round use, and lodgers' rooms are to be included. Excluded are strip or Pullman kitchens, bathrooms, open porches, balconies, halls or foyers, half rooms, utility rooms, unfinished attics or basements, or other unfinished space used for storage. A partially divided room is a separate room only if there is a partition from floor to ceiling, but not if the partition consists solely of shelves or cabinets.[1]

Moreover, the survey asks respondents the following two-part question to measure rooms:[2]

a. **How many separate rooms are in this house, apartment, or mobile home?** *Rooms must be separated by built-in archways or walls that extend out at least 6 inches and go from floor to ceiling.* INCLUDE bedrooms, kitchens, etc. EXCLUDE bathrooms, porches, balconies, foyers, halls, or unfinished basements. Number of rooms: _____

b. **How many of these rooms are bedrooms?** Count as bedrooms those rooms you would list if this house, apartment, or mobile home were for sale or rent. If this is an efficiency/studio apartment, print "0." Number of bedrooms: _____

The measurement development process emerges in the first two steps of the research process—determining the purpose and developing the focus of the research. The end product from the development stages, the variables, answers the question, what do we want to know. For example, if researchers are interested in the average commute time for workers in cities with populations over 500,000, they would want to create variables to measure this concept. The characteristics that define the variables develop from an understanding of the remaining parts of the research process—how we are going to measure what we want to know. How does the city planner measure recycle efforts, how does the hospital administrator measure emergency department efficiency, or how does the nonprofit development officer measure the characteristics of the organization's donors? To measure variables, researchers need to understand the purpose and focus of the research, its research design, the data collection process, and data analysis techniques. Moreover, researchers developed these in tandem in order to create valid and reliable variables that measure the concepts of interest. In the end, good measures are those that are simple, valid, and reliable. This chapter discusses the characteristics and development of measures as well as the tests available to researchers to help establish measurement reliability and validity.

3.2 Characteristics of Measurements

The steps in the research process are all related. The purpose of the research is linked to the research design, and the research design is related to the type of statistical techniques employed to describe variables and evaluate their relationships. The variables and their measurement characteristics are no different. Finally, the definitions for measures must fit the purpose, research design, and statistical analysis. For example, if the purpose of the research is to describe what is happening and to generalize these findings to a larger population, the researcher must randomly select a large sample and rely on quantifiable measures. However, if exploring what is happening is the researcher's purpose, then qualitative measures might be more practical.

Quantitative variables are those with numbers that are inherent to their definition, such as weight, height, distance, square footage, etc. The number truly represents the concept; for example, tonnage of recycled materials, number of patients, or dollars of donations. All of these numbers (five tons, 400 patients, $200,000) associated with these concepts (tonnage, patients, dollars) have a true meaning that is the same to everyone.

Beyond the numbers, public and nonprofit administrators are also concerned with perceptions, behaviors, characteristics, quality, opinions, and rankings, all of which are inherently subjective. What one person values as very good customer service, another individual might rank as average. Variables such as race/ethnicity, level of agreement, occupation, gender, marital status, and happiness, to name a few, are qualitative. Qualitative measures take on two forms—quantifiable and nonquantifiable. Typically, researchers assign numerical labels to qualitative measures where a common list of attributes applies to the majority of respondents, such as gender, marital status, or race. Researchers assign numbers as labels because statistical software packages read numbers, not words. Although these measures are not truly quantitative, assigning numerical labels allows the computer to count (i.e., quantify) the numbers quickly.

Nonquantifiable qualitative measures are those for which numbers cannot be assigned because there is no systematic interpretation; interpretation is often based on the researcher's understanding and analysis of what someone else said or behaved. For example, Habitat for Humanity gathers qualitative data when they ask new home owners to describe how their lives have changed as a result of living in a new home. Researchers cannot quantify or label such descriptions in a consistent manner to determine how many respondents said this or how many respondents said that. Typically, qualitative data are collected through participant observation, personal interviews, and focus groups (a small group of people interviewed at the same time). Researchers look for commonalities among the qualitative information gathered and narrate a story based on their analysis of the information. They explain what is happening and how it is happening, using prose rather than numbers. This approach is similar to your analysis of a political debate. Suppose you watch and take notes on a debate among the presidential candidates from one party (the one you most favor). In your head or on a piece of paper you sort through the information you collected and observed; for instance, you consider their behaviors and arguments, as well as your interpretation of what each candidate really meant. Based on the information and the analysis, you decide for whom to vote.

When measures are quantifiable, they are either discrete or continuous, classified as nominal, ordinal, or ratio, and are always mutually exclusive and exhaustive. Researchers who understand measures, their definitions, capabilities, and inabilities are better able to establish reliability and validity.

3.2.1   Discrete or Continuous

Numbers used to code information are either discrete or continuous. Discrete numbers are characterized by whole numbers; that is, there are no data points represented between each number. For example, we may code political party affiliation as follows:

1 = Democrat
2 = Republican
3 = Independent
4 = Other

Here there are no halves or quarters, just whole numbers that serve as labels for qualitative data. In addition, there is an interruption between the whole numbers. Discrete variables can also represent quantitative measures; for example, the number of children, the number of vehicles owned, and so on. Typically, discrete measures are popular with researchers in public and nonprofit research because, more often than not, the information collected is quantifiable, qualitative data.

Continuous data, on the other hand, embody continuity; there is no interruption between the whole numbers. The data and the number of increments between each whole number are infinite, for example, tonnage of recycled materials yields pounds and ounces, and monetary donations are measured in dollars and cents. The ounces and cents represent the continuity between the whole numbers.

3.2.2   Mutually Exclusive and Exhaustive

The attributes or categories representing measures must be mutually exclusive—nonoverlapping—and exhaustive. A mutually exclusive category means that only one attribute applies to an individual observation. In addition, the list of attributes should include all possible responses. For example, a question about age must provide all of the categorical increments that represent the different ages. The mutually exclusive and exhaustive categories could look something comparable to this:

☐ <18   ☐ 18–25   ☐ 26–33   ☐ 34–41   ☐ 42–49   ☐ 50+

Here, the response categories are mutually exclusive, where no one observation (person) would fall into more than one category. In addition, the list of categories is exhaustive. Although the list contains six options, people of all ages are able to find and select an option that applies to them. However, the following example is not exhaustive or mutually exclusive:

☐ ≤18   ☐ 18–25   ☐ 25–33   ☐ 33–41   ☐ 41–49   ☐ 49–57

In this case, the response categories overlap. If a respondent is 33, which category would she select? Moreover, the categories are not exhaustive. If a respondent is 62, which category would he choose? These are common mistakes when defining concepts and establishing measures. These mistakes threaten the reliability of the measures and hence the research. How would the measures for our three administrators be exhaustive and mutually exclusive?

3.2.3 Levels of Measurement

In general, there are three types or levels of data. Each level has different characterisics that provides different information—from basic categorical labels (low-level data) to robust numbers (high-level data). The lowest level of data is nominal, followed by ordinal, and ratio is the highest level.

Nominal measures possess the least amount of information. That is, the numbers assigned to the attributes or categories of the variable are discrete and represent a label with no intrinsic value—no one number is larger than the others. In addition, the exclusive and exhaustive rules apply. A few examples of nominal-level measures include gender, political party affiliation, marital status, race, religion, region of the country, and employment status. Beyond counting the number of responses and calculating the percentage for each category, mathematical operations—addition, subtraction, multiplication, and division—are not possible with nominal-level measures.

The next highest measurement is ordinal. In addition to possessing the characteristics of nominal data (mutually exclusive, exhaustive, and discrete), ordinal measures are ranked or ordered. Here, subtle differences are added such that one category ranks higher than the others. For example, undergraduate college student class status is ordinal, with classifications ranging in order from freshman to senior. Education level is ordered from less than a high school diploma to a Ph.D., and agreement includes ordering such as strongly agree, agree, somewhat agree, somewhat disagree, disagree, and strongly disagree. Similar to nominal data, mathematical operations do not make sense with ordinal data.

The highest level of measurement is ratio. Examples of ratio measures include income, distance traveled to work, number of children, etc. The first two examples are continuous measures, whereas the third illustration is a discrete measure. Regardless of its continuity, the distance between ratio numbers is measurable and meaningful. For example, the difference between two children and four children is two. Also, the ratio of two values is meaningful because ratio data have an inherent zero; for example, four children are twice as many as two children. These measurable meanings and inherent zeros common to ratio data are absent in nominal and ordinal data. Therefore, ratio-level measures are the highest level of data because they possess all the characteristics—mutually exclusive, exhaustive, rank ordering, meaningful distance, and an inherent zero—and mathematical operations of all types are possible.

What type of data should be used? The answer depends on the focus and purpose of the research—what we want to know, what the constructs are, and what statistical approaches are used. In addition, the decision depends on the researcher's desire for precision and accuracy. The best approach is to collect the highest level of data because real numbers are simply more telling than other levels of data; however, a trade-off exists between precision of measures and accuracy of data: the more precise or specific the measure, the less accurate the data. This is particularly true when asking questions about sensitive information, for instance, questions about income, weight, height, and age. Research that asks for ratio-level responses might be less accurate because some people prefer to round up for height and income, and round down for weight and age. To improve accuracy, researchers alter the level of measurement, sacrificing precision from higher-level data for more accurate responses yielded from lower-level measures. For example, rather than asking respondents to provide their age, researchers can ask respondents to check the appropriate box as illustrated below.

☐ <18   ☐ 18–25   ☐ 26–33   ☐ 34–41   ☐ 42–49   ☐ 50+

3.3   The Development of Variables

Researchers develop variables to capture the concepts of interest. They can be vague or specific; some variables are easy to convert into measurable variables, whereas others are not. Nevertheless, all variables have a unique definition and attributes. The attributes are the elements that make up the variable, and the researcher defines the attributes using experts, the literature, and measurement characteristics.

In the final research document, the researcher explains the variable names and definitions. In addition, where longitudinal data are collected, the analysts must communicate any changes to the definitions or changes in the wording of a survey question.

The list of attributes that makes up the variable depends on what is being measured and the measurement level. For example, if the measure is education level, the researcher could include the following ordinal level attributes: no highschool diploma, highschool diploma, associate's degree, bachelor's degree, and master's degree. However, if the researcher is interested in comparing two groups, one with and the other without a baccalaureate degree, he or she would inquire only about those two, nominal attributes—bachelor's degree and no bachelor's degree.

Creating the list of attributes is not that easy, however. The changes that occur in society or the nature of social constructs lead to conflicts among researchers as to what should or should not be included in the list of attributes. That is, classifications are based on individualistic perceptions. For example, individuals in same-sex long-term relationships who are not married because the state denies them that opportunity might classify themselves as partnered. Therefore, the attributes of single and married fail to capture those who classify themselves differently. The same is true with variables such as gender, ethnicity, sexuality, and nearly every other variable based on individual perceptions and classifications.

Consider the U.S. Census Bureau has changed the definition and attributes of race over time. For example, in 1850, color, not race, was measured using three attributes: white, black, and mulatto. By 1880, it added Chinese and Indian to the list; Japanese, quadroon (one-quarter black), and octoroon (one-eighth black) were added in 1890.[3] The 1980 Census Enumeration Form no longer used the label color or race; rather the form simply asked:[4]

| 4. Is this person —

Fill one circle. | o White
o Black or Negro
o Japanese
o Chinese
o Filipino
o Korean
o Vietnamese
o Indian (Amer.)
   Print
   Tribe ⟶ | o Asian Indian
o Hawaian
o Guamanian
o Samoan
o Eskimo
o Aleut
o Other – *Specify* |

In addition, the 1980 form asked about a person's Spanish/Hispanic origin or descent, but the question was not asked immediately before or after the race question; it was question number seven. The 2000 Census Enumeration Form placed the two questions together, asking about Spanish/Hispanic origin first, followed by race:[5]

5 Is Person 2 of Hispanic, Latino, or Spanish origin?

☐ No, not of Hispanic, Latino, or Spanish origin

☐ Yes, Mexican, Mexican Am., Chicano

☐ Yes, Puerto Rican

☐ Yes, Cuban

☐ Yes, another Hispanic, Latino, or Spanish origin – *Print origin, for example, Argentinean, Colombian, Dominican, Nicaraguan, Salvadoran, Spaniard, and so on.*

6 What is Person 2's race? *Mark (X) one or more boxes.*

☐ White

☐ Black, African Am., or Negro

☐ American Indian or Alaska Native — *Print name of enrolled or principal tribe.*

☐ Asian Indian	☐ Japanese	☐ Native Hawaiian
☐ Chinese	☐ Korean	☐ Guamanian or Chamorro
☐ Filipino	☐ Vietnamese	☐ Samoan
☐ Other Asian – *Print race, for example, Hmong, Laotian, Thai, Pakistani, Cambodian, and so on.*		☐ Other Pacific Islander – *Print race, for example, Fijian, Tongan, and so on.*

☐ Some other race – *Print race.*

In addition, the census form allowed respondents to select one or more options in the 2000 Census to better measure individual classifications and perceptions, rather than being forced to identify with only one category, as was the case on the 1980 census form.

The race example is one of many where changing perceptions and classifications result in changes to the definitions. Individual perceptions dictate the classification of items, and at the same time the classification of items shape individual perceptions. This affects the creation of variables in two very different ways. First, the way in which a researcher defines a variable is based on the person's perceptions and classifications of what the literature and his or her expertise reveal. Second, a participant's responses are rooted in his or her own perceptions and classifications, which may be different from the researcher's and the literature.

Regardless, researchers develop the most parsimonious—simplest—measure possible in order to count items en masse. The measure may not capture the concept in its entirety, but the easiest way for researchers to yield reliable and valid information is to use simple measures. For example, the long form from the 2000 Census asks about marital status and lists the following options: now married, widowed, divorced, separated, and never married. The list does not include partnered or common-law marriage; the addition of both would add complexity to the concept of marital status. A married person may consider himself or herself partnered when partnered is trying to capture same-sex relationships. In addition, a married person with a marriage license from a state government may consider his or her marriage a common-law marriage because, by law, he or she is married. "Partnered" and "common-law" marriage could be listed in tandem with "married"; however, certain states do not recognize common-law or same-sex marriages, so the definition of the concept "marital status" would change. Finally, the five original categories are somewhat overlapping, particularly "separated" and "married." If an individual is married but currently separated, then his or her perceptions, not the researcher's definition, guide the respondent's selection.

Some concepts are easy to translate to measurable variables. For example, suppose a nonprofit director is interested in donation patterns and defines the concepts as yearly donations by marital status of the donor. These concepts are translated into the measurable variables of annual donations and marital status, where the variable donation is a ratio variable and marital status is a nominal variable.

3.3.1 Summated Scales and Indexes

Other concepts, such as efficiency, urban sprawl, accountability, and productivity are more difficult to convert into measurable variables. For instance, efficiency of an emergency department could be measured by the amount of time it takes for patients to get through the emergency department. This makes sense, but does this capture efficiency? Most likely, the stakeholders would be interested in the mortality rates, the number of patients seen, types of diagnoses, number of staff, day of the week, and so forth; not just the amount of time.

Complex concepts most likely require more than one variable to measure the phenomenon. To do this, researchers create indexes and scales. Both index and scale attempt to measure the phenomenon of interest, but each does so differently. An index uses ratio measurements, whereas a scale relies on ordinal- or nominal-level measures. Generally, indexes use existing (secondary) sources of information (prices of goods, stock prices, number of crimes) collected by others, but scales rely on primary sources of data, those from interviews and questionnaires.

The Consumers Price Index (CPI) and the Dow Jones Industrial Average (DJIA) are examples of indexes. The CPI, used to gauge inflation, is calculated based on the prices of more than 200 consumable goods, for example, coffee, milk, rent, men's apparel, women's jewelry, car insurance, prescription drugs, movie tickets, tobacco, funerals, just to name a few. The prices of these goods are generally independent of one another, but considered collectively, they construct the price index. The DJIA tracks stock prices of 30 companies.[6] The DJIA "serves as a measure of the entire U.S. market, covering such diverse industries as financial services, technology, retail, entertainment, and consumer goods."[7]

The Economist Intelligence Unit developed its own quality-of-life index to better measure worldwide quality of life (socioeconomic quality). The index includes the following indicators: material well-being, health, political stability and security, family life, community life, climate and geography, job security, political freedom, and gender equality. Each indicator has a definition and a source. For example, health is defined as life expectancy, and the information comes from the U.S. Census Bureau. The United Nations supplies the divorce rate per 1000 people, which measures family life. This index acquires its information from existing sources.

Much of the information gathered in social science research is low-level data and is not conducive to index creation. As an alternative, researchers develop scales. For example, the Quality of Life [Scale],[8] developed by Ferrans and Powers, draws on ordinal level measures to monitor the quality of life in patients with certain illnesses such as cancer, arthritis, diabetes, and spinal cord injuries.[9] These patients are asked a series of questions before and three times subsequent to rehabilitation. The patients' scales are examined over time to determine the changes in the quality of life with the hope that the quality of life improves during after rehabilitation.

When designing an index or a scale, researchers begin by defining the construct of interest and creating a list of variables called indicators. Researchers use experts, the literature, and common sense to build these indexes and scales. For example, the Bureau of Labor Statistics, the organization responsible for the CPI, surveyed more than 30,000 individuals and families over a 2-year period, 2001 through 2002, to create the current list of items included in the CPI.[10]

Once the list of indicators is created, the next step is to decide if each item carries the same weight—the same level of importance. For example, a college student's grade point average (GPA) is weighted. A three-credit course carries more weight than a one-credit course; therefore, a weight is added to the calculation of the GPA. Suppose Lynn takes five classes this semester and gets two As and three Bs. If all the classes are weighted the same, her GPA is a 3.4 [(4+4+3+3+3)/5]. However, two of the courses are four credits, two others are two credits, and the fifth class is three credits. She receives the following grades in each course, and her new GPA of 3.53 is higher because the As now carry more weight than the Bs.

Grade	Credits (Weight)
A	4
A	4
B	3
B	2
B	2

In the end, the weight is assigned to the variables to denote the importance of measuring the concept of interest. Once the concepts are developed into measurable variables, researchers must test these variables to ensure measurement reliability and validity.

3.4   Reliability

A good measure is reliable and valid. A measure is reliable when it is repeatedly consistent or dependable, generating accurate information at an aggregate level. For example, the first thing Pat does in the morning is step on the scale to measure his weight. The scale reads 145 pounds, the same weight as yesterday and the day before. This is consistency.

There is more to reliability than consistency, however. Other researchers should yield the same finding for the same phenomenon; the results should be uniform. Say, Pat's roommate, Sam, weighs 155. In the morning, Sam steps on the scale and finds the scale reads 155. He weighs himself the next day, and again the scale reads 155. The measure is uniform. A different researcher, in this case the roommate, uses the same measure—a bathroom scale—and finds consistent results.

In sum, a reliable measure is one where the same results (equivalent) are generated repeatedly (consistent), in different situations and by different researchers (uniform).

What if Pat steps on the scale today and finds the scale reads a weight of 148 pounds, when he really weighs 145 pounds? Does this mean the scale is any less reliable? It depends. Perhaps Pat's order of events today differed from those events of yesterday, such as eating breakfast or wearing heavier clothing. These factors, which are outside the ability of the researcher to control, create error. The data collection conditions change over time and create error; error is why Pat weighs more.

Error derives from inconsistent conditions, which exist with most social science measures administered in an uncontrolled setting or collected over time. Although researchers can have the best, most consistent, uniform measures, the conditions in which these measures are collected create degrees of unreliability. For example, the knowledge level of respondents is a condition researchers cannot control. Unreliable data results from asking people about the quality of the local park, when they do not use the park. Researchers control for the lack of knowledge by adding options to questionnaires, for instance, "don't know," "does not apply," or "have not used the service." The same applies to telling the truth. Lynn may consistently report her age as 29 when she is really 37; this creates unreliable data. Beyond asking multiple questions about the same concept, a researcher can do little to minimize dishonest responses. In any event, these conditions create unavoidable errors in the individual data points. If many of the individual observations are unreliable, then the overall reliability of the measure is affected.

Researchers establish reliability by testing the measures prior to collecting the data. Researchers conduct pilot tests using focus groups or a subset of a sample, or by asking colleagues and other experts in the field. In all instances, researchers incorporate the feedback obtained from these methods into the improvement of the measure, its definition, and attributes.

The test–retest method, parallel forms, and the interrater technique are simple mathematical approaches researchers use to estimate the reliability of one-question/one-concept measures. Researchers using multiple indicators to measure one concept (indexes and scales) rely on sophisticated statistical approaches such as the split-half method or the alpha coefficient to evaluate the reliability of their scales. However, these two methods are beyond the scope of this text.

The test–retest reliability approach is where the researcher administers the same questionnaire/survey/test twice but at different times. For example, suppose the city council is interested in overall citizen satisfaction with the city's services. The council creates a 25-question survey about basic services. Prior to sending out the questionnaire, the council administers the survey twice, at different times, to a small group of citizens. The test–retest approach compares the scores of the first questionnaire to those of the second. Reliable measures yield similar scores. As researchers, keep in mind that the type of question as well as the relevance of the question affects reliability. If questions are opinion-based, and an event occurs between the test and retest such that the event changes the respondent's answer, the scores could be different. Therefore, as a rule of thumb, researchers do not wait too long to administer the retest. On the other hand, sometimes waiting to retest can be useful in determining the longevity or permanence of an impact or viewpoint.

Parallel forms, or alternative forms, test the reliability of at least two different questionnaires. For example, to minimize the potential for cheating, one professor administers three different versions of an exam to one class of undergraduate students. Similar scores, or grades, suggest the tests are reliable. This approach is useful for standardized tests where versions change from year to year.

The interrater technique tests the reliability of two or more trained observers who collect data by viewing a situation. For example, two observers rate the interest level of students enrolled in a research methods course. Using a series of questions created by the researchers, the raters observe the class and score the level of interest. The analysts test for reliability by comparing the observers' scores. Similarly rated scores (a high percentage of agreement) suggest reliability; however, if the scores are different (a low percentage of agreement), then the questions are not reliable, and should be reworked and retested. This approach could be useful to estimate the reliability of the federal government's race-neutral profiling program called SPOT—Screening Passengers by Observation Techniques. The program began at Boston's Logan Airport and expanded to Warwick, Rhode Island, and Portland, Maine in 2004.[11] According to the TSA (Transportation Security Administration), security officials are trained in "behavior detection techniques [to spot] dangerous passengers by a pulsing [carotid] artery, how much they sweat, blink, and changes in voice."[12] The list of anxious behaviors, called the *scorecard*, is much longer, but TSA will not reveal all the behaviors they observe. In order for such a program to be reliable, the raters' scores should be similar; that is, a significant number of raters must be able to correctly identify a terrorist. The TSA acknowledges that, at least in Warwick, terrorists are yet to be identified, but SPOT "routinely turns up undocumented aliens and passengers who are carrying illegal drugs or have [outstanding] arrest warrants."[11] A downside, however, is that the standards that increase consistency among raters may promote blind spots (consistent inaccuracies) as well; this is an aspect of validity.

Where significant differences exist in any of these reliability tests, the researcher must reexamine the measures, definitions, and attributes included to find better, more reliable, measures.

3.5 Validity

A valid measure captures the concept being studied; that is, the measure is a good fit. Researchers cannot prove validity, but they can provide evidence to suggest that the measure is as close to the concept as possible. Unfortunately, the researcher's subjectivity can dictate the analysis process to yield valid measures. Fortunately, the research community gets the last say. Researchers analyze the research or conduct their own research to question the measurement validity claimed by others.

Returning to the bathroom scale example, we can ask, is the scale Pat and Sam use valid? Does the scale measure weight and do so correctly? The previous section established reliability; however, Pat turned down the scale a few pounds. Although the scale consistently and uniformly measured weight, it is not valid because the measurement tool was altered—the scale measures weight less five pounds.

Researchers create valid measures by establishing one of three different types of validity: face, content, or criterion. A measure that achieves face validity does so because the researcher says it is valid. Researchers are able to establish face validity by being experts in their fields, as well as consulting other experts and the literature. Therefore, where validity is claimed on the basis of expertise the credentials of the researcher or "fact provider" should be investigated before accepting measures for their face value. The city manager, nonprofit director, and hospital administrator are all experts in their fields. As such, they argue that the measures they use to capture tonnage of recycled materials, donations, or emergency efficiency are valid.

A content-valid measure suggests that the measure is able to capture all the meanings (context) of the concept. For example, the attributes associated with the quality of a service should include all levels of quality, not just outstanding, excellent, and very good. The practitioners measuring tonnage of recycled materials, donation dollars, and emergency room efficiency validate these measures by demonstrating that, in fact, the measures do capture tonnage, dollars, and efficiency. In the end, all measures must be face and content valid.

Researchers can test the validity of their measures using certain criteria. They establish criterion validity in one of two ways: through concurrent validity or predictive validity. Concurrent validity is determined when the new measure is tested against an existing measure of the same concept. If the measures are similar (not significantly different), then the new measure is valid. Pat checks the validity of the bathroom scale against the doctor's scale (we assume Pat has not altered the scale and the scale measures Pat's weight as 145 pounds). The doctor's scale reads 145, the same as Pat's scale. Two researchers, in this case Pat and the doctor, produced the same findings for the same phenomenon (weight) in different settings with different weight measures (scales). If the hospital administrator creates a new measure of efficiency because the old measure is too complex, then the administrator compares the results of the new measure to the old measure. If the measure holds up and is similar, then the researcher has established concurrent validity.

Predictive validity is achieved when a measure created for predictive purposes does in fact predict, within reason, what is going to happen. Researchers are not able to validate their model's predictability until the time of the prediction elapses. The city manager can estimate the tonnage of recycled materials that will be produced next month, the nonprofit director can predict next year's stream of revenue from donations, and the hospital administrator can estimate how efficient the emergency department will be today given the number of staff on hand. If their predictions are valid, then the estimators should be similar to the actual results.

3.6 Summary

Variables capture and measure qualitative or quantitative concepts of interest and are directly related to the purpose of the research. All measures should be simple, mutually exclusive, and exhaustive. Moreover, where quantitative measures are present, researchers use discrete or continuous numbers to describe nominal-, ordinal-, and ratio-level variables. Finally, measures that encapsulate the concept, and do so with consistency and uniformity, are valid and reliable. To ensure that the concept is really being measured, researchers rely on experts and the literature. In addition, researchers use simple tests to check for equivalency, consistency, and uniformity to establish reliability. Both reliability and validity are equally important to researchers when constructing measures, and collectively valid and reliable measures assist researchers in exploring, describing, or explaining what is happening. Moreover, researchers should explain, in detail to the reader, why the measures are valid and reliable. Without these explanations, consumers of research are left wondering about the usefulness of the measures and significance of the research as a whole.

Key Terms

Content validity	Interrater reliability	Qualitative
Continuous	Mutually exclusive	Quantitative
Criterion validity	Nominal	Ratio
Discrete	Ordinal	Reliability
Exhaustive	Parallel forms	Test–retest
Face validity	Predictive validity	Validity

Exercises

1. For each of the following variables, determine the type and level of data and then list all the possible attributes.
   a. Gender
   b. Marital status
   c. Occupation
   d. Annual income
   e. Commute time

2. Create a scale or an index for each of the following concepts. Be sure to provide variable definitions as well as the type and level of data used.
   a. Job performance of professors
   b. Satisfaction with the public transit system
   c. Quality of life in your state
3. Your local government's park and recreation department has hired you to create measures for the local park system. Explain the process you would use to develop valid and reliable measures.
4. Evaluate the measures in the report used in exercise number three from Chapter 2. Does the author mention and establish measurement validity and reliability? Explain. Beyond what the author claims, do the variables seem to measure what the author claims he or she are measuring? Have the measures been used by others? Were the measures created by the researcher or by someone else?
5. Think back to the most recent research you conducted for your organization. What variable were used? How were the variables defined? What were their attributes? Do you think the variables are valid and reliable? Explain. What could you do to establish validity and reliability? Explain.

Recommended Reading

DeVellis, R. F. (2003). *Scale Development: Theory and Applications.* Second edition. Thousand Oaks, CA: Sage Publications.

U.S. Census Bureau (2002). *Measuring America: The Decennial Censuses from 1790 to 2000.* http://www.census.gov/prod/www/abs/ma.html.

Endnotes

1. U.S. Census Bureau (2006). Design and Methodology: American Community Survey, pp. 6–7. Available at: http://www.census2010.gov/acs/www/Downloads/tp67.pdf/ pp. 6–7.
2. U.S. Census Bureau (2008). American Community Survey, p. 5. Available at http://www.census.gov/acs/www/SBasics/SQuest/SQuest1.htm or http://www.census.gov/acs/www/Downloads/SQuest08.pdf.
3. U.S. Census Bureau (2002). Measuring America: The Decennial Censuses From 1790 to 2000. http://www.census.gov/prod/www/abs/ma.html.
4. U.S. Census Bureau (1980). Census Enumeration Form, p. 3. Available at http://usa.ipums.org/usa/voliii/tEnumForm.shtml.
5. U.S. Census Bureau (2000). Census Enumeration Form, p. 3. Available at http://usa.ipums.org/usa/voliii/tEnumForm.shtml.
6. For the current list of companies, visit http://www.djindexes.com/mdsidx/index.cfm?event=showAvgStats.
7. http://www.djindexes.com/mdsidx/index.cfm?event=showAvgMethod.

8. Ferrans and Powers refer to the scale as an index. Some researchers use the terms index and scale interchangeably, and this is inappropriate. Given the level of data used, the Quality of Life Index should be labeled the Quality of Life Scale, as it is in the text.

9. See http://www.uic.edu/orgs/qli/index.htm for more information on the Quality of Life Index.

10. Bureau of Labor Statistics. Frequently asked questions. http://www.bls.gov/cpi/cpifaq.htm. Accessed November 19, 2007.

11. DePaul, T. (2006, January 17). At T.F. Green, Security Screeners Watch Behavior to Detect Terrorists. Transportation Security Administration. http://www.tsa.gov/public/display?content=090005198019fbf0 accessed July 5, 2006.

12. DePaul (2006). Donnelly, S. B. (2006, May 17). A new tack for airport screening: Behave yourself. Time.com. http://www.time.com/time/nation/article/0,8599,1195330,00.html accessed July 5, 2006.

Chapter 4

Research Ethics

4.1 Introduction

Ethics is a system of moral principles recognized by particular groups or individuals. In research, ethics are formed by federal government guidelines as well as an individual researcher's set of beliefs. The most important rule to follow as a researcher is to be true to the research process. From beginning to end, researchers must be honest and revealing about the process of developing and carrying out the research. Ethical researchers explain without altering what other researchers say, design relevant studies, define and collect valid and reliable information, never fabricate data or results, never overgeneralize findings or draw sweeping conclusions, and when data are collected from human subjects, the human subjects are to be afforded all the rights and protections guaranteed by law.

This chapter serves two different purposes. First, it explains the importance of maintaining ethical standards throughout the entire research process, focusing on illustrations of ethical violations at each phase of the research process. This section of the chapter is important to all researchers—current students and practitioners. Second, the chapter focuses on the rights of human subjects and the protections afforded to them through government rules and regulations. This portion of the chapter is most useful to those students currently enrolled in a research methods course or to those college students who are currently working on a research project where the data are collected from human subjects.

4.2 Ethics in the Research Process

When beginning a research project, philosophies, values, and beliefs guide the researcher and the researcher's interests help him decide what to research. As helpful as these beliefs and values are, they should not influence the rest of the research process; researchers maintain objectivity throughout the process. If a researcher believes a program is good for society or good for a municipality, then he may allow those beliefs and values to influence the research process. For example, suppose a city council wants to create performance measures for the local public transportation system. Perhaps they regard public transportation as a method to preserve scarce resources, reduce dependency on foreign oil, and stimulate downtown development. Or maybe the chair of the transportation commission has persuaded (i.e., bribed) some council members to find positive outcomes. Thus, no weakness is found in the new measures, and the council recommends the expansion of the public transportation system. This is not ethical research. When a researcher knowingly deceives the readers of the research, the stakeholders, or the public, then the researcher and the research is unethical. In the end, the researcher's interests, beliefs, and opinions guide the development of the research questions, but the researcher should remain objective to ensure that the research and its findings are accepted in the research community.

In a few instances, researchers have fabricated data and results. For example, at the University of Maryland's Department of Pediatrics, three researchers intentionally fabricated data for a study that received more than $1 million from the National Institutes of Health and was published in the journal *Pediatrics*.[1] However, according to the lead researcher, Dr. Donald Wilson, all of the fabricated data were removed from the study prior to analysis and publication in the scholarly journal.[2] Unfortunately, the research team did not reveal any of this information in the publication. The fabrication was not revealed until a research coordinator from the university discovered and reported it two and a half years later.[2]

Researchers often publish studies that offer findings about the effectiveness of programs, the implications of policies, or the need for more programs. However, the findings must emerge from a properly conducted research model, one that maintains validity and reliability. Moreover, the statistical analysis and the interpretation of the results must be appropriate.

Consider decision makers like Dr. Debbie Kuboto. She works as a pharmacist for Kaiser, a medical insurance provider based in California. Dr. Kuboto, as well as other pharmacists at Kaiser, is responsible for sifting through medical studies on pharmaceuticals to create the company's formulary—the lists of medications the company will cover. After reading two studies claiming a new antidepressant, Cymbalta, to be superior to other antidepressants, Dr. Kuboto questioned the research methods. The patients in the treatment group of the experiment who took Cymbalta received twice the recommended dose, and the group taking another antidepressant did not have enough people to determine effectiveness. Subsequently, Dr. Kuboto recommended that the drug should not be added to Kaiser's formulary.[3]

This was not the first time Dr. Kuboto questioned research. When reading about an epilepsy drug called Lyrica in the journal *Neurology*, Dr. Kuboto noticed the fine print—literally, a section of the article in smaller print. Although the article and four others authored by Pfizer scientists declared Lyrica to be an effective drug to treat epilepsy pain, the small print said, "the trial excluded patients who had not responded to Neurotin."[3] Neurotin is a drug used to treat epilepsy and is Lyrica's competition. In other words, the researchers for Lyrica created a research model to find positive results.

Researchers have also misinterpreted results by making gross overgeneralizations. For example, one study suggests that each year 1400 college students ages 18 to 24 die in alcohol-related traffic and unintentional injury deaths.[4] The authors generalized data collected by the National Center for Education Statistics (NCES) to college students. For example NCES estimates 31% of those aged 18 to 24 are in college as full- or part-time students in 2- or 4-year colleges. The authors argue that since 31% of 18–24-year-olds in the United States are college students, they also "estimate that 18–24-year-old college students experience 31% of the traffic and other unintentional injury deaths experienced by the 18–24-year-old population."[5] They propose that college and noncollege 18–24-year-olds are similar in their driving patterns, particularly in regard to drunk driving. Without providing other evidence that the two groups are similar, such generalizations are unacceptable.

In another example of overgeneralizations, the U.S. government spent millions of dollars combating human trafficking because experts from the U.S. State Department estimated that annually, approximately 50,000 humans are being smuggled into the United States. However, since 2000, new estimates suggest that a total of 1362 humans have been trafficked into the United States.[6] How did these experts get the estimate so wrong? They used human trafficking estimates from other countries, particularly third world countries, to predict the number of humans smuggled into the United States.

Also, researchers must not intentionally harm human subjects. Worldwide rules and regulations, discussed later in this chapter, were established after the Nazi war crime tribunals, and the United States expanded these regulations for researchers in the United States after the Tuskegee syphilis study. Yet with all the rules and regulations, research has harmed, and in extreme cases killed, human subjects. Although death is an unlikely result, it does happen. For example, in 1996, a 19-year-old student volunteer at the University of Rochester died after undergoing a bronchoscopy.[7] In 1999, a subject involved in a University of Pennsylvania gene therapy study died at the age of 18.[8] And as recently as 2001, an employee at Johns Hopkins University volunteered for an asthma study. After inhaling hexamethonium, the subject became ill with a cough that became so severe that doctors placed her on a ventilator, but she later died from organ failure.[9]

The above examples of unacceptable and unethical behavior illuminate potential problems researchers face throughout the entire research process. Although professional societies, research boards, and reviewers and editors of journals advocate for ethical behavior in the research process, there are no standards to apply or regulations to follow when conducting research, except when human subjects are used.

4.3 Protection of Human Subjects

Although ethics is important at all stages of the research process, the ethical use and treatment of human subjects is the only regulated part of the research process. This is not because human subjects are the focus of so many research projects; rather, regulations exist because researchers have violated the rights of human subjects so many times. In the United States, the federal government sets these regulations, and institutions receiving federal funding and/or conducting research, including colleges and universities, have committees that interpret and enforce these regulations.

According to the federal government, a human subject is "a living individual about whom an investigator conducting research obtains: (1) data through intervention or interaction with the individual or (2) identifiable private information."[10] The protection of human subjects is, however, a rather new phenomenon. Beyond the long-accepted Hippocratic Oath, governments around the globe did not create ethical codes, laws, and regulations to protect the interests of human subjects until 1947 when the Nuremburg Code was established.[11]

The Nuremburg Code was a result of the war crime atrocities committed by the Nazis who forced their prisoners to be subjects of many experiments. At Auschwitz alone, one Nazi physician, Carl Clauberg, used a nonsurgical mass sterilization technique on women, and another physician, Horst Schumann, experimented with x-ray sterilization using men and women. Other experiments included the planned starvation and extermination of the prisoners to study the effect of starvation on the human body and the intentional injection of contagious diseases to test the effectiveness of certain medications.[12] To protect human subjects from future mayhem, the Nuremburg Code established the following ten principles:[13]

1. Voluntary and informed consent must be obtained.
2. Experiments should benefit society.
3. Human trials should be preceded by animal experimentation.
4. Experiments should not be conducted where there is a risk of injury and suffering.
5. Experiments should not be conducted where there is an a priori knowledge of death or disabling injury.
6. The risk of experiments should not exceed the benefit or importance to society.
7. Preparations and facilities should be provided to protect subjects.
8. Only qualified personnel should conduct experiments.
9. Human subjects have the liberty to end the experiment at any time.
10. The researcher should terminate the experiment at any stage if the continuation is likely to result in injury, disability, or death.

The United States is not without its own blemishes when it comes to unethical research. The well-known, controversial, government-run Tuskegee Syphilis Study, which began in 1932 and ended 40 years later, well after the adoption of the

Nuremberg Code, is particularly infamous. The experiment involved 600 black men from Macon County, Alabama; 399 of the men had syphilis and 201 did not have syphilis. During this study the U.S. Public Health Service (now the Department of Health and Human Services) withheld adequate treatment to learn more about the disease and how it affected blacks, and to justify treatment programs.[14]

In July 1972, Peter Buxtun, a venereal disease investigator from the Public Health Service (PHS), blew the whistle by forwarding his concerns, once expressed to PHS in 1968, to the media. Subsequently, the study ended, Congressional investigations opened, and a class-action lawsuit began.[15] Although an advisory panel learned the men volunteered freely for the study, the panel cited evidence that the men were never told of the study's real purpose, the connection between sexual behavior and the disease, or given an opportunity to leave the study once penicillin—the drug of choice to cure syphilis—hit the market in 1945.

Because of the Tuskegee Study, Congress passed the National Research Act in 1974, which created a commission called the National Commission for the Protection of Human Subjects of Biomedical and Behavioral Research. This commission studied, created, and established regulations and guidelines to protect human subjects from similar events. As a result, Institutional Review Board (IRB) procedures were established in Title 45, Part 46 (45CFR46) of the Code of Federal Regulations in 1974[16] and the Belmont Report was published in 1979.[17] Each is discussed in turn.

4.3.1   *Institutional Review Boards*

Institutional Review Boards (IRBs) are established at colleges and universities, and federal government agencies responsible for conducting research. The purpose of an IRB is to review proposed research where data, in any form, are collected from human subjects.[18] The boards evaluate the benefits and risks of the research, the type of information collected, the proposed collection process, and from whom the data will be collected. Before those researchers associated with colleges, universities, or government institutions can collect any data from human subjects, the research, its process, and means of data collection are reviewed by members of the IRB committee. The following discussion focuses on IRBs at colleges and universities.

At colleges and universities, the human subjects committee reviews all research that uses human subjects. Three different review categories exist: exempt, expedited, or full review. The type of review depends on the amount of risk posed to the human subjects; however, federal regulations are very loose, leaving the final decision to the committee.

A full review of the research proposal is necessary when the data collection process or reporting of results (i.e., identification of the human subject) poses more than minimal risks to the human subject. In these instances, all members of the IRB evaluate the research proposal and decide if the benefits of the research to society outweigh the risks imposed on the human subjects.

Most of the research conducted by public and nonprofit administrators that uses human subjects poses no risk, so it is either exempt from a full review or it is subject to an expedited review. In both cases, only one or two members of the IRB review the proposal. What type of research is classified as exempt or expedited? The federal government's regulation guidelines (45CFR46) suggest that research is exempt from full review when human subjects are involved in one or more of the following:

1. Education settings involving education practices, strategies, instruction techniques, curricula, or classroom management; for example, teaching or course evaluations.
2. Educational tests such as cognitive, diagnostic, aptitude, or achievement tests, survey procedures, interview procedures, or observation of public behavior. If the human subjects can be identified, if disclosure of responses poses criminal, liable, or financial risk to the human subjects, or if they are public officials—elected, appointed, or candidates—the research is not exempt from full review, although it may be expedited. Again, this depends on interpretation of 45CFR46 by colleges and universities.
3. Collection of existing publicly available data, documents, records, pathological specimens, where human subjects were used by a different researcher.
4. If the information recorded by the researcher is conducted in such a way that the subject cannot be identified, directly or through identifiers.
5. Research designed to examine costs and benefits to public programs.
6. Research intended to evaluate taste and food quality and consumer acceptance.

Fortunately, when administrators conduct research for their organizations, the research is not subject to any review as long as the researcher and organization are not affiliated with a college or university.

Regardless of the type of review, the committee evaluates the risks posed to and anticipated benefits received by the human subjects, the process of informed consent, and the research methodology including the selection of human subjects. Most of the language in the federal regulations regarding IRBs is vague and does not call for review of a research proposal's scientific validity. However, the regulations do require IRBs to assess risks not only in relation to anticipated benefits, but also in regard to the significance of the knowledge generated from the research. This ambiguous language in the federal regulations often places the methodological approaches of natural scientists against those of social scientists, particularly those in public administration.

Social scientists and natural scientists differ in their opinion as to what is or is not sound methodological research. In fact, even among the different types of social science researchers—political scientists, economists, and public administrators—methodological disputes exist. These differences create a challenging review process, as different members from the scientific community are involved. For example, natural scientists conduct experimental research in controlled laboratory settings whereas policy analysts, public administrators, and planners conduct case studies, program evaluations, or citizen surveys. These methods of collecting data are considerably different from controlled laboratory settings and are seemingly less theoretical and more subjective. For these reasons, natural scientists view the methods employed by public administrators as unsound and inadequate, and the findings as contributing little to no value to the world of research.

Beyond the differences between social scientists and natural scientists, other conflicts of interest exist. For example, Campbell et al. finds that 94% of medical faculty serving on IRB committees also conducted research and 47% were consultants for the medical industry.[19] Consequently, paid consultants serving on the IRB might be more apt to approve a study to maintain the consulting relationship. Moreover, competing interests may result in an IRB member delaying the review process of a competitor's proposal. However, the conflicts of interest may benefit the research process. For example, "direct experience may facilitate a deeper understanding of the types of human subjects concerns that may arise in industry-funded studies."[20]

Setting aside the differences of methodological approaches and conflict of interests, the purpose of the IRB is to protect the rights of human subjects. The board accomplishes this by applying the three principles established in the Belmont Report.

4.3.2   The Belmont Report

The National Research Act of 1974 (PL 93-348) created a commission—the National Commission for the Protection of Human Subjects of Biomedical and Behavioral Research—that argued that the Nuremberg Code and other similar codes were "inadequate to cover complex situations ... [that were] frequently difficult to interpret or apply."[21] That is, these codes were unclear as to the definitions and differences between practice and research. As a result, the Belmont Report, written by the commission, differentiates between practice and research where practice is "designed solely to enhance the well being of the patient ... [and] ... to provide diagnosis, preventive treatment, or therapy to the patients." Research, on the other hand, is "designed to test [a] hypothesis, permit conclusions to be drawn, and thereby develop or contribute to generalizable knowledge."[22] The research undergoes a review where both practice and research are performed collectively.

The Belmont Report established three ethical principles germane to the study of human subjects: (1) respect, (2) beneficence, and (3) justice. The application of these principles is carried out through informed consent, risk-benefit assessment, and the selection of research subjects. Each of the principles is discussed in turn and a summary of these principles is presented in Table 4.1.

4.3.2.1   Respect

The principle of respect represents autonomy. As such, research participants have the right to know what the research is about, and participants must agree to participate

Table 4.1 Guiding Principles of the Belmont Report

Principle	Application	Process
Respect	Informed consent	Provide necessary information Participant comprehension Voluntary participation
Beneficence	Assessment of risks and benefits	Explain and evaluate risk/ benefit ratio
Justice	Selection of subjects	Equal and fair selection

by signing a consent form. The consent form must provide information such as the purpose of the research, the research procedure, the risks and anticipated benefits, and the selection process. Moreover, the principle investigator must inform the research subject that participation is voluntary—free from coercion or influence—and the subject can withdraw from the research at any time. In addition, researchers must provide the human subjects with an opportunity to ask questions. All of this information provided by the researcher assists the human subject in making an informed decision.

The burden or obligation to ensure that the human subject comprehends the research, its process, risks, and benefits, as well as understands that participation is voluntary, falls to the researcher. In addition, the IRBs take on a certain level of responsibility because they approve the informed consent form. What should the researcher include in the consent form? The federal government's regulation code (45CFR46) lists the following eight basic elements of informed consent that must be provided when consent is necessary:

1. A statement of the study, its purpose, the amount of time the subject can expect to be involved, a description of the procedures, and identification of any experimental procedures.
2. A description of risks.
3. A description of the benefits.
4. A disclosure statement of alternative treatments that may be more beneficial to the subject.
5. An explanation of how confidentiality will be maintained.
6. Where more than minimal risk is involved, details should be provided about compensation and available medical treatments, should injury occur.
7. Contact information on whom subjects can call to find out more about the research and subjects' rights.
8. A narrative explaining that participation is voluntary, and no consequences exist for not participating.[23]

When using interviews and surveys that pose no risk to the participants, similar to the ones used by public and nonprofit administrators, participants do not have to sign a consent form. In this case, the respondent's action—completing and returning the questionnaire or not—connotes informed consent. However, all researchers, regardless of affiliation with a college or university, should provide the participant with similar information included in the consent form. In the directions or in the cover letter that accompany the questionnaire, the researchers communicate their credentials, the purpose of the research, the selection process (i.e., randomly from the voters' registration list), the confidentiality of the data, and that participation is voluntary. Chapter 8 discusses these items in more detail.

The presence of a consent form does not guarantee protection, however. For example, the National Institutes of Health (NIH) investigated the gene therapy research mentioned earlier in this chapter, conducted at the University of Rochester, that killed a student volunteer. The NIH investigation spanned the nation and found "more than 650 dangerous adverse reactions had [been] previously kept secret, including several deaths."[8] Moreover, the lawsuit filed against the University of Rochester on behalf of the deceased states that the Food and Drug Administration (FDA) found multiple violations including, but not limited to, changing the FDA-approved consent form "by removing information concerning the death or illness of several monkeys during a similar study."[24] In another example, researchers in the asthma experiment (also mentioned earlier in the chapter) did not provide enough information about the medication being tested. The researchers "referred to hexamethonium as a 'medication' and did not mention that hexamethonium used by inhalation was experimental."[9] In fact, the FDA never approved hexamethonium for inhalation and the principal investigator, Alkis Togias, did not conduct a thorough review of the literature; he failed to uncover studies from the 1950s that revealed the toxicity from inhaling hexamethonium.[9]

Regardless of the federal rules and regulations on informed consent, Arthur Caplan, director of the Bioethics Center at the University of Pennsylvania, argues that informed consent does not work. He suggests the necessary information to protect human subjects is kept from patients and researchers alike due to "trade secrets, financial conflicts of interest, and overloaded review committees."[8] Caplan also suggests that those serving on IRBs are overwhelmed. For example, research conducted in 1998 by James Bell and Associates estimates that 40% of the funded NIH research is conducted by 10% of the institutions receiving funding[25]—that is a lot of research to review.

4.3.2.2 Beneficence

Beneficence is the second principle of the Belmont Report and rests on the obligation of posing no harm to the human subject, and minimizing risks and maximizing anticipated benefits. The Belmont Report defines risks as the probability of harm and benefits as anticipated benefits. Researchers consider risks and benefits for the individuals involved, their families, and society as a whole. Where risks arise, they must be justified and outweighed by anticipated benefits. Quantifying risks and benefits into a ratio is a difficult task; for that reason, the researcher explains and the review board assesses, each risk and benefit.

4.3.2.2 Justice

The third principle set forth by the Belmont Report is that of the justice principle, which preserves the idea of equality. This principle argues, "equals ought to be treated equally"; that is, subjects should not be denied benefits where benefits are due and risks should not be disproportionately imposed on individuals. Moreover, certain classes—for example, patients, persons confined to institutions, or children—should not be selected because of easy access. Rather, participants should be selected fairly and should be from groups likely to receive the benefits.

All three principles are important, but the application and implementation of informed consent covers all three, and is most relevant to the research performed by practitioners. Few, if any, research projects conducted by administrators pose more than a minimal risk to the participants. In addition, the information that emerges from the research helps the organization improve its services, performance, transparency, and the like; all of which are beneficial to the stakeholders, clientele, or community as a whole.

The U.S. Department of Health and Human Services (HHS) offers helpful tips on informed consent, particularly what to include in the consent form or cover letter.[26] IRBs must approve the informed consent form or cover letter prior to the researcher collecting data from the human subjects. In then end, consent must be obtained in a manner that is not coercive.

4.4   Summary

Administrators are responsible for conducting research that investigates policies, problems, and ideas that are important to the organizations, clients, and communities which they serve. And, as researchers, these administrators maintain ethical standards by being objective and truthful. Researchers must never intentionally deceive decision makers or be intimated or influenced by political interests or political pressures. Researchers set aside philosophical or political beliefs as they develop their research plan, collect and analyze the data, and draw conclusions. In addition, researchers explain the "how" and "why" details of the research process. That is, they explain how the variables are defined and why they are measured this way rather than that way; how the research is designed and why this method is more conducive than another method; how the data are collected and analyzed, and why the collection and analysis processes are more useful than others are. In addition, although a board does not review the research conducted by administrators and practitioners, the administrator must honor the rights of human subjects by providing the necessary information in the directions or cover letter of the questionnaire. In the end, researchers have an ethical responsibility to provide assurances to the research community that their research upholds the highest standards.

Key Terms

Belmont Report	Full review	National Research Act
Beneficence	Human subjects	Nuremburg Code
Confidentiality	Inform consent	Respect
Exempt review	Institutional Review Board	Tuskegee Syphilis Study
Expedited review	Justice	Voluntary

Exercises

1. Write a generic letter that would accompany a questionnaire where the identity of the participant is known (i.e., the surveys are coded to know who completed the survey). Be sure to include the necessary information that informs human subjects of their benefits in and risks of participation as well as their rights as human subjects.
2. Write an analysis examining the IRB process at your college or university. In doing so, consider the following questions: What is the process a researcher has to go through when using human subjects in her research? Does the IRB differentiate between exempt, expedited, and a full review? If so, what is the application process for getting the research reviewed? Is there enough information provided to the researcher to determine what to do? Does the IRB provide a different set of standards for student researchers? If yes, how are they different from those standards that apply to faculty?
3. Compare the U.S. Department of Health and Human Services consent tips and checklist to your college's IRB offers. How are they similar? How are they different? What recommendations, if any, could you offer the IRB for improving its process?
4. According to the United States Code, participation in the United States Census is mandatory; a person could be fined up to $100 for refusing or neglecting to answer (i.e., skipping) any question and up to $500 for knowingly providing false information.[27] Does this seem to violate the Code of Federal Regulations, particularly the section on the rights and protections of human subjects? Explain.
5. In the most recent survey distributed by your organization, did it guarantee the protections and ensure the rights of human subjects? Explain. What would you advise the organization to do differently the next time?

Recommended Reading

American Association for Public Opinion Research (2005). Protection of Human Participants in Survey Research: A Source Document for Institutional Review Boards. Available at: http://www.aapor.org/default.asp?page=news_and_issues/aapor_statement_for_irb.

Council of Graduate Schools (2006). *Graduate Education for the Responsible Conduct of Research*. Washington, DC: Council of Graduate Schools.

Council of Graduate Schools (2003). *On the Right Track: A Manual for Research Mentors*. Washington, DC: Council of Graduate Schools.

Lee-Treweek, G. and Linkogle, S. (2000). *Danger in the Field: Risk and Ethics in Social Research*. London: Routledge.

Maloney, D. (1984). *Protection of Human Research Subjects: A Practical Guide to Federal Laws and Regulations*. New York: Plenum Press.

Romm, N. R. A. (2001). *Accountability in Social Research: Issues and Debates*. New York: Kluwer Academic/Plenum Publishers.

Sieber, J. E. (1992). *Planning Ethically Responsible Research: A Guide for Students and Internal Review Boards*. Newbury, CA: Sage Publications.

Steneck, N. H. (2003). *ORI Introduction to the Responsible Conduct of Research*. Washington DC: Department of Health and Human Services, Office of Research Integrity.

Endnotes

1. McCain, R. S. (2003a, December 5). Researchers fake AIDS study data. *The Washington Times*. http://www.washtimes.com/national/20031204-113809-8229r.htm, accessed December 5, 2003.
2. McCain, R. S. (2003b, December 9). Falsified data not included in AIDS study, officials say. *The Washington Times*. www.washingtontimes.com accessed January 6, 2006.
3. Mathews, A. W. (2005, August 24). Detective work: Reading the fine print, insurers question studies of drugs. *The Wall Street Journal*, p. A1. www.online.wsj.com accessed August 24, 2005.
4. Hingson, R. W. et al. (2002). Magnitude of alcohol-related mortality and morbidity among U.S. college students ages 18–24. *Journal of Studies on Alcohol*, 136–144.
5. Hingson, R. W. et al. (2002), p. 138.
6. Markon, J. (2007, Sept. 23). Human trafficking evokes outrage, little evidence. *Washington Post*. p. A01.
7. Massachusetts Institute of Technology News Office (1996, April 10). Student dies at Rochester in MIT-based study. http://web.mit.edu/newsoffice/1996/print/wandeath-0410-print.html, accessed January 6. 2006.
8. *News Weekly* (2000, August 12). Bioethics: Gene therapy business: the tragic case of Jesse Gelsinger. http://newsweekly.com.au/articles/2000aug12_bio.html, accessed January 6, 2006.
9. Savulescu, J. and Spriggs, M. (2002). The hexamethonium asthma study and the death of a normal volunteer in research. *Journal of Medical Ethics*, 28: 3–4. http://jme.bmjjournals.com/cgi/content/full/28/1/3 accessed December 15, 2005.

10. United States Department of Health and Human Services, Code of Federal Regulations, Title 45, Public Welfare Part 46, Protection of Human Subjects, p. 7. Code found at http://www.hhs.gov/ohrp/humansubjects/guidance/45cfr46.htm. Accessed August 5, 2005.

11. For a complete timeline of laws related to the protection of human subjects visit http://history.nih.gov/01Docs/historical/2020b.htm.

12. Information obtained from the Auschwitz-Birkenau Memorial and Museum online at http://www.auschwitz-muzeum.oswiecim.pl/html/eng/historia_KL/eksperymenty_ok.html. Accessed October 24, 2005.

13. Trials of War Criminals before the Nuremberg Military Tribunals Under Control Council Law No. 10, Vol. 2, pp. 181–182. Washington, DC: U.S. Government Printing Office, 1949. See: http://history.nih.gov/laws/pdf/nuremberg.pdf.

14. The National Center for HIV, STD, and TB Prevention (2005). The Tuskegee Timeline. U.S. Department of Health and Human Services, Centers for Disease Control and Prevention. http://www.cdc.gov/nchstp/od/tuskegee/time.htm. Accessed October 24, 2005.

15. The National Center for HIV, STD, and TB Prevention (2005). The Tuskegee Timeline. U.S. Department of Health and Human Services, Centers for Disease Control and Prevention. http://www.cdc.gov/nchstp/od/tuskegee/time.htm. Accessed October 24, 2005. Wikipedia, Tuskegee Syphilis Study, http://en.wikipedia.org/wiki/tuskege_experiment. Accessed October 24, 2005. Shweder, Richard A. (2004). Tuskeggee re-examined. Spiked Essays at http://www.spiked-online.com/Articles/0000000CA34A.htm. Accessed October 24, 2005.

16. Title 45, Public Welfare Part 46, Protection of Human Subjects can be found at http://www.hhs.gov/ohrp/humansubjects/guidance/45cfr46.htm.

17. Visit http://www.hhs.gov/ohrp/humansubjets/guidance/belmont.htm for the Belmont Report in its entirety.

18. The Code of Federal Regulations, Title 45: Public Welfare, Part 46: Protection of Human Subjects (45CFR46) was created and revised June 23, 2005.

19. Campbell, E. et al. (2003). Characteristics of medical school faculty members serving on institutional review boards: Results of a national survey. *Academic Medicine, 78*, 8, 831–836.

20. Campbell, E. et al. (2003), p. 834.

21. Find the Belmont Report at www.hhs.gov/ohrp/humansubjects/guidance/belmont.htm.

22. Belmont Report, p. 3.

23. Department of Health and Human Services. (2005, June 23). Code of Federal Regulations, Title 45 Public Welfare, Part 46 Protection of Human Subjects. www.hhs.gov/ohrp/humansubjects/guidance/45cfr46.htm. Accessed October 24, 2005.

24. Sherman, Silverstein, Kohl, Rose, and Podolsky Law Offices (2000). Gelsinger et al. versus Trustees of the University of Pennsylvania, et al. http://www.sskrplaw.com/links/healthcare2.html, accessed January 6, 2006.

25. Randal, J. (2001). Examining IRBs: Are review boards fulfilling their duties? *Journal of the National Cancer Institute, 93*, 19, 1440–1441. http://jncicancerspectrum.oxfordjournals.org accessed January 6, 2006.

26. The tip sheet can be found at http://www.hhs.gov/ohrp/humansubjects/guidance/ictips.htm.

27. United States Code, Title 13 Census, Chapter 7 Offenses and Penalties, Subchapter 2 Other Persons, Section 221 Refusal or neglect to answer questions; false answers. http://www.access.gpo.gov/uscode/title13/chapter7_subchapterii_.html.

Chapter 5

Research Designs

5.1 Introduction

Chapter 2 presented the research process and discussed the first two steps—developing the purpose and focus of the research. The remaining chapters, including this one, center on the last three steps of the research process: developing and executing the research plan through data collection, data analysis, and writing the report. The research plan entails selecting and developing a research design as well as determining the sources of data. A data collection tool or mechanism emerges from the research plan that the researcher administers to collect the data, and in the fourth step, the researcher analyzes the data. Each step of the research process overlaps another step. Therefore, in order for researchers to conduct research properly, they must have knowledge of research designs, data collection mechanisms, and data analysis techniques. This chapter presents some of the different research designs that practitioners use to explore, describe, or explain concepts of interest. More importantly, this chapter discusses each research design in the context of design validity.

5.2 Validity

Researchers set out to explore, describe, or explain some phenomenon of interest, and their analyses, conclusions, and recommendations influence the decision-making process. Given this power of persuasion on the world at large, the research must be valid. Valid research allows the researcher to make claims of causality and generalize the findings to a larger population. The validity of a design improves when researchers really measure what they say they are measuring—the concepts of interest—when they employ the proper statistical procedures, and when they use appropriate research designs.

Generalizations or causation claims are possible only with certain types of research designs; there are trade-offs among all the different research designs. The designs most conducive for describing and generalizing the findings to a larger group typically are inadequate for linking cause and effect. Alternatively, the designs used to improve causality are less capable of generalizing. Finally, some designs lack both the ability to generalize and suggest cause and effect, but are still useful for decision making.

Researchers are better able to infer (i.e., generalize) research findings to a larger population when the participants are randomly selected from the population being studied (Chapter 7 discusses sampling). Random selection means that each element has the same probability of being selected, and is common among polling organizations who call, at random, hundreds and sometimes thousands of people to inquire about their behaviors, opinions, and perceptions. Using the information gathered from a few, polling organizations generalize to the masses. For example, in November 2007, a *USA Today*/Gallup Poll said, "most Republicans are unfamiliar with [Rudy] Giuliani's precise positions on abortion (55%) and gay civil unions (74%)."[1] From the 430 randomly selected Republican or Republican-leaning voters, they generalized their findings to *all* Republicans.

Researchers interested in explaining causality—where one variable, the independent variable, forces another, the dependent variable, to change—must establish time order and statistical association, eliminate alternative explanations and spurious relationships, and use random assignment. Time order exists when the change in the independent variable occurs before the change in the dependent variable. For example, if the researcher claims that a change in the independent variable causes the dependent variable to change, then the change in the independent variable must occur prior to the change in the dependent variable. Moreover, a statistical association between the independent and dependent variable is necessary to ascertain causality.

Consider the following statement: More education leads to a better standard of living. The researcher analyzes the association between these two variables and finds that a positive association exists. That is, as one variable increases (decreases), the other variable increases (decreases). Further investigation reveals that educational attainment (i.e., graduation) occurs prior to making a standard income; so, education attainment is the independent variable and standard of living, measured by income, is the dependent variable. Because the researcher has established time order and a statistical association between educational attainment and income, can he say that education causes an improvement in the standard of living?

Research that establishes time order and reveals a statistical association between two variables does not mean that the two variables are causally related. The analyst must still eliminate alternative explanations (i.e., other variables) that might cause the dependent variable to change. For example, other independent variables such as gender, race, region of the country, or occupation might cause income to change. In addition, another variable altogether might cause both the independent and dependent variables to change. This creates a spurious relationship between the original independent variable and dependent variable. For instance, a person's gender might influence educational attainment and income, making gender the independent variable, and education and income the dependent variables.

To establish causality, researchers conduct experiments where they randomly assign participants, units, or observations to treatment and control groups. Researchers collect data from each group before, and subsequent to, the experiment; these are called the pretest and posttest, respectively. Random assignment occurs when each subject has an equal chance of being selected. For example, some elementary school administrators are interested in implementing a new math program that is supposed to improve the math skills of fourth graders. They assign each student a number from 1 to 50, because there are 50 fourth graders, and places the numbers, 1 through 50, in a hat. Then, one of the administrator randomly selects a number from the hat, and the student with the matching number is assigned to the treatment group. The administrator draws again and assigns the student with the matching number to the control group. This process continues until all 50 students are assigned to a group.

Next, each student takes a math skills test prior to implementing the new program. At the end of the program, the test is administered again. The use of the experiment allows the administrators to test for differences between the two groups as well as identify changes in the scores from within each group. Random assignment is important when making claims of causality, because without it selection or assignment bias may be present and weaken the strength of the design. For example, rather than randomly assigning the students, the administrators feel that those students with poorer math skills would benefit more from the program, so they assign the students with the poorer math skills to the treatment group. The presence of selection bias through nonrandom assignment threatens the ability to test for cause and effect—in this case, to test for the effect of the program on math skills.

Therefore, randomization, through either selection or assignment, improves the validity of any research design; its absence creates biased results. Explanatory research relies on random assignment to improve the ability to suggest causality, whereas descriptive research uses random selection to generalize to larger populations. Exploratory research lacks random assignment or random selection; therefore, such studies lack many aspects of validity.

5.3   Research Designs

This section focuses on specific research designs that are most popular among practitioners in public administration. Moreover, this part of the chapter discusses the usefulness and weakness of each design. The terminology used throughout this section stems from the terms associated with an experiment—a treatment group, a control group, a pretest, a posttest, and randomization. Although the absence of one or more of these elements threatens the validity of the research, researchers design such studies without these elements because they are not conducive to the purpose of the research—to explore or describe.

To provide illustrations, we demonstrate how one program—the math program introduced earlier—can be studied using a variety of different designs. The administrators have a number of ways to design the study—case studies, one-group comparison studies, and two-group comparison studies—and the design depends on the purpose—to explore, describe, or explain the impact of the program.

5.3.1 Case Studies

Case studies take on multiple meanings in the research arena. The more classical definition of a case study is that of a one-shot case study where researchers collect information about a phenomenon of interest—the case or treatment—at one point in time using some tool—the test—to collect the information. The popular terminology found in research papers is a cross-sectional design, rather than a one-shot case study and surveys, interviews, or focus groups are used to gather information for these designs.

For example, the federal government collects a variety of information through the census questionnaire, polling organizations interview registered voters to estimate who among the presidential candidates is more popular, and cities use surveys to assess citizen satisfaction levels with city services. All of these examples measure some phenomenon of interest at one point in time. The researcher does not need to use a pretest or a control group because these designs are descriptive in nature.

Let us apply the case study framework to the math program example. The school administrators use a case study design to evaluate the effectiveness of the math program, as Figure 5.1 illustrates. The school officials add the program to lesson plans and implement the program at the beginning of the school year. At the end of the 8-week program, the students take a test measuring math skills. The result reveals an average test score of 70.

Although the math program is 8 weeks long, the school officials are testing the students only once, at the end of the program; therefore, the study is cross-sectional.

Figure 5.1   Illustration of a one-shot case study design.

However, given the absence of any pretest and comparison (i.e., control) group there is no way for school officials to measure the change (e.g., improvement) in the students' math skills. Therefore, they cannot say if this math program *really* works (i.e., significantly improves math skills). What does an average score of 70 mean? What were the scores prior to participating in the program? The school administrators would have to use a different design to determine success.

The other more popular definition of a case study is an in-depth examination of one organization, group, or program, sometimes called program evaluations, needs assessments, cost-benefit analysis, and so forth. These evaluations analyze information gathered from different sources; for example, from surveys, interviews, and focus groups, as well as archival information. Researchers collect the data at once (a cross-sectional design) or over a period of time (a longitudinal design). For example, a drug rehabilitation organization interested in studying the effects of their rehab program would want to know which patients stay sober and for how long. To examine the program, the researchers decide to use a longitudinal design rather than a cross-sectional design because the focus of the study is patient progress. Therefore, the administrators of the program agree to interview each person six times after completing the program. The interviews take place 2 weeks after the program ends, then every 30 days for the next 3 months, followed by every 6 months, then every year for 2 years. Figure 5.2 depicts this design. Here the researchers are able to follow the same participants over time to study the effectiveness of the program. This is an example of a panel study.

All case study designs lack a control group as well as pretests so they are unable to suggest cause and effect. With case studies, researchers are unable to establish time order or eliminate alternative explanations and spurious relationships. In addition, when case studies lack randomization (assignment or selection), findings from case studies cannot not be inferred to other organizations, programs, or larger populations because the findings are too specific. Nevertheless, these case studies, without randomization, generally serve as best practice models, lessons learned, or recommendations for others in similar situations.

5.3.2   One-Group Comparison Studies

The school administrator decides that a better option to test the effectiveness of the math program is to test the students before and after the implementation of the

Figure 5.2   Illustration of a longitudinal case study.

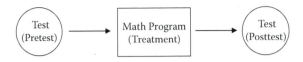

Figure 5.3   Illustration of a pretest–posttest research design.

program. Figure 5.3 illustrates this design, called a pretest–posttest design. In these designs, the researcher gathers the same data prior and subsequent to the implementation of the treatment. Such designs are useful to illuminate changes within the group being tested and establish time order.

If the math program worked as intended (i.e., improved math skills), then the scores on the posttest should be higher than the scores in the pretest, and they are. The scores before the program averaged 65, but the scores after the program averaged 70, a five-point increase. However, the time-ordered numerical improvement of five points is not enough to suggest cause and effect; a statistical association must also be present. The scores on the posttest need to be *significantly* higher than the scores of the pretest to suggest real improvement. Statistical tools, presented later in the book, determine if the difference between the two tests is significant. Consequently, the difference between the results of a pretest–posttest design does not imply significance until researchers run the proper tests.

The approaches used in a pretest–posttest design vary by researcher and depend on the purpose of the research and the dimension of time. When researchers are interested in a longitudinal design, they collect additional information for multiple periods both before and after the treatment. This design is practical for analysts who study policy changes. For example, suppose a city has a high percentage of citizens who are delinquent on paying their property taxes. To decrease the number of delinquent tax bills, the city implements a new program that allows those likely to default on their tax bills the option of paying monthly installments rather than paying twice a year. To analyze the impact of the program, the city's research analyst studies 10 years of property tax data, 5 years before the implementation of the program and 5 years after the implementation. Figure 5.4 shows this design. The researcher compares the two sets of data and finds the delinquency rate decreases; the program reduced delinquent payments. Again, the change between the "before" and "after" must be statistically significant in order for the program to be considered a success, and statistical tests calculate the significance.

The pretest–posttest design establishes time order by identifying changes from the first test to the second, but the lack of a control group limits the analysis; researchers cannot compare between groups. Therefore, researchers cannot eliminate alternative

Figure 5.4   Research design over time.

explanations or spurious relationships that might explain the changes for the time before the treatment to the time after the treatment.

Moreover, the presence of a pretest affects the results of the posttest. For example, in the case of the fourth grade math skills test, some students might simply do better the second time around, regardless of the effect of the treatment. The anxiety associated with taking a second test is reduced due to the experience of taking the test once before; student concentration level improves which leads to better scores. In addition, the exposure to the pretest might give participants the ability to know what to look for or pay attention to particular information throughout the treatment, which also may result in increased scores on the posttest.

5.3.3 Two-Group Comparison Studies

Both the case study and pretest–posttest designs lack a control group—a group not exposed to the treatment. The addition of a control group allows researchers to compare the results between groups, which isolates the impact of the treatment. This improves the ability of the researcher to suggest cause and effect by eliminating alternative explanations and spurious relationships.

The two-group posttest-only design, illustrated in Figure 5.5, compares two groups at one point in time. This design consists of a treatment group and a control group. Researchers gather the necessary (and same) information from both groups using a data collection tool—for instance, a test that is conducted at the end of the treatment (a posttest)—analyze the data by comparing the differences between the control group and the treatment group.

For example, the school administrators decide to use this design to test the effectiveness of the math program. To do this, they randomly divide the fourth-grade students into two groups. One group participates in the math program, while the other group, the control group, does not. At the conclusion of the math program, all the students take the same test, the posttest. The scores for the treatment group averaged 70 and the control group averaged 67. The administrators wonder if the three-point difference between the groups is large enough to warrant claims

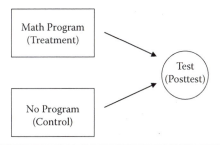

Figure 5.5 Illustration of a two-group posttest only cross-sectional design.

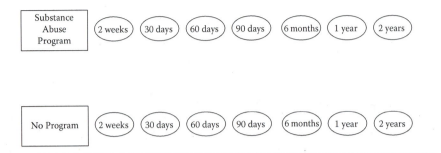

Figure 5.6   Illustration of a two-group posttest only longitudinal design.

of effectiveness—that the program caused higher scores. A statistical test discussed later in this book will reveal the answer to their question.

When long-term effects are of interest, researchers collect information at multiple intervals after the completion of treatment; that is, multiple posttests are conducted. Figure 5.6 presents this design using the rehabilitation program example. Researchers follow individuals with substance abuse problems who are trying to get and remain sober. One group has access to a program, the treatment, and the other group does not have access, but both groups are court ordered to get sober. Two weeks after the program finishes, researchers follow up with both groups. They do this repeatedly for 2 years. Over the long run, a successful program would yield better results (i.e., significant) than the control group.

These examples, however, illustrate that researchers cannot compare changes within each group because the design lacks a pretest. For example, the school officials did not measure the students' math skills prior to executing the treatment, and as a result, they cannot determine the real effect of the math program on math skills because better scores between the groups are not necessarily attributed to the math training treatment. Increased scores might result from the treatment group having disproportionately more students than the control group with inherently better math skills. Therefore, there is no way to know the true effect of the treatment, which restricts the ability to link cause and effect. When the design lacks random selection or assignment and a pretest, the study takes on an exploratory design, which is difficult to suggest cause and effect or generalize to other populations or places.

To improve these designs, researchers add a pretest to the design, creating an experimental design. The experimental design, shown in Figure 5.7, is cross-sectional design and includes a control group, a treatment group, a pretest, and a posttest. When researchers are interested in time, they add time intervals to both sides, using multiple pretests and posttests. Figure 5.8 depicts this design.

The school administrators decide to test the effectiveness of the math program using this experimental design. To conduct the experiment for the math program, they randomly assign students to the two groups, and each group completes the math skills pretest. At the conclusion of the 8-week math program, all the fourth-grade

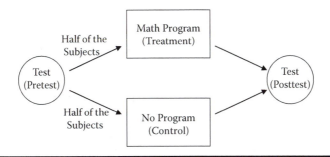

Figure 5.7 Illustration of an experimental research design.

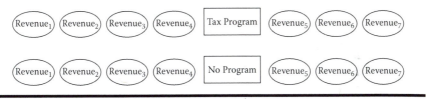

Figure 5.8 Research design over time.

students take the test again. With the four tests—two pretests and two posttests—they are able to identify differences between and within the groups. For example, by examining the pretests of both groups, they can determine if the two groups have similar (not significantly different) math skills. In addition, the posttest scores are analyzed to determine a difference exists and if so that it might be caused by the treatment. Overall, the experiment establishes time order and statistical associations, and eliminates potential alternative explanations and spurious relationships.

The school administrators also are able to compare within the groups, identifying changes from the pretest to the posttest. The analysis of the control group's pretest and posttest helps identify the effect of taking the test twice. If scores of the two test from the control group are similar (not significantly different), then the threat of multiple test exposure is minimized and the change in the treatment group's test scores is more likely to be attributed to the math program rather than exposure to the test. Overall, the administrators analyze all four tests to determine the effectiveness of the math skills program.

5.3.4 Recap

The sections above did not present all the research designs available to researchers, but it did discuss those that are most popular among practitioners, particularly case studies. Overall, researchers shape their designs to fit the purpose of the research. When researchers want to describe and generalize the findings beyond the sample, they select participants at random. On the other hand, researchers interested in establishing cause and effect randomly assign subjects to a control and treatment group and conduct pretests and posttests. The absence of any one of these elements minimizes the researcher's ability to link cause and effect, but these are generally more conducive to the manager.

5.4　Threats to Validity

Throughout the presentation of the different designs, certain problems have been noted that limit the validity of a study, particularly the lack of pretests, control groups, randomization, and/or the effect of a pretest and selection bias. However, other threats compromise the validity of research.

For example, events, maturation, and attrition threaten the validity of longitudinal studies. As events unfold and people mature over time, opinions, perceptions, and behaviors can change. Moreover, those studies that follow the same subjects over time are susceptible to the threat of attrition where participants discontinue their involvement from one period to the next.

Although the controlled setting of an experiment improves a researcher's ability to link cause and effect, the controlled conditions can threaten the ability of the findings to be generalized. The conditions could be so restrictive that researchers are virtually unable to generalize the results to the outside, uncontrolled world. Researchers simply do not know what will happen or the effects on others in the uncontrolled environment.

Another threat is the voluntary nature of human subject participation. Regardless of the randomness of the selection or assignment process, participation is voluntary. For example, psychology departments at universities conduct many studies that use student volunteers. To encourage participation, psychology professors might offer extra credit or mandate participation as part of the course requirements. In any event, the students participate in these studies, and the findings are generalized to groups beyond these students. However, researchers have no way of knowing if the volunteers are similar to or representative of the nonvolunteers or the population to which the researchers generalize the findings. In a recent news article, one professor argued that generalization from college students to a nonstudent population is not valid because "[c]ollege students aren't representative by age, wealth, income, educational level, or geographic location."[2] In addition, when the professor compared studies that use student research subjects to studies that use nonstudent research subjects, he found that more than half of the studies he analyzed produced "contradictory results" and where results trended in the same direction, the differences were two times as great.

Overall, researchers are unable to control for the unknown, and many presume that those willing to participate in a study are similar to those who do not want to participate. This assumption, coupled with the difficulty to measure perceptions, limits the overall validity—generalizations and claims of causality—of any study.

As Chapter 2 stated, the practical world is drastically different from the theoretical world. In the practical world, practitioners want to understand their organizations by understanding their employees and the direct and indirect beneficiaries of the organization's services; there is no unknown. That is, the managers know who (employees, stakeholders, donors, patients, clients) or what (performance, needs, quality, usage) they want to study. Therefore, the research conducted by managers is not designed to maintain validity because the questions administrators ask and answer focus on and are directly applied to some aspect of the organization. Research helps practitioners discover what is happening (descriptive), what to expect (predictive), and what to do or how to react (prescriptive).

For example, research reveals to the city manager that 20% of the households in the city recycle. Using this information, the manager can predict, with some certainty, that next year a similar percentage of households will recycle, all else being equal. However, because the research uncovered underperforming recycling efforts, the city manager can create a new policy to increase the number of households that recycle. Likewise, a nonprofit director can put a new development plan in action to improve donations next year because the research showed decreased donations, particularly from males between the ages of 35 to 50.

5.5   Summary

Research designs are an essential part of the research process and link directly to the purpose of the research. If researchers want to explore ideas without generalizing or establishing cause and effect, they use exploratory research designs, such as case studies. Elements such as control groups, pretests, and random selection or assignment are added to the designs to strengthen validity. As a result, researchers can better understand cause and effect.

Practitioners ask and then answer the most pressing and time-sensitive questions by conducting research that is designed to fit the organization. Most often, these designs are not experiments nor do the designs have control groups and/ or pretests; rather, the designs most conducive for managers are cross-sectional (i.e., case studies). In the end, our responsibility is to create and conduct useful, credible, cost-effective research efforts that benefit our organizations and the public we serve. Working with research designs that are best able to capture what we want to research enables us to do exactly that.

Key Terms

Case study	Longitudinal	Time order
Causality	Nonspurious relationship	Treatment group
Control group	Pretest	Selection bias
Cross-sectional	Posttest	Validity
Experiment	Random assignment	Voluntary
Generalization	Random selection	

Exercises

1. Explain the role randomization plays in generalization and causality. What happens to a researcher's ability to generalize or link cause and effect without randomization?
2. How does the voluntary nature of subject participation affect the generalization and causality of research designs? What, if anything, could you do to improve a research designs ability to generalize and link cause and effect?
3. Using the article analyzed in Chapters 2 and 3, examine the author's research design. What type of research design does the research use? Does the design fit the purpose of the research? Are the conclusions appropriate, given the purpose and research design? Could the researcher's improve the design to better fit the purpose and conclusions? Explain?
4. Consider some of the recent research projects conducted by your organization. What research designs were employed? Do you think a better research design could have been used? Why or why not?

Recommended Reading

Campbell, D. T. and Stanley, J. C. (1963). *Experimental and Quasi-Experimental Designs for Research*. Boston, MA: Houghton Mifflin Company.
Cook, T. D. and Campbell, D. T. (1979). *Quasi-Experimentation: Design and Analysis Issues for Field Settings*. Boston, MA: Houghton Mifflin.
Yin, R. K. (2004). *The Case Study Anthology*. Thousand Oaks, CA: Sage Publications.

Endnotes

1. From http://www.gallup.com/poll/102685/Conservative-Values-Republicans-Prefer-Giuliani.aspx. Accessed November 13, 2007.
2. Bialik, C. (2007, August 10). Too many studies use college students as their guinea pigs. *Wall Street Journal*, B1.

Chapter 6

Data Collection

6.1 Introduction

Collecting data is the transition point in the research process. The concepts that were developed and defined into variables in the previous steps of the research process are measured in the data collection step. That is, the variables become data. Researchers collect data by distributing questionnaires, conducting interviews, or collecting existing data. These are primary and secondary sources of data. For example, a city manager interested in the median income levels of surrounding cities would find this information from the U.S. Bureau of the Census. These data are primary sources for the Census Bureau (it collects the data) but secondary for the city manager (she is using sources collected by someone else). This chapter presents a variety of data collection methods, as well as the validity, reliability, strengths, and weaknesses of each.

6.2 Primary Sources

Primary sources of data are those collected by the researcher. For example, managers may count tonnage of recycled materials, donations collected, or number of patients entering the emergency department. They can study the number of potholes filled, observe traffic flow during rush hour, or examine workflow variations of the organization's employees. They can administer surveys to or conduct interviews with the organization's employees, stakeholders, or users of the services to understand their needs, perceptions, opinions, and reactions. With data from observing situations or asking people questions, administrators must understand and follow the rules associated with questionnaire construction discussed in chapter 8. Before discussing the rules, first we focus on the different ways to collect primary data. Therefore, this section focuses on interviews (face-to-face interviews or phone interviews) and self-administered questionnaires (mail, e-mail, onsite, or Web-based surveys).

6.2.1 *Interviews*

Interviews are one-on-one information-gathering conversations between a trained interviewer and research subjects. Researchers conduct interviews either in-person (face-to-face) or on the phone using structured or unstructured questionnaires.

Face-to-face interviews can be one-on-one interviews—between the interviewer and respondent—or transpire in a small group, called a focus group. Both use unstructured interviews that rely on qualitative, open-ended questions where respondents provide the answers rather than choosing one from a predetermined list. In the one-on-one interview, the open-ended nature of questioning allows for in-depth probing, spontaneous follow-up questions, and lengthy conversations that the participant, not the interviewer, dominates. In the focus group, the interviewer plays the role of a facilitator asking vague questions of the whole group, generally of 10 or fewer respondents. The participants' responses beget additional conversations and questions that yield detailed, qualitative information. The researcher records the interviews and focus groups using a recording device (voice or video).

Given the high cost and length associated with unstructured face-to-face interviews and focus groups, only a small number of subjects are used. The focus groups are more time efficient as the researcher can collect information from 10 participants at once. Overall, the complexity of interpreting and analyzing the qualitative data collected from interviews as well as the small sample size, threatens the validity of the research, making such interviews conducive for exploratory research. That is, researchers using unstructured interviews are less likely to generalize or link cause and effect. However, these interviews serve the administrator particularly well when interested in improving services and understanding community needs.

Structured interviews use a questionnaire to gather more quantifiable information that is most useful in descriptive research. The structured format consists of both closed questions (those where respondents select responses from a predefined list of options) and open-ended questions (those that do not restrict respondents to a list of responses). The interviews transpire in a room, at an onsite location, or over the phone. Given the preplanned, unchanging structure of the interview, a larger number of subjects can participate because not as much information, note taking, follow-up questioning, or conversation is necessary to complete an interview. Moreover, a larger sample helps to improve the validity of the research. Some interviews using structured questionnaires can take 30 or more minutes to administer. For example, the Bureau of Justice Statistics measures crime by interviewing randomly selected respondents. Through a long telephone interview, interviewers ask respondents numerous questions about crime and victimization. Box 6.1 presents two pages of the Crime Victimization Survey used by the Bureau of Justice.

One of the major advantages of any interview is the presence of the interviewer, but this can threaten the reliability of the data. The interviewer helps clarify questions where complexities exist; however, such involvement may jeopardize the precision and usefulness of the research. For example, a subject may not fully understand the question and may ask the interviewer for clarification. In the process of explaining, the interviewer provides an illustration to the respondent that is not provided to other subjects. Other participants who did not receive such an illustration may interpret the question differently and respond accordingly. The interviewer has influenced the responses, creating biased data.

In addition, the presence of an interviewer might cause respondents to change their answers because of social desirability. That is, the respondents might be embarrassed about their answer, they may think their response is controversial, or they may not want to offend the interviewer who might have a different opinion; as such, the respondents provide an answer they think the interviewer wants to hear. The presence of social desirability threatens the reliability of the data.

Researchers minimize the effects of social desirability in an interview setting by using interviewers who resemble the participants; for instance, women interviewing women and men interviewing men. When questions are so personal or private that respondents are likely to change their responses regardless of the interviewer, self-administered surveys are more effective because they reduce the threats of social desirability. Studies show that positive responses to seemingly private issues increase as the survey becomes more private; that is, "yes" responses to personal questions are the lowest with face-to-face interviews but increase with phone interviews, and are the highest among anonymous, self-administered questionnaires.[1]

When the researcher requires a large number of interviews, many well-trained interviewers are employed to gather data. For example, the U.S. Bureau of the Census interviews over 50,000 people a month for the Current Population Survey. The Census Bureau employs about 6000 field representatives, all of whom go through a rigorous training program. The training program consists of 20 hours of home study and three and a half to four and a half days of classroom training that "includes ... special emphasis on the labor force concepts to ensure that the new [field representatives] fully grasp these concepts before conducting interviews. In addition, a large part of the classroom training is devoted to practice interviews that reinforce the correct interpretation."[2]

In the end, all interviewers, not just those from the Census Bureau, must be properly trained prior to performing an interview. They have to know about the subject matter, how to interpret answers, and enter and code the information. Moreover, all interviewers are trained to be consistent in documenting their responses

BOX 6.1 ILLUSTRATION OF A QUESTIONNAIRE USED IN A PHONE INTERVIEW[3]

HOUSEHOLD RESPONDENT'S COMPUTER CRIME SCREEN QUESTIONS

FIELD REPRESENTATIVE – *Read introduction.*

INTRO: The next series of questions are about YOUR use of a computer. Please include ALL computers, laptops, or access to WebTV used at home, work, or school for PERSONAL USE *or* for operating a home business.

45c. During the last 6 months, have YOU used a computer, laptop, or WebTV for the following purposes *(Read answer categories 1–4) –*

Mark (X) all that apply.

100
1 ☐ For personal use at home?
2 ☐ For personal use at work?
3 ☐ For personal use at school, libraries, etc.?
4 ☐ To operate a home business?
5 ☐ None of the above – *SKIP* to Check Item D

45d. How many computers do you have access to for personal use or for operating a home business?

101
0 ☐ None
1 ☐ 1
2 ☐ 2
3 ☐ 3
4 ☐ 4 or more

45e. Do YOU use the Internet for personal use or for operating a home business?

102
1 ☐ Personal use
2 ☐ Operating a home business
3 ☐ Both
4 ☐ None of the above

45f. Have you experienced any of the following COMPUTER-RELATED incidents in the last 6 months *(Read answer categories 1–6) –*

Mark (X) all that apply.

103
1 ☐ Fraud in purchasing something over the Internet?
2 ☐ Computer virus attack?
3 ☐ Threats of harm or physical attack made while online or through E-mail?
4 ☐ Unrequested lewd or obscene messages, communications, or images while online or through E-mail?
5 ☐ *(Only ask if box 4 is marked in Item 45c)* Software copyright violation in connection with a home business?
6 ☐ Something else that you consider a computer-related crime?–*Specify* 🡦
_____
7 ☐ No computer-related incidents –*SKIP* to Check Item D

45g. Did you suffer any monetary loss as a result of the incident(s) you just mentioned?

104
1 ☐ Yes
2 ☐ No – *SKIP* to 45i

45h. How much money did you lose as a result of the incident(s)?

105
$_____.00 Amount of loss
x ☐ Don't know

45i. Did you report the incident(s) you just mentioned to *(Read answer categories 1–5) –*

Mark (X) all that apply.

106
1 ☐ A law enforcement agency?
2 ☐ An Internet Service provider?
3 ☐ A Website administrator?
4 ☐ A Systems Administrator?
5 ☐ Someone else? – *Specify* 🡦
_____
6 ☐ None of the above

HOUSEHOLD RESPONDENT'S CHECK ITEMS D AND E

CHECK ITEM D Who besides the respondent was present when the screen questions were asked? *(If telephone interview, mark box 1 only.)*

555
1 ☐ Telephone interview – *SKIP* to 46a
Personal interview – *Mark all that apply.*
2 ☐ No one besides respondent present
3 ☐ Respondent's spouse
4 ☐ HHLD member(s) 12+, not spouse
5 ☐ HHLD member(s) under 12
6 ☐ Nonhousehold member(s)
7 ☐ Someone was present – Can't say who
8 ☐ Don't know if someone else present

CHECK ITEM E *If self-response interview, SKIP to 46a*

Did the person for whom this interview was taken help the proxy respondent answer any screen questions?

556
1 ☐ Yes
2 ☐ No
3 ☐ Person for whom interview taken not present

FORM NCVS-1 (5-10-2001)

Page 7

HOUSEHOLD RESPONDENT'S COMPUTER CRIME SCREEN QUESTIONS

FIELD REPRESENTATIVE – *Read introduction.*

INTRO: **The next series of questions are about YOUR use of a computer. Please include ALL computers, laptops, or access to WebTV used at home, work, or school for PERSONAL USE** *or* **for operating a home business.**

45c. During the last 6 months, have YOU used a computer, laptop, or WebTV for the following purposes *(Read answer categories 1–4)* –

Mark (X) all that apply.

> 100
> 1 ☐ For personal use at home?
> 2 ☐ For personal use at work?
> 3 ☐ For personal use at school, libraries, etc.?
> 4 ☐ To operate a home business?
> 5 ☐ None of the above – **SKIP** *to Check Item D*

45d. How many computers do you have access to for personal use or for operating a home business?

> 101
> 0 ☐ None
> 1 ☐ 1
> 2 ☐ 2
> 3 ☐ 3
> 4 ☐ 4 or more

45e. Do YOU use the Internet for personal use or for operating a home business?

> 102
> 1 ☐ Personal use
> 2 ☐ Operating a home business
> 3 ☐ Both
> 4 ☐ None of the above

45f. Have you experienced any of the following COMPUTER-RELATED incidents in the last 6 months *(Read answer categories 1–6)* –

Mark (X) all that apply.

> 103
> 1 ☐ Fraud in purchasing something over the Internet?
> 2 ☐ Computer virus attack?
> 3 ☐ Threats of harm or physical attack made while online or through E-mail?
> 4 ☐ Unrequested lewd or obscene messages, communications, or images while online or through E-mail?
> 5 ☐ *(Only ask if box 4 is marked in Item 45c)* Software copyright violation in connection with a home business?
> 6 ☐ Something else that you consider a computer-related crime?–*Specify* ⟋
> _____
> _____
> 7 ☐ No computer-related incidents –**SKIP** *to Check Item D*

45g. Did you suffer any monetary loss as a result of the incident(s) you just mentioned?

> 104
> 1 ☐ Yes
> 2 ☐ No – **SKIP** *to 45i*

45h. How much money did you lose as a result of the incident(s)?

> 105 $ _____ .00 Amount of loss
> x ☐ Don't know

45i. Did you report the incident(s) you just mentioned to *(Read answer categories 1–5)* –

Mark (X) all that apply.

> 106
> 1 ☐ A law enforcement agency?
> 2 ☐ An Internet Service provider?
> 3 ☐ A Website administrator?
> 4 ☐ A Systems Administrator?
> 5 ☐ Someone else? – *Specify* ⟋
> _____
> _____
> 6 ☐ None of the above

HOUSEHOLD RESPONDENT'S CHECK ITEMS D AND E

CHECK ITEM D
Who besides the respondent was present when the screen questions were asked? *(If telephone interview, mark box 1 only.)*

> 555
> 1 ☐ Telephone interview – **SKIP** *to 46a*
> Personal interview – *Mark all that apply.*
> 2 ☐ No one besides respondent present
> 3 ☐ Respondent's spouse
> 4 ☐ HHLD member(s) 12+, not spouse
> 5 ☐ HHLD member(s) under 12
> 6 ☐ Nonhousehold member(s)
> 7 ☐ Someone was present – Can't say who
> 8 ☐ Don't know if someone else present

CHECK ITEM E
If self-response interview, **SKIP** *to 46a*

Did the person for whom this interview was taken help the proxy respondent answer any screen questions?

> 556
> 1 ☐ Yes
> 2 ☐ No
> 3 ☐ Person for whom interview taken not present

to questions asked by respondents. When a respondent asks questions or needs clarification, a simple change in the tone of the interviewer's voice, emphasis on a particular word, or additional explanations can lead or cause respondents to answer a specific way; perhaps, in a different way if the respondents were to read the question themselves. Finally, interviewers are supposed to be nice to the respondent, but not involved; that is, the conversation should be about the interview with no small talk.

No matter how well trained the interviewers are, some stray from protocol. As a way to reduce these problems, some researchers randomly record the interviews or conduct random follow-up phone calls to confirm the interview, the information collected, and the behavior of the interviewer. All of these methods are costly in both time and money, but necessary to authenticate the information.

6.2.2 Self-Administered Surveys

Self-administered surveys are those where no interviewer is present and the respondent completes the form. Researchers distribute self-administered surveys to research subjects via mail or e-mail, through a Web page, or at an onsite location. Subsequently, the respondents complete the questionnaire on their own and return it to the researcher, or in the case of a Web-based survey, submit it via the Internet. Surveys sent through the mail system are mail surveys, whereas those distributed at a particular location are onsite surveys. Questionnaires included as an attachment to an e-mail are e-mail surveys, whereas the link for a Web-based survey is sent to respondents via e-mail. Table 6.1 presents the differences among the various forms of self-administered surveys, and Box 6.2 presents two pages of the 2008 American Community Survey conducted by the U.S. Census Bureau.

Mail surveys are useful when researchers have access to addresses or names. The researcher includes a cover letter and a self-addressed, postage-paid envelope. Beyond the costs associated with copying the survey and stuffing envelopes, the major disadvantages of mail surveys include not getting the survey to the correct person and the low return/response rates. Compared to interviews, mail surveys are relatively cheap, but paper and postage costs add up quickly, particularly with larger samples or where many follow-up reminders are distributed.

Researchers distribute onsite surveys to the people entering the site location. At the onsite location, the respondents fill out the questionnaire and return it to the researcher. Onsite surveys are most useful when the target population is immediately available and directly associated with the organization by way of using its services; such as client-based satisfaction. Onsite surveys provide instant cooperation and rapid distribution and turn-around. The researcher reaches many respondents in one place at one time. This allows researchers to shift costs from conducting expensive individual face-to-face interviews from a smaller sample size to gathering more data from a larger sample size. Finally, the onsite administrator can answer

Table 6.1 Differences Among Surveys

	Face-to-Face	Phone Survey	Onsite Survey	Mail Survey	Web Survey
Anonymity	No	No	No	Yes	Yes
Complexity	Yes	No	No	Yes	Yes
Confidentiality	Yes	Yes	Yes	Yes	Yes
Convenience	None	Yes	Yes	Yes	Yes
Cost	Expensive	Expensive	Inexpensive	Inexpensive	Inexpensive
Data entry error	n/a	Yes	Yes	Yes	Yes
Interviewer	Yes	Yes	Depends	No	No
Interviewer effects	Yes	Yes	Yes, if present	No	No
Length	Long	Short	Short	Short	Short
Response rate	n/a	n/a	n/a	20–70%	20–70%
Response set bias	Limited	Limited	Limited if interviewer is used	Increases	Increases
Sample size	Small	Varies	Varies	Varies	Varies
Skip patterns okay	Yes	Yes	Yes, if interviewer is used	Limited or avoided	Not necessary
Type of data	Qualitative	Quantitative	Quantitative	Quantitative	Quantitative
Type of question	Open	Open and closed	Closed	Closed	Closed

BOX 6.2 ILLUSTRATION OF A SELF-ADMINISTERED MAIL SURVEY[4]

questions, provide clarification, or read the survey to those with disabilities or poor reading skills.

E-mail surveys are inexpensive and take less time to distribute and collect than onsite and mail surveys and require no copying or stuffing envelopes. In addition, no postage or return envelopes need to be included in the distribution process. E-mail surveys are very inexpensive. However, not everyone has access to e-mail, which can pose problems when a researcher is seeking a representative sample. Consequently, researchers should use e-mail surveys only when the entire target population being researched has access to e-mail; for example, university administrators studying student and/or faculty opinions. However, when certain portions of the

Housing

➡ **Please answer the following questions about the house, apartment, or mobile home at the address on the mailing label.**

1 **Which best describes this building?** Include all apartments, flats, etc., even if vacant.
- ☐ A mobile home
- ☐ A one-family house detached from any other house
- ☐ A one-family house attached to one or more houses
- ☐ A building with 2 apartments
- ☐ A building with 3 or 4 apartments
- ☐ A building with 5 to 9 apartments
- ☐ A building with 10 to 19 apartments
- ☐ A building with 20 to 49 apartments
- ☐ A building with 50 or more apartments
- ☐ Boat, RV, van, etc.

2 **About when was this building first built?**
- ☐ 2000 or later – *Specify year*

  [ ]
- ☐ 1990 to 1999
- ☐ 1980 to 1989
- ☐ 1970 to 1979
- ☐ 1960 to 1969
- ☐ 1950 to 1959
- ☐ 1940 to 1949
- ☐ 1939 or earlier

3 **When did PERSON 1 (listed on page 2) move into this house, apartment, or mobile home?**

Month   Year
[ ]   [ ]

A Answer questions 4 – 6 if this is a HOUSE OR A MOBILE HOME; otherwise, SKIP to question 7a.

4 **How many acres is this house or mobile home on?**
- ☐ Less than 1 acre → *SKIP to question 6*
- ☐ 1 to 9.9 acres
- ☐ 10 or more acres

5 **IN THE PAST 12 MONTHS, what were the actual sales of all agricultural products from this property?**
- ☐ None
- ☐ $1 to $999
- ☐ $1,000 to $2,499
- ☐ $2,500 to $4,999
- ☐ $5,000 to $9,999
- ☐ $10,000 or more

6 **Is there a business (such as a store or barber shop) or a medical office on this property?**
- ☐ Yes
- ☐ No

7 **a. How many separate rooms are in this house, apartment, or mobile home?** Rooms must be separated by built-in archways or walls that extend out at least 6 inches and go from floor to ceiling.
- INCLUDE bedrooms, kitchens, etc.
- EXCLUDE bathrooms, porches, balconies, foyers, halls, or unfinished basements.

Number of rooms
[ ]

b. How many of these rooms are bedrooms? Count as bedrooms those rooms you would list if this house, apartment, or mobile home were for sale or rent. If this is an efficiency/studio apartment, print "0".

Number of bedrooms
[ ]

8 **Does this house, apartment, or mobile home have –**

	Yes	No
a. hot and cold running water?	☐	☐
b. a flush toilet?	☐	☐
c. a bathtub or shower?	☐	☐
d. a sink with a faucet?	☐	☐
e. a stove or range?	☐	☐
f. a refrigerator?	☐	☐
g. telephone service from which you can both make and receive calls? Include cell phones.	☐	☐

9 **How many automobiles, vans, and trucks of one-ton capacity or less are kept at home for use by members of this household?**
- ☐ None
- ☐ 1
- ☐ 2
- ☐ 3
- ☐ 4
- ☐ 5
- ☐ 6 or more

10 **Which FUEL is used MOST for heating this house, apartment, or mobile home?**
- ☐ Gas: from underground pipes serving the neighborhood
- ☐ Gas: bottled, tank, or LP
- ☐ Electricity
- ☐ Fuel oil, kerosene, etc.
- ☐ Coal or coke
- ☐ Wood
- ☐ Solar energy
- ☐ Other fuel
- ☐ No fuel used

population lack access to e-mail, researchers rely on multimethod data collection approaches where e-mail, mail, and onsite surveys are distributed. The major problem with e-mail surveys is getting back the completed survey. The responsibility of the respondent increases with e-mail surveys; the respondent has to properly download, fill out, save, and return the survey. The added responsibility requires more effort than opening an envelope that comes in the mail or filling out a survey onsite, and the increased effort is likely to reduce response rates.

Researchers can use Web-based technology to create Web surveys. This technology is available for purchase from companies; for example, Survey Monkey or Zoomerang are two very popular companies organizations use to create Web-based surveys. Once the survey is ready for distribution, the researchers send out the survey's link through e-mail or by a postcard in the mail to the respondents. By clicking the link or entering the Web address, respondents are taken immediately to the survey, where they click or type answers until the survey is complete. From the viewpoint of the researcher, Web surveys are advantageous because the researcher is not required to manually process the returned information (i.e., code, enter, and clean the data); the software automatically codes and enters the data into a database as the respondent answers the questions. In addition, less responsibility falls to the participant; the respondent does not have to download or save the survey or return the survey through mail or e-mail. The reduction in the responsibility of the respondent improves response rates.

Finally, researchers can design Web-based questionnaires to minimize respondent errors such as skipping questions or selecting more than one option when only one was necessary. That is, the survey can be created in such a way to ask one question at a time and advance to the next question only if the respondent answers the current question. In addition, the survey software can unselect the option when another option for the same question is selected. However, forcing respondents to answer opinion-based questions may result in less differentiation (e.g., more neutral responses) or higher quit rates than mail surveys where respondents can easily skip a question. Web surveys are appropriate as the only data collection tool when all potential respondents have access to the Internet, similar to those conducted within organizations for interoffice surveys. When a proportion of the population of interest lacks access to the Web, researchers use a multimethod data collection process.

Although researchers find the process for distributing self-administered surveys easy, cheap, and convenient, they also understand the difficulty with the distribution process. Major problems associated with all self-administered surveys include getting the survey to the correct person, getting back the completed survey, and different interpretations of question meaning. The distribution list for an organization, which researchers use for the names and addresses, changes regularly as respondents change jobs, move, go on vacation, or die. On occasion, researchers may find as many as 5% of the addresses listed could be incorrect, which is an unknown statistic to the researcher until the unopened envelope is returned with a stamp that says "Return to Sender" or that the addressee or address is unknown. Finally, respondents may interpret the questions, portions of a question, and/or responses differently. Chapter 8 discusses these interpretation issues at length.

Sometimes it does not matter if the survey gets to the wrong person, as long as the survey arrives at the correct address or job title. For example, if the target population is residents of a community, facilities managers, or chief operating officers, researchers can address the envelopes generically; for instance, "Current Resident," "Current Facilities Manager," or "Current Operating Officer." Unfortunately, respondents perceive generic addressees and salutations as less personal; these perceptions are likely to reduce response rates.

Although getting the survey to the correct person is challenging, the biggest challenge for researchers when it comes to self-administered mail, e-mail, and Web surveys is time. Researchers wait days and sometimes weeks for respondents to return completed surveys. As researchers wait for returning surveys, the remaining steps of the research process—data analysis and communication of the findings—are put on hold. Researchers cannot begin to analyze the data until enough surveys have been received, which can take four to six weeks. Generally, researchers try to improve response rates by sending follow-up reminders, sending the survey in its entirety again, or phoning the respondents where researchers have the respondents' phone numbers. Chapter 7 presents strategies to improve response rates, but all of these efforts increase costs and postpone the analysis of the data and communication of the findings.

Nonresponses create problems for researchers and threaten the quality of data. For example, researchers do not know who the nonrespondents are nor do they know if nonrespondents are similar to the respondents.[5] However, if the respondents resemble (are similar to or representative of) the target population, then researchers consider the returned data to be representative of the sample—that is, had the non-respondents participated, their answers would be similar to those who did respond. Therefore, the nonresponses are not as threatening to the reliability and validity of the data when the respondents are similar to the nonrespondents. Where the respondents are dissimilar to the target population, researchers assign weights to the responses to make them more representative. The next chapter discusses the use of weights in the sampling process.

Overall, self-administered surveys are more beneficial than interviews when respondents are asked personal, private, or sensitive questions, particularly about opinions or when resources (e.g., time and money) are limited. In fact, sometimes, researchers gather information that is more reliable from self-administered surveys because there is no interviewer effect; the absence of the interviewer reduces social desirability. However, when complexities exist, such as difficult questions or unclear directions, the responsibility of understanding what is being asked falls to the respondents, which threatens the reliability of the measures.

6.3 Secondary Sources

So far this chapter has focused on collecting primary data. Primary data collection reveals information about a specific group of people, typically an organization's clientele, residents of a community, and so forth. Sometimes, however, primary data collection is both inefficient and redundant—data may already exist. As a result, researchers generally check on the availability of existing information before venturing out to collect original data.

When students ask how to find data and statistics, I say "Google it or ask the reference librarian." Today, finding databases and information is far easier than it was 20 or even 10 years ago. In fact, the availability of numerous Internet search engines makes searching for information almost too easy, and even fun and interesting. For example, if we want to find vital statistics such as infant mortality or life expectancy, how would we locate these? Not too long ago, we would ask the reference librarian, and she would point us to the government document section of the library where a sourcebook entitled *Health, United States* would be sitting on the shelf. Today, an Internet search of "vital statistics" reveals a long list of results, about 1.8 million links, but the Centers for Disease Control's (CDC) vital statistics link is among the first on the Google list. Clicking the link provides access to hundreds of statistics as well as reports and the sourcebooks distributed by the CDC. Global databases are also available on the Web. For example, the World Health Organization provides vital statistics for 193 member countries.

The Internet provides easy access to plenty of free data, mainly from government organizations. Some organizations, like the Census Bureau, offer entire databases, whereas others, for example, the Federal Bureau of Investigation, supply aggregate data. A few institutions provide interactive query systems where responses from a database are transformed into user-defined tables. Table 6.2 lists just a few of the many sites on the Internet that post databases and statistics.

As stated in Chapter 2, anyone can post anything on the Internet. As a result, all sources of data, even government sources, must be evaluated prior to their use, and the researcher is the one responsible for this evaluation. Researchers assess the data by investigating the survey questions, sampling methodology, and the organization that produced the information. Theories of measurement and sampling guide the researcher's evaluation of the measures, variables, survey, and sampling techniques. To evaluate each, researchers ask the following questions about measurements and sampling methods: ·

- What are the variables?
- How are the variables measured?
- Are the questions worded appropriately? Or do the questions violate measurement theory?
- Who or what is the target population and who is included in the sample?
- What are the specifics of the sampling procedures? Probability or nonprobability?
- What is the sample size?
- What is the level of confidence?
- Does the researcher report the sampling error? If so, what is it?
- Do the researchers use weights to make the sample more representative?
- Does the sampling methodology meet external validity standards?
- Can the sample be generalized to the target population? Why or why not?
- Who collected the data? How are they trained? Are they paid employees or volunteers?

- How are the data coded?
- How are the aggregate data reported?
- How old are the data? How often are the data updated?

Finally, readers inquire about the organization conducting the research, those responsible for distributing the survey and collecting and reporting the data. Some research organizations have known political agendas and others do not. Several research institutes claim to be apolitical or nonpartisan, but employ staff or have donors who embrace particular ideologies. Moreover, some research groups say very little, if anything, about their organizations. Regardless of the organizations' mission or political agenda, the mission or agenda should not take precedence over or compromise measurement and sampling theories; their own researchers must employ rigorous and appropriate methods. Researchers want to be sure that the organization is legitimate, and its research is unbiased and uncompromised. They accomplished this by asking and answering the questions listed above in the context of the following questions about the organization:

- Who is the organization or person collecting the data?
- Is the same person or organization distributing the data (i.e., did someone else collect the data for the organization)? If so, investigate the responsible party using these questions.
- Does the person or organization have authority or expertise in this area?
- What are the credentials of the staff designing the measures and sampling techniques?
- What is the organization's mission? If one is provided, read the "About Us" link on the Web site.
- Is the organization partisan or apolitical?
- Are there sponsors of the organization?
- Does the organization have a board? If so, who are the members?
- Will the board's membership influence or compromise the data collection process (i.e., threaten validity and reliability of the research)?
- Who funds the organization? Donors, taxpayers, grant monies, others? Do these donors have a political agenda?

The research produced by politically motivated organizations is acceptable only when the research methods are rigorous and appropriate. Problems occur, however, when the organization or other groups begin to exaggerate their claims through improper interpretation or analysis of the data as illustrated in Chapter 4, where researchers exaggerated human trafficking statistics and inappropriately generalized drinking and violence statistics from one group to another.

Table 6.2 Sources for Data and Statistics Available on the Internet

Data and/or Statistics Source	Web Site Address
Federal Government Sources	
Bureau of Economic Analysis	http://www.bea.gov/
Bureau of Justice Statistics	http://www.ojp.usdoj.gov/bjs/
Bureau of Labor Statistics	http://stats.bls.gov/
Bureau of the Census	http://www.census.gov/
Bureau of Transportation Statistics	http://www.bts.gov/
Business Data and Statistics	http://www.business.gov/topic/Business_Data_and_Statistics
Centers for Disease Control and Prevention	http://www.cdc.gov/datastatistics/
Department of Agriculture, Economic Research Service	http://www.ers.usda.gov/Data/
Department of Commerce, STAT-USA	http://www.stat-usa.gov/
Economic Report of the President	http://www.gpoaccess.gov/eop/index.html
Economics and Statistics Administration	https://www.esa.doc.gov/
Energy Information Administration	http://www.eia.doe.gov/
Environmental Protection Agency	http://www.epa.gov/epahome/Data.html
Federal Reserve Board	http://www.federalreserve.gov/econresdata/default.htm
Federal Reserve Economic Data	http://research.stlouisfed.org/fred2/
FedStats	http://www.fedstats.gov/
Internal Revenue System, Tax Statistics	http://www.irs.gov/taxstats/index.html
National Agricultural Statistics Service	http://www.nass.usda.gov/index.asp
National Association of State Election Directors	http://www.nased.org/membership.htm
National Center for Education Statistics	http://nces.ed.gov/
National Center for Health Statistics	http://www.cdc.gov/nchs/Default.htm
National Science Foundation	http://www.nsf.gov/statistics/

Office of Management and Budget	http://www.whitehouse.gov/omb/
Office of the Clerk, Election Information	http://clerk.house.gov/member_info/election.html
Securities and Exchange Commission, EDGAR	http://www.sec.gov/edgar.shtml
Social Security Data and Research	http://www.ssa.gov/policy/
Statistical Abstract	http://www.census.gov/prod/www/statistical-abstract.html
Uniform Crime Report	http://www.fbi.gov/ucr/ucr.htm
USA.gov General Data and Statistics	http://www.usa.gov/Topics/Reference_Shelf/Data.shtml
White House Briefing Room	http://www.whitehouse.gov/news/fsbr.html

International Sources

International Databases, Bureau of the Census	http://www.census.gov/ipc/www/idb/
International Monetary Fund	http://www.imf.org/external/data.htm
United Nations Statistical Databases	http://unstats.un.org/unsd/databases.htm
The World Bank	http://www.worldbank.org/
World Health Organization	http://www.who.int/research/en/

Research Institutes

Community Research Institute	http://www.cridata.org/
National Center for Charitable Statistics	http://www.nccs.urban.org/

Universities

Census data	http://fisher.lib.virginia.edu/collections/stats/histcensus/
Inter-University Consortium for Political and Social Research (ICPSR)	http://www.icpsr.umich.edu/ICPSR/access/index.html
Research Resources from Yale University Library	http://www.library.yale.edu/ia-resources/datasrc.html
Statistical Resources on the Web from The University of Michigan Library	http://www.lib.umich.edu/govdocs/stats.html

Definitions, sample sizes, and data collection tools change over time, which is another reason why researchers should investigate the sources of information. For example, the Census Bureau has been conducting the Current Population Survey every month since 1940. Changes have been made as a result of increased demand for additional data as well as technological improvements, budget cuts, and policy changes. For instance, in 1994 the survey was rewritten "to better take advantage of technology."[6] Because of budget cuts, the sample size was reduced from approximately 56,000 to 50,000 in 1996 but increased to 60,000 in 2001 to improve estimates required by the State Children's Health Insurance Program, known as SCHIP.[7]

The crime statistics produced by the Federal Bureau of Investigation (FBI) provide another example of changing definitions and sample sizes. Police organizations around the country submit their crime data to the FBI, and the FBI aggregates (sums up) the information by type of crime, weapon used, characteristics of the criminal, the state in which the crime occurred, and so on in its annual *Uniform Crime Report*. Nevertheless, the FBI cautions users of the data in the following disclaimers. The first disclaimer cautions researchers when analyzing crime statistics over time and the second notifies researchers about the FBI estimates.

1. Data users should exercise care in making any direct comparison between data in this publication and those in prior issues of *Crime in the United States*. Because of differing levels of participation from year to year and reporting problems that require the FBI to estimate crime counts for certain contributors, the data are not comparable from year to year. In addition, this publication may contain updates to data provided in prior years' publications. Therefore, for example, the 2004 data in last year's publication may not match the 2004 data in this publication.[8]

2. Because not all law enforcement agencies provide data for complete reporting periods, the FBI includes estimated crime numbers in these presentations. The FBI estimates offenses that occur within each of three areas: metropolitan statistical areas (MSAs), cities outside MSAs, and nonmetropolitan counties. The national program computes estimates by using the known crime figures of similar areas within a state and assigning the same proportion of crime volumes to nonreporting agencies or agencies with missing data. The estimation process considers the following: population size of agency; type of jurisdiction, e.g., police department versus sheriff's office; and geographic location.[8]

Researchers need to understand these types of disclaimers when searching for information. Moreover, when using secondary data that come with warnings, researchers must disclose these same warnings in their own research.

6.4   Summary

When comparing interviews to self-administered surveys, self-administered surveys have an inherent advantage: they are less likely to suffer from social desirability and more likely to have better comprehension. That is, respondents can read the question as many times as necessary before answering or they may skip and come back to the question later, whereas in phone interviews respondents are less likely to have the interviewer repeat the question more than once. However, phone interviews provide better coverage and faster turn-around times than self-administered surveys. Given the advantages and disadvantages of all the modes of data collection, a multimode approach is often advocated for and used by researchers. Researchers use a combination of different types of surveys to measure a concept, because not everyone can be reached on the phone or through mail or e-mail. For example, the Census Bureau uses a combination of phone and face-to-face interviews to collect the unemployment data for the Current Population Survey.

Using secondary sources of data is acceptable and more efficient in both time and money. Prior to including the data, a thorough examination of the source is necessary, however. The definition of variables, the data collection tool, and the sampling methodology should also be thoroughly investigated.

Key Terms

E-mail surveys	Onsite surveys	Secondary data
Face-to-face interviews	Mail surveys	Self-administered surveys
Interviewer bias	Phone interviews	Social desirability
Onsite interviews	Primary data	Web-based surveys

Exercises

1. Explain the advantages and disadvantages of the different types of self-administered surveys. When is one more or less conducive than the others are?
2. What are the benefits and weaknesses of having an interviewer present in the data collection process?
3. Find statistics or a dataset provided by a government bureau, nonprofit organization, or research institute. What information, if any, does the organization supply in reference to its measures and sampling techniques? As a researcher, do you have enough confidence in its measures or statistics to use the information in a related research project? Explain.
4. How does you organization collect information? What are some of the advantages and disadvantages of these methods? Do you believe there is a better way?

Recommended Reading

Dillman, D. A. (2006). *Mail and Internet Surveys: The Tailored Design Method*. New York: Wiley.

Dillman, D. A. (1978). *Mail and Telephone Surveys*. New York: Wiley.

Sudman, S. and Bradburn, N. M. (1974). *Response Effects in Surveys: A Review and Synthesis*. Chicago: Aldine Publishing Company.

Endnotes

1. Sudman, S. and Bradburn, N. M. (1974). *Response Effects in Surveys: A Review and Synthesis*. Chicago: Aldine Publishing Company.
2. U.S. Bureau of the Census (2002). Current Population Survey Technical Paper 63RV Design and Methodology. Appendix F, pp. 190–191. http://www.census.gov/prod/2002pubs/tp63rv.pdf.
3. U.S. Department of Justice, Office of Justice Programs, Bureau of Justice Statistics, Crime Victimization Survey, 2003. Available at http://www.ojp.usdoj.gov/bjs/cvict.htm.
4. U.S. Census Bureau. American Community Survey, 2008. Available at http://www.census.gov/acs/wwwsbasics/squest/squest1.htm.
5. See validity section in Chapter 5 and the section on error in Chapter 7.
6. U.S. Bureau of the Census (2002). Technical Paper 63RV, foreword. http://www.census.gov/prod/2002pubs/tp63rv.pdf.
7. Ibid, pp. 2–5.
8. U.S. Department of Justice, Federal Bureau of Investigation, Uniform Crime Report, Methodology. 2005. http://www.fbi.gov/ucr/05cius/about/table_methodology.html.

Chapter 7

Sampling

7.1 Introduction

When researchers decide to collect their own data, not only do they have to select the mode of data collection but they also have to determine whom to interview or to whom the questionnaire must be issued. If a hospital, city, or nonprofit organization is interested in the opinions of their clientele, should it collect as much information as possible from its entire client population, or should it use a sample of this population? Collecting information from the entire population when it is larger than 1000 would be extremely time consuming and costly. Consider the 2000 Census conducted by the United States Census Bureau; it cost $4.5 billion to count the entire U.S. population—281,421,906 people.[1]

The federal government has substantial resources available (i.e., it has an entire bureau devoted to the census, which employs 12,000 people regularly, and 860,000 temporary employees to help with the 2000 census),[2] other organizations do not. Because of the time and money constraints associated with collecting data from an entire population, the best approach is to collect data from a sample that is representative of the target population. For example, the Gallup Poll News Service surveyed 1001 adults 18 and older to inquire about acceptable ways for presidential candidates to raise money.[3] According to the U.S. Census *American FactFinder*, there are over 209 million people aged 18 years and older.[4] How is a sample size of 1001 acceptable to generalize to a population of 209 million? This chapter answers this question by discussing the different sampling methods, and the confidence, accuracy, and errors in the sampling process. However, before discussing some of the different sampling techniques available to researchers, we begin with some definitions.

7.2 Some Definitions

A sample is a representative subset of units of the population. Elements or units refer to the unit of analysis, and are the people, places, or objects from which researchers obtain their data. The population is the group of interest to which the study's findings will be generalized; for example, all public administration students from accredited institutions, tenured professors from RUVH institutions (research university with very high research activities), nonprofits with assets worth $100 million or more, or Americans. Most often, however, researchers do not have access to the entire population of interest; therefore, they develop a sampling frame. The sampling frame is the list of elements that is accessible to the researcher; for example, a list of cities with population more than 100,000, nonprofit organization board members, college alumni lists, or voter registration lists. Therefore, sampling is the process of selecting elements from the sampling frame.

Researchers analyze the information collected in aggregate (whole) form to determine statistics, that is, percentages, averages, standard deviations, and medians. For example, in the Gallup Poll mentioned earlier, 75% of the units in the sample responded that it is unacceptable for presidential hopefuls to accept money from lobbyists. Researchers use these statistics to draw conclusions about the sample and make inferences and generalizations about the population. The use of proper sampling techniques improves the validity of the findings—the researcher's ability to generalize sample findings to the target population. Figure 7.1 illustrates this principle.

From the population, researchers draw a representative sample, collect data, run statistical analyses, calculate the findings, and draw conclusions. These findings and conclusions are generalized back to the population of interest. For example, the Gallup Poll claims the following in its report:

> More than three-quarters of Americans say that raising campaign money from contributions made by Washington lobbyists is unacceptable. Two-thirds of Americans say that candidates who accept money from Washington lobbyists cannot change the way things are done in Washington.[3]

Gallup uses the broad, all-encompassing term "Americans" rather than "respondents." They say, for example, "more than three-quarters of Americans" and "two-thirds of Americans." They are generalizing the findings from 1001 adults to all Americans because, they argue, their sample is representative of the population.

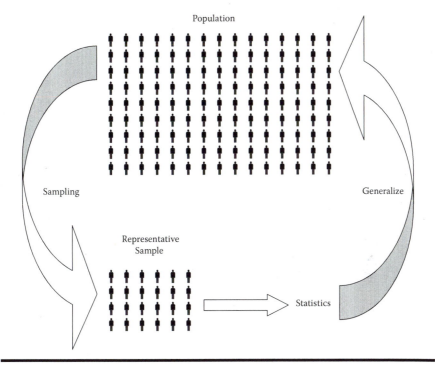

Figure 7.1   Illustration of sampling.

Overall, the factors that improve validity, particularly that of generalizations, include sample selection and the sample size. We examine each of these factors in turn.

7.3   Sample Selection

Sample selection involves probabilities, that is, the chance that something will be selected and this probability is known. When a referee flips a coin at a sporting event, the probability of one of the teams winning the coin toss is one half (.50), or 50%. A one-in-six chance exists of rolling a six on a die, and the probability of one's getting an N35 for the first ball of a bingo game is .013 or 1.3%. Each of these events produces an equal, or uniform, probability of occurrence—a one-in-two chance for the coin toss, a one-in-six chance for the die, and 1 in 75 chance for any bingo ball.

The same selection uniformity applies to sample selection when researchers use probability sampling; the probability of selecting one element from the population is known. Moreover, random selection provides the means to achieve a probability sampling; random selection maintains validity, allowing researchers to generalize sample statistics to the target population. Nonprobability sampling, on the other hand, does not ensure that every unit has the same probability of being selected (i.e., the probability is unknown or unequal); here, researchers select units based on convenience. This approach increases the threat of selection bias, which weakens validity and affects the ability of the researcher to generalize the findings.

7.3.1 Probability Sampling

Four basic types of probability sampling exist: simple random sampling, systematic sampling, stratified sampling, and cluster sampling. Researchers use simple random sampling to randomly select units from the sampling frame, without restriction (the researcher selects any element) and without replacement (once the element is selected, it does not go back into the population for another chance of being selected). This sampling method is most useful when the population is homogeneous. The process is as simple as placing all the elements of the sampling frame in a hat and picking one unit after another until the desired sample size is achieved. Suppose the sampling frame consists of the following elements and we want to randomly select seven:

01. Abby	05. Elaine	09. Irene	13. Mike	17. Quentin
02. Bill	06. Fred	10. James	14. Nicky	18. Robert
03. Carl	07. George	11. Kim	15. Oliver	19. Sophie
04. Donna	08. Hope	12. Lynn	16. Pam	20. Tony

We write each of these names on its own piece of paper and place all of them in a hat. Next, we randomly select one name at a time. For the first selection, each unit has the same chance or probability of being selected in each round—a 1-in-20 chance. The next selection has a 1-in-19, and so forth. We continue selecting elements from the hat until we achieve the sample size of seven. This random approach selects the following individuals: Hope, Sophie, Abby, Lynn, Tony, Fred, and Robert.

Imagine writing each number or name on a piece of paper and drawing the appropriate sample size from a sampling frame with 100, 1000, or even 1 million elements. This would take a lot of time. To speed up the process for projects using large samples, researchers rely on random number tables or generate their own set of random numbers. This approach begins with researchers assigning a number to each unit in the sampling frame, for example, assigning 01 to 20 to the elements as mentioned earlier. If the sampling frame consists of 1000 units, each is numbered from 0001 to 1000. Next, researchers use an existing table, as illustrated in Table 7.1, to select their sample. They move up, down, or across to select each unit, using the same number of digits as the highest number in the sampling frame. For example, to select seven individuals from the list using a random number table, we use two digits and move across from left to right until we find a number with the last two digits of 20 or less. The first number listed, 86367, is not useful because its last two digits are 67, and we need something smaller than 21. The next number to the right of 86367 is 97442. Again, this number is not useful; its last two digits

Table 7.1   Random Number Table

86367	97442	96088	**64710**	**56520**	31135	**93712**	99161	67852
35450	30751	20693	47132	95791	15848	31995	22970	22577
47829	87584	**74307**	58256	89935	**50419**	85719	71253	13535
97412	62527	85173	47898	65150	69662	**11508**	13170	83569
16655	**59217**	80415	90408	61041	50823	40175	74389	64787
15540	86063	47349	92190	70371	72365	20267	13035	72025
12285	25398	45050	63079	91583	92583	34077	75524	18116
47093	70898	51936	74164	74708	62656	78306	11741	49969
76845	79454	89812	37230	76941	59511	69888	60165	78375
82129	96884	30108	91350	74746	34961	63675	64295	13230
46470	55536	33846	77194	84818	23835	97741	36802	97615
96467	41067	94478	55589	38106	16705	51178	80352	15131
61664	52054	24832	26051	20786	99117	33217	94212	12964
32800	65163	38667	42399	40924	75348	37214	30918	26128
17290	86225	22563	61038	13516	11656	78334	85519	78240
30833	11096	99392	24403	49076	36557	40309	73846	77361
72068	79619	54196	84511	60382	58832	19448	98573	77825
69061	67745	36423	74469	53553	50675	78619	22006	85362
12145	37991	17334	26131	64647	65386	10950	43666	73719
77257	81275	44264	54394	68987	46794	80553	33396	97486
74150	50634	32124	71255	49749	82154	88581	33264	39419
15798	77284	21440	10865	49389	80611	64559	42504	99691
81803	23472	16943	75205	15208	39796	48093	41965	78336
22126	22717	12634	68649	14507	62376	84695	85651	76007
37650	37071	11936	20212	97266	49653	58069	90435	81212
42089	76194	30954	21041	69283	71448	69075	64320	88828
69242	31981	39963	13359	40562	14189	15688	18754	77633
50892	21047	49203	62840	35077	59585	62895	74782	57223
38021	31863	64359	27535	40435	23527	17347	87147	22541
51145	28408	20303	71744	60783	83341	99167	56303	63057
11033	17671	73123	56160	16111	57885	82986	56374	60859
50213	50565	63024	91001	39084	50557	14244	38760	58129
21223	92701	52320	39576	84038	43915	75689	40974	83165
82269	60258	30193	27477	40301	43841	60590	97159	35873
22761	81500	25958	89117	84972	16661	78545	37483	84222
97884	33629	95429	34497	55141	37615	60607	43457	24931
55223	91836	46992	43484	73381	89839	99925	16499	34970
62554	61944	26645	88029	93492	12917	60563	88062	15065
65133	96920	46887	64158	90410	34453	62549	55611	39002
50790	52680	56822	48667	27713	12477	90897	88372	44962
47313	88570	15205	34909	87219	40641	79902	38787	17504
81218	60750	69987	96522	22651	24060	34854	60758	42421
32264	41548	27378	16735	14925	51265	16806	39894	83577
56297	41468	10404	27735	86175	78707	27378	91852	96810

are 42. We proceed across until we find 647**10**. The last two digits are 10, so we select element number 10, that is, James. The process continues until we find another useful number, 565**20**. Using the last two digits, Tony is selected. We repeat this process until we reach the desired sample size, that is, in this case, five more times. In the end, we select elements numbered 10, 20, 12, 07, 19, 08, and 17.

01. Abby	05. Elaine	09. Irene	13. Mike	**17. Quentin**
02. Bill	06. Fred	**10. James**	14. Nicky	18. Robert
03. Carl	**07. George**	11. Kim	15. Oliver	**19. Sophie**
04. Donna	**08. Hope**	**12. Lynn**	16. Pam	**20. Tony**

If a number repeats itself, as 19 and 12 did in the preceding illustration, then the repeated number is skipped and the next useful number is used. If the sample size is larger than the number of random numbers listed, then the process uses another set of digits. For example, if the sample size is 500 and there are not enough numbers on the table to reach this sample size, then we can use a combination of the digits. That is, the first time through the random number table, the middle three digits can be drawn on; the second time through, the last three digits are used, and so on. This process is repeated until the researcher is able to arrive at the desired sample size.

Sometimes, elements of the sampling frame might already be assigned numbers such as invoice numbers, check numbers, or student numbers. In these cases, a random number table might not be useful. Instead, researchers can create their own set of random numbers using a random-number-generating program. Appendix 7.1 provides an illustration of generating random numbers in Microsoft Excel.

Another type of random sampling is systematic sampling. Rather than randomly selecting each element, researchers systematically select elements from a list; that is, every kth element is selected. This method is useful when the distribution of probabilities is uniform and the target populations are homogeneous. When predetermined lists are used, the kth unit is determined by dividing the total sampling frame by the sample size; in our example, we divide 20 by 7, so we select every third element on the list. If the sampling frame is 1000 and sample size is 100, every 10th element is selected until 100 elements have been picked. To begin, we start at a random location on the list; we do this by pointing to the list, drawing a number from a hat or better still, generating a random number in Microsoft Excel (see Appendix 7.1 for this process). For our example, we use Excel, and it produces the number 11. Therefore, we start at 11 and count every third element as illustrated here:

01. Abby	05. Elaine	**09. Irene**	13. Mike	**17. Quentin**
02. Bill	**06. Fred**	10. James	**14. Nicky**	18. Robert
03. Carl	07. George	11. Kim	15. Oliver	19. Sophie
04. Donna	08. Hope	**12. Lynn**	16. Pam	**20. Tony**

Using this process, Nicky, Quentin, Tony, Carl, Fred, Irene, and Lynn are selected. Systematic sampling is easier than simple random sampling because researchers do not have to rely on random number tables or generate their own random numbers; however, systematically selecting elements from a set list ties the researcher to the arrangement or order of elements (i.e., alphabetical order). Systematic sampling and simple random sampling are useful only when the target population is homogeneous. The following might transpire when the population is heterogeneous.

The administration of a university is interested in studying its faculty's perceptions of governance. The university samples 271 of its 922 faculty members using a systematic random sample. Once the sampling is complete, it finds that 80% of the responses are from the faculty in the College of Liberal Arts and Sciences, the university's largest unit. Furthermore, it discovers that there are no responses from the College of Interdisciplinary Studies, the university's smallest unit. The differences in representation result in selection bias, which weakens the validity of the study. To control for the potential threat of selection bias, researchers can do one of two things: use a stratified random sample or use weights to make the sample more representative.

A stratified random sample is one in which researchers separate the elements by strata, determine the makeup of each stratum in relation to the total number of elements in the sampling frame, and then multiply the proportion by the sample size to achieve the appropriate number of elements from each stratum to be sampled. The strata are based on some characteristic such as gender, race, region of the country, student status, or a university's organizational chart.

The university's administration samples the faculty, this time using a stratified sampling technique. First, the sampling frame is separated by college, the strata as shown in columns 1 and 2 of Table 7.2. Next, the administration calculates the

Table 7.2   Illustration of a Stratified Sampling Technique

Strata	Number of Faculty	Percentage of Faculty (%)	Sample (n = 271)
College of Community and Public Service	62	6.7	18
College of Education	68	7.4	20
College of Health Professions	35	3.8	10
College of Interdisciplinary Studies	18	2.0	5
College of Liberal Arts and Sciences	577	62.6	170
College of Nursing	36	3.9	11
College of Engineering and Computing	48	5.2	14
College of Business	78	8.5	23
Total	922		271

proportion of faculty per college by dividing the number of faculty for the respective college by the total number of faculty, shown in column 3 of the table. Finally, the proportion is multiplied by the study's sample size (a predetermined number calculated with a formula discussed later in this chapter) to yield the number of faculty to be randomly selected from each college, listed in the last column of Table 7.2. Therefore, the administration randomly selects and surveys 170 professors in the College of Liberal Arts and Sciences, 5 from Interdisciplinary Studies, 18 from the College of Community and Public Service, and so on until each college has been equally represented based on the proportion of the stratum. The sample size for each stratum is listed in the last column of Table 7.2. The threat of selection bias is reduced because the faculty members are equally represented by college.

The last type of probability sampling is cluster or multistage sampling. Cluster sampling uses a top-down hierarchical approach and is useful when the sampling frame is difficult to research and expensive to obtain. The hierarchical approach begins by breaking down the entire target population into clusters or groups. These clusters can be further broken down into additional groups: for example, from a state, to counties, to cities, and finally to neighborhoods. Once the clusters have been established, researchers randomly select clusters and collect information from all of the units in that cluster. Suppose we want to conduct face-to-face interviews with school district superintendents across the state of Michigan. Rather than randomly selecting superintendents from across the state and traveling across the state to interview the subjects—a process that would be rather time consuming and expensive—we could use cluster sampling. We divide the state into clusters (using counties) and randomly select eight counties as illustrated by the gray shaded areas in Figure 7.2. Once the clusters have been randomly selected, we conduct interviews of all the superintendents in those counties.

Although cluster sampling is cheaper than other types of random sampling techniques, selection bias will be more prevalent, especially in cases where heterogeneous populations exist. Moreover, large populations can be overlooked. In the Michigan example, three of the four largest counties—Kent, Oakland, and Wayne—are not included in the sample, and these three counties represent 38% of the state's population. Therefore, where populations are large and diverse, cluster sampling is inappropriate because the sample will lack representation of the different groups and threaten the validity of the research. Overall, cluster sampling will be useful and potentially less expensive when the population is homogeneous and uniformly distributed.

When the elements of the sample do not represent their respective proportions in the target population, researchers add weights to balance the sample. For example, the administration of the university wants to look beyond colleges and consider faculty rank—assistant, associate, or full professor—when studying perceptions of faculty governance. In doing so, the administration finds that the sample underrepresents both assistant and associate professors.

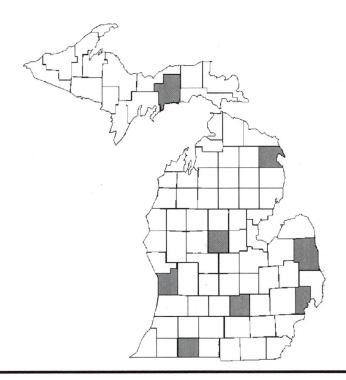

Figure 7.2 Illustration of Cluster Sampling.

Table 7.3 Assignment of Weights for Disproportionate Samples

Rank	Number of Faculty	Percentage of Faculty (%)	Expected Sample Size	Actual Sample Size	Weight
Professor	192	20.8	56	91	0.62
Associate professor	338	36.7	99	90	1.10
Assistant professor	392	42.5	115	90	1.28
Total	922	100.0	271	271	

Table 7.3 presents the faculty rank, number of faculty, expected and actual sample size, and the weight. As column 2 of the table illustrates, 21% of the population is comprised of professors, but faculty with the rank of professor make up 34% of the sample. Rather than trying to increase the sample size for assistant and associate professors, the administration adds weights to make the sample representative of the target population. The weight is used to correct the disproportionate distribution of the results and is calculated by dividing the expected sample size by the actual sample size (column 4 of Table 7.3 divided by column 5). The weight, in the

Table 7.4 Illustration of Applying Weights to Responses

Rank	Actual Sample	Frequency	Percentage	Weight	Weighted Frequency	Weighted Percentage
Professor	91	27	29.7	0.62	17	18.4
Associate professor	90	36	40.0	1.10	40	44.2
Assistant professor	90	54	60.0	1.28	69	76.8
Total	271	117	43.2		126	46.4

last column of Table 7.3, for a group that is overrepresented in the actual sample size will be less than 1, whereas the weight for a group that is underrepresented will be greater than 1.

How do researchers apply weights to the data? The weight is multiplied by the aggregate data to yield a new result, one that proportionately represents the target population. For example, say, the university's administration asks its faculty members if they believe the university's president is doing a good job running the institution. Of the 90 faculty members ranked as assistant professor, 54 said the president is doing a good job. In addition, 36 of the 90 associate professors and 27 of the 91 full professors also responded "yes" to the question. The third column of Table 7.4 lists the frequency (i.e., the number) of positive or "yes" responses. However, because the sample does not appropriately represent the faculty by rank, the frequency is multiplied by its respective weight (column 3 multiplied by column 5). This process yields a new weighted frequency, listed in column 6. Overall, the use of weights corrects the disproportionate representation of samples; the frequencies of the underrepresented groups increase, and the frequencies of the overrepresented groups decrease.

7.3.2 Nonprobability Sampling

Sometimes, researchers do not always have access to a sampling frame or do not know how many elements make up the target population. As a result, researchers use nonprobability sampling techniques. These techniques begin with the researcher, through expertise and judgment, building a sampling model of convenience—a convenience sample—and selecting elements from a population of an unknown size. Nonprobability sampling is common in exploratory research and is generally less expensive and time consuming than conducting a probability sample. However, the findings and results from nonprobability sampling techniques are more difficult to generalize; the nonrandom selection process threatens the design's validity.

For example, suppose the university's administration is interested in its students' food preferences. They hire student researchers to select students walking through the doors at the student center. The student center is used because the restaurants are centralized in this location and, besides the cafeterias in the dorms, it is the only place on campus for students to get food. On any given day, the researchers do not know how many in the entire student body will enter the student center; therefore, the probability of selection is unknown. To decrease the threat of selection bias, researchers could establish a systematic approach so that every 10th student who walks into the student center is selected. However, the probability of selection is still unknown.

Besides the systematic approach, researchers can build certain assurances into their sampling technique to achieve a representative number, or quota, of the different elements of the known population. For the university's survey, if the desired sample size is 500, and student body is 55% female and 45% male, then the researchers can plan to gather responses from 275 females and 225 males. However, when they begin to select the element based on its characteristics rather than separating all the elements into strata and then randomly selecting the elements, the data are threatened by selection bias because of the unknown probability associated with not knowing the size of the target population.

7.3.3 Recap

Overall, sampling saves money; it is less expensive to collect data from 1000 subjects than from 1 million. Sampling saves time; it is faster to collect data from 1000 elements rather than from 1 million. There are many variations of the earlier techniques mentioned, and some researchers combine different methods. However, deciding which method to use goes beyond the factors of time and money and rest on what the manager wants to know.

7.4 Sample Size

When sampling the target population, the confidence researchers have in the accuracy (level of error) of the statistics is linked to the size of the probability sample. Consequently, the sample size depends on the population size (large or small), the homogeneity of the data, the type of data collected (categorical or ratio), as well as the confidence and accuracy levels of the statistics. Moreover, researchers calculate the confidence and accuracy levels of the statistics only when they use probability sampling techniques. However, nonprobability samples have no confidence or accuracy levels.

The confidence level represents the probability that the population parameters are contained within a range of two data points. For example, in a normal bell-shaped curve shown in Figure 7.3, the majority of the data points, 68%, fall within ±1 unit (i.e., standard deviation) from the mean, 95% of the data are within the ±2 standard deviations, and 99%, within ±3 standard deviations.

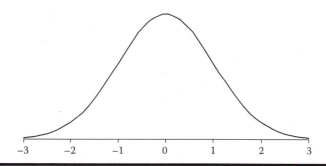

Figure 7.3   The Standard Normal Curve.

What does this mean? Say, the average age for a graduate research methods class is 35 years, with a standard deviation of 4 years. Assuming a normal distribution, we can say the following:

■ 68% of the students are between the ages of 31 and 39 years.
  – mean ± 1 standard deviation.
  – 35 ± 4.
■ 95% are between the ages of 27 and 43 years.
  – mean ± 2 standard deviations.
  – 35 ± (2 × 4).
■ 99.7% of the population is between the ages of 23 and 47 years.
  – mean ± 3 standard deviations.
  – 35 ± (3 × 4).

These numbers, ±1, ±2, ±3, are standardized scores, each representing a probability of confidence. Generally, researchers use whole numbers for confidence levels, such as 90%, 95%, and 99%. The standard scores for these levels are ±1.645, ±1.96, and ±2.575, respectively.

Accuracy is defined as the level of error associated with a sample; the smaller the level of error, the more accurate the statistics. The numerical unit of the margin of error is the same as that of the data. That is, data expressed in percentages report margin of error percentages and continuous data produce a nonpercent, continuous margin of error.

You may have heard or read about the confidence and accuracy levels (the sampling errors) associated with polling organizations. For example, the Gallup News Poll, presented earlier, asked 1001 respondents about acceptable ways to raise funds for presidential campaigns. It says:

> For results based on the total sample of national adults, one can say with *95% confidence* that the maximum margin of *sampling error* is ±4 percentage points.[3]

What does this mean? If researchers collected information from the entire population and compared it to the information collected from a sample, then the findings from the sample would resemble the population. In the preceding illustration, the organization is confident that their statistics resemble the population 95% of the time. In addition, the statistics vary 4% in either direction. For example, from the survey, they find that 80% of the respondents believe presidential candidates should refuse campaign contributions from Washington lobbyists. Given the sampling error, this ranges from 76 to 84%, and the probability that the entire population would feel the same way is 95%. Therefore, they are 95% confident that 76 to 84% of Americans believe presidential candidates should not accept money from lobbyists.

Sometimes margins of errors are reported in nonpercent units. For example, Table 7.5 presents median household incomes and their respective margins of error by state. The median household income for the state of North Carolina is $40,729, with a margin of error of ±321 dollars. Hawaii has a median income of $58,112, with a margin of error of ±1,969 dollars. The same interpretation applies to the nonpercent interval margin of errors. The median household income for the population of North Carolina is between $40,408 and $41,050, whereas the range for Hawaii is $56,143 to $60,081.

Besides the confidence level and accuracy (margin of error), calculating the sample size also depends on the size of the population (large or small). There are two formulas for large populations and two for small populations. Populations with more than 20,000 units are considered large because the sample sizes are roughly the same for any population over 20,000. Therefore, our discussions and illustrations are based on the formulas for large populations.

The final factor researchers use to calculate the sample size is the type of data being collected. The two basic types of data, categorical and continuous, have two separate formulas, and each is based on the variability of the data. We begin with the formula for categorical data.

Researchers use two proportions to measure the variability of categorical data: for example, those who are for and against an issue, and those who support a cause and those who do not. When more than two categories exist, such as race, region of the country, or religion, the categories are reduced to two, such as white and nonwhite, south and not south, or Republican and not Republican. These proportions are substituted in the following formula to calculate the sample size for large populations.

$$ n = \frac{\left[z_{\alpha/2} \right]^2 p(q)}{e^2} \tag{7.1} $$

where

n = sample size
$z_{\alpha/2}$ = level of confidence
p = proportion for
q = proportion against
e = margin of error (as a percentage)

Table 7.5 Illustration of Margin of Errors for Continuous Data, Median Household Income by State, 2005

Rank	State	Median Income	Margin of Error	Rank	State	Median Income	Margin of Error
1	New Jersey	61,672	±526	26	Indiana	43,993	±503
2	Maryland	61,592	±595	27	Nebraska	43,849	±762
3	Connecticut	60,941	±812	28	Iowa	43,609	±520
4	Hawaii	58,112	±1,969	29	Ohio	43,493	±340
5	Massachusetts	57,184	±694	30	Oregon	42,944	±582
6	New Hampshire	56,768	±999	31	Kansas	42,920	±732
7	Alaska	56,234	±1,807	32	Maine	42,801	±969
8	Virginia	54,240	±540	33	Florida	42,433	±272
9	California	53,629	±324	34	Texas	42,139	±247
10	Delaware	52,499	±1,416	35	Missouri	41,974	±360
11	Minnesota	52,024	±366	36	Idaho	41,443	±841
12	Rhode Island	51,458	±1,374	37	North Dakota	41,030	±705
13	Colorado	50,652	±553	38	North Carolina	40,729	±321
14	Illinois	50,260	±338	39	South Dakota	40,310	±890
15	New York	49,480	±422	40	South Carolina	39,316	±614
16	Washington	49,262	±644	41	Montana	39,301	±965
17	Nevada	49,169	±890	42	Tennessee	38,874	±481
18	Utah	47,934	±946	43	New Mexico	37,492	±749
19	Wisconsin	47,105	±394	44	Kentucky	37,369	±479
20	Wyoming	46,202	±1,518	45	Oklahoma	37,063	±566
21	Michigan	46,039	±449	46	Alabama	36,879	±529
22	Vermont	45,686	±1,196	47	Louisiana	36,729	±575
23	Georgia	45,604	±438	48	Arkansas	34,999	±599
24	Pennsylvania	44,537	±392	49	West Virginia	33,452	±801
25	Arizona	44,282	±646	50	Mississippi	32,938	±615

Source: United States Census, 2005 American Community Survey.

The researcher selects the margin of error (*e*) and level of confidence ($z_{\alpha/2}$; we will always use the 95% level of confidence [±1.96] for our calculations), and uses previous studies or available statistics to establish the proportions. When the proportions are unknown, researchers use the most conservative estimate of 50% for and 50% against the issue or 50% of one race and 50% of another race. For example, suppose we want to determine the sample size with which we would be 95% confident that the information collected would vary 3% of the time (i.e., a ±3 margin of error). We know that 50% of the population is against the issue for which we are sampling and 50% are in favor of it. Substituting these numbers in Formula 7.1, we calculate a sample size of 1068 (always round up):

$$n = \frac{1.96^2(.50)(.50)}{0.03^2} = 1067.11$$

By decreasing the accuracy (i.e., increasing the margin of error) from ±3% to ±4%, the sample size is reduced to 601. Table 7.6 illustrates the change in sample size at different margins of error, assuming a 95% confidence level.

Moreover, to improve the accuracy (decrease the margin of error) from 3% to 2%, an additional 1333 elements must be surveyed. Ultimately, the trade-off is between resources (e.g., money and time) and accuracy; the larger the sample, the more expensive and accurate the research. However, to most researchers the cost savings associated with surveying 1068 rather than 2401 might be worth the sacrifice of 1% change in accuracy. This is particularly true of those researchers associated with smaller organizations that cannot afford more elaborate research studies.

The sample size decreases when proportions differ from a 50/50 split, as depicted in Table 7.7, where sample sizes are listed for different proportions and margins of

Table 7.6 Sample Sizes for Various Margins of Error Assuming a 95% Level of Confidence

Margin of Error (e)	Sample Size	Change in Sample Size to Improve Error by 1%
9%	119	
8%	151	32
7%	196	45
6%	267	71
5%	385	118
4%	601	216
3%	1068	467
2%	2401	1333
1%	9604	7203

Table 7.7   Sample Sizes for Various Margins of Error and Proportions

Margin of Error (%)	p/q				
	90/10	*80/20*	*70/30*	*60/40*	*50/50*
1	3,458	6,147	8,068	9,220	9,604
2	865	1,537	2,017	2,305	2,401
3	385	683	897	1,025	1,068
4	217	385	505	577	601
5	139	246	323	369	385
6	97	171	225	257	267
7	71	126	165	189	196
8	55	97	127	145	151
9	43	76	100	114	119
10	35	62	81	93	97

error. For example, the 80/20 split with a 3% margin of error yields a sample size of 683, which results in 385 fewer interviews or surveys than the 50/50 split.

Equation 7.2 is used to calculate the sample size when data are continuous. The formula is as follows.

$$n = \left[\frac{z_{\alpha/2}\sigma}{e} \right]^2 \qquad (7.2)$$

where

n = sample size
$z_{\alpha/2}$ = level of confidence
σ = standard deviation
e = margin of error (as a nonpercent interval)

Unlike Equation 7.1, in which the variability is comprised of proportions (p^*q), here the variability is the standard deviation (σ) of the population. As with proportions, if previous studies were conducted, then researchers would know the standard deviation, but when the standard deviation is unknown, researchers estimate it. To estimate the standard deviation, the difference between the highest and lowest value is determined, and then this value is divided by four. Researchers select a margin or error (e), a nonpercent interval that is acceptable for the sample findings. For example, suppose we want to be 95% confident that the population average income is within $500 of the average income from the sample range. Moreover, we find previous research suggesting an income standard deviation of $7500. We substitute the numbers in Formula 7.2 and calculate a sample size of 865:

$$n = \left[\frac{(1.96)7500}{500} \right]^2 = 864.36$$

If we are willing to sacrifice accuracy, then we can increase the error (e.g., to $750 or even $1000), which will yield smaller sample sizes (e.g., of 385 and 217, respectively).

Formula 7.1 is the one used to determine the sample size where the data are categorical. Where the data are continuous, Formula 7.2 is used. Where the study uses both types of data, the sample size (n) for each formula is calculated, and the formula with the largest sample size is selected. Typically, Formula 7.1 yields a larger sample size. Overall, both equations allow researchers to be as confident and accurate as they would prefer. That is, as confidence and accuracy increase, so does the sample size. In addition, as the population becomes less homogeneous (i.e., the larger its variability), the sample size increases. For example, the Washington Post–Kaiser Family Foundation–Harvard University survey of political independents used a sample of 2140 people to achieve a margin of error of ±3%.[5] However, the sample was broken down into subsets based on party affiliation, each with a sample size and respective margin of error. There were 1014 independents (with an error margin of ±4%), 542 Democrats (margin of error equal to ±5%), and 462 Republicans (margin of error equal to ±5%). As shown in this illustration, the larger the margin of error, the smaller the sample size.

Where populations are very small—fewer than 1000 units—the sample size should be at least half of the population size when margins of error of 3% or smaller are required. Moreover, when studying populations smaller than 500, it is recommended all the units in the population should be included; the information gathered ends up being easier to analyze, and is more accurate and more authoritative than from a small sample of an already small population. Table 7.8 provides a partial list of sample sizes for small populations using proportions. As the population size increases, the sample sizes become similar, particularly at a 3% (or larger) margin of error. A full list of sample sizes is provided in Appendices 7.2 and 7.3.

7.5 Error

Research organizations predicted that the United States would have a President Landon and a President Dewey. If the polling institutions were right, Alf Landon would defeat Franklin Roosevelt in the 1936 presidential race, and Harry Truman would lose the presidential election to Thomas Dewey in 1948. In fact, the *Chicago Daily Tribune* was so certain Dewey would win, it printed the next day's issue before the final tally was in, as shown in Figure 7.4. Why were these organizations

Table 7.8 Sample Size for Small Populations Using Proportionate Data Using 95% Confidence

Margin of Error (%)	Population Size								Large Population Sample Size
	1,000	2,000	3,000	4,000	5,000	10,000	15,000	20,000	
1	906	1,656	2,287	2,825	3,289	4,900	5,856	6,489	9,604
2	707	1,092	1,334	1,501	1,623	1,937	2,070	2,144	2,401
3	517	697	788	843	880	965	997	1,014	1,068
4	376	462	501	523	537	567	578	583	601
5	278	323	341	351	357	370	375	377	385
6	211	236	246	251	254	260	263	264	267
7	165	179	185	187	189	193	194	195	196
8	131	140	143	145	146	148	149	149	151
9	107	112	115	116	116	118	118	118	119
10	88	92	94	94	95	96	96	96	97

Note: The formula for calculating the sample size where the population is small is

$$n = \frac{(z_{\alpha/2})^2 [p(1-p)]N}{(z_{\alpha/2})^2 [p(1-p)] + (N-1)e^2}$$

where N denotes the population size.

Figure 7.4 *Chicago Daily Tribune*, **November 3, 1948.**[6]

wrong when they had been right before? They were wrong because of sampling and nonsampling errors.

Sampling error occurs naturally (i.e., by chance) and is the difference between the measures yielded from the sample and the real results that would occur if all the elements of the population were surveyed. The researcher controls for the sampling error through the sample size (i.e., the larger the sample, the smaller the error). Nonsampling error, on the other hand, results from the improper collection or usage of the sampling data; researchers, not chance, are to blame for the presence of nonsampling error. For example, a nonrandom, unrepresentative, biased sample creates error as does a poorly designed survey question or survey instrument (survey construction is discussed in Chapter 8). In addition, nonsampling error increases when subjects skip questions or refuse to participate. Finally, data entry errors produce nonsampling error. Box 7.1 illustrates the sampling and nonsampling errors associated with the Consumers Price Index (CPI).

Some famous nonsampling errors include the Hawthorne and Rosenthal effects in addition to the predictions of the 1936 and 1948 presidential races as mentioned earlier. The Hawthorne effect describes intentional changes in subjects' behaviors because they know they are involved in a study. We often refer to this as social desirability, which was discussed in previous chapters. Subjects will answer questions, particularly about behaviors, in a way they believe is socially acceptable or desirable. Some examples include participants saying that they only watch 1 hour of television a day, when they really watch 4 hours; graduate students claiming they studied for 4 hours when it was only 1 hour; and patients telling their dentist that they floss once a day. The Rosenthal effect, however, is a result of the experimenter's behaviors and expectations. The experimenter, including the interviewer,

---

**BOX 7.1   SAMPLING AND NONSAMPLING ERRORS
FOR THE CONSUMER PRICE INDEX[7]**

Sampling errors. Because the CPI measures price change based on a sample of items, the published indexes differ somewhat from what the results would be if actual records of all retail purchases by everyone in the index population could be used to compile the index. These estimating or sampling errors are limitations on the precise accuracy of the index, not mistakes in calculating the index. The CPI program has developed measurements of sampling error, which are updated and published annually in the *CPI Detailed Report*. An increased sample size would be expected to increase accuracy, but it would also increase CPI production costs. The CPI sample design allocates the sample in a way that maximizes the accuracy of the index, given the funds available.

    Nonsampling errors. These errors occur from a variety of sources. Unlike sampling errors, they can cause persistent bias in the measurement of the index. Nonsampling errors are caused by problems of price data collection, logistical lags in conducting surveys, difficulties in defining basic concepts and their operational implementation, and difficulties in handling the problems of quality change. Nonsampling errors can be far more hazardous to the accuracy of a price index than sampling errors. The Bureau of Labor Statistics (BLS) expends much effort to minimize these errors. Highly trained personnel ensure the comparability of quality of items from period to period; collection procedures are extensively documented. The CPI program has an ongoing research and evaluation program to identify and implement improvements in the index.

---

can unintentionally manipulate the subjects, particularly through the researchers' or interviewers' actions and attitudes, to elicit an answer or obtain a result.

    Many researchers argue that errors in the aforementioned presidential election predictions resulted from the use of nonprobability sampling. For the 1936 election, the *Literary Digest* distributed 10 million ballots to voters across the country. The names were acquired from phone lists of subscribers to the *Digest* as well as automobile owners. In the 1930s, many voters did not own telephones or automobiles, so the sampling frame was biased, because it was not representative of the voters. However, the pollsters at the *Literary Digest* claimed otherwise. They argued that they went out of their way to get less-affluent voters, surveying most registered voters and systematically selecting others, for example, every third person in Chicago. So, what went wrong in 1936? Voluntary participation was the problem. Of the 10 million people who received the survey, 2.3 million people responded. No matter how random and representative the sampling procedure, voluntary participation threatens the validity of any research design.[8]

The error in the 1948 election is blamed on a demographic shift not accounted for in the sampling procedure. Pollsters used decade-old demographic information to guide their sampling process in the election. By 1948, the demographics of the United States were much different from the decade before. The mean center of the population moved southwest from Sullivan County, Indiana, to Richland County, Illinois, as more people moved from the Midwest and Northeast to the western part of the United States.[9] Therefore, too many people were sampled in areas losing population, whereas too few were included from the West.

Overall, representative samples are best achieved when researchers use a probability sample. A large sample with a small sampling error maintains reliability and validity, which helps generalize the findings to other settings, times, and people. However, the accuracy of and confidence in the data are diminished when participation is voluntary, when nonresponses are present, poor question quality exists, data entry errors occur, and/or improper sampling techniques are used. One or more of these nonsampling errors are most likely to be present in any research project.

7.6 Reaching Respondents and Improving Response Rates

A major problem researchers face in the data collection process is reaching respondents. For example, organizations conducting phone interviews need to find a phone number, call the person, ask for the appropriate person in the household, and secure the subject's participation. Similar issues arise with self-administered surveys—the researchers have to locate the correct address and trust that the respondent opens the mail, responds to the survey, and returns it by a particular date.

Unfortunately, the sampling techniques miss some elements of the population. With phone interviews, the elements most missed are those with unlisted numbers, those who do not have a landline phone, and those who screen their calls. To reach those with unlisted numbers, researchers use random digit dialing—a computer program generating lists of numbers. This is not a cure-all, as some of the generated numbers are not useable—they are business numbers, fax numbers, unassigned numbers, or numbers of households with multiple phone lines. However, answering machines, caller identification, and call blocking as well as the federal *Do Not Call List* decreases the likelihood that someone will answer the phone.

According to the Pew Research Center, 78% of households have answering machines, 51% have caller ID, and 18% subscribe to privacy managers (i.e., call blocking).[10] However, they argue that the majority of these households with caller ID do not use it to screen calls, suggesting that the reliability and validity of the data remain representative and generalizable.

Table 7.9   Characteristics of Households without a Landline Phone[11]

Household Characteristic	Percentage of Households	
	With Only Cell Phone	*With No Phone*
Central city dweller	8.1	7.2
Nonmetro city dweller		7.0
Rented dwelling	12.8	10.9
Multiunit dwelling	12.6	10.1
18–24 years old	20.1	12.6
Hispanic	7.3	10.2
Black non-Hispanic		8.8
Not married adults	11.1	7.7
Adults with less than high school degree		11.9

Source: Tucker, C., Brink, J. M., and Meekins, B. (2007), *Public Opinion Quarterly, 71*, p. 10.

Moreover, their research reveals that only 37% of the respondents claim they screen calls most or all of the time. As for the individuals who screen their calls, the Pew Center claims these people are the most difficult to get to answer the phone; that is, the organization has to call 20 or more times to get the "difficult" ones to answer. After 20 or more calls, perhaps respondents feel the only way for the organization to stop calling is to answer the phone and participate; they feel coerced. In the end, the organization bullies respondents into participating, creating a lack of enthusiasm and interest on the part of the respondent. How valid and reliable do you suppose are these responses?

Who are other potential respondents overlooked by researchers? Researchers also miss people without a landline or cell phone. Table 7.9 lists the percentage points of certain households with only a cell phone and those with no phone altogether. Studies estimate that 11% of the households are without a landline phone.[11] Who are these people without a landline phone? The authors say they are likely to be uneducated (less than a high school education), central city dwellers who rent, Hispanic, young (18–24 years old), or unmarried adults.[11]

As with phone interviews, potential respondents are missed when researchers distribute surveys at an onsite location, through the mail or e-mail or via the Web. Onsite surveys miss those who do not visit the site at the time of the interview. The distribution process of mail surveys misses those who have a post office box or have moved with no forwarding address. E-mail and Web-based surveys do not get to respondents with no Internet access—they resemble those who do not have a landline. Researchers use weights to correct for the undercoverage of certain groups, but if the target population is any of these groups, which often it is in public and nonprofit administration, researchers miss a large piece of the population.

Once researchers are able to get respondents to answer their phones or open their mail, the next step is to get the respondents to participate. The literature provides 11 different ways to improve response rates for self-administered surveys, but the first 6 also apply to interviews:[12]

1. Include a monetary incentive or other form of compensation.
2. Keep the length of the survey/interview short.
3. Send out a prenotification letter.
4. Send a follow-up reminder.
5. When possible, include endorsements and/or sponsors.
6. Always guarantee confidentiality.
7. Address the letter with a personal salutation.
8. Sign the letter with pen, not a stamp.
9. Include a postage-paid, self-addressed envelope for the survey's return.
10. List the return address on the survey.
11. Provide a deadline for completion.

The list is relatively self-explanatory, but for self-administered surveys, response rates are improved when the survey is short and guarantees confidentiality. These are the first things respondents notice—the cover letter addressing confidentiality and the length of the survey.

A prenotification letter helps improve response rates. These letters inform subjects about an impending survey or interview, when it will arrive or occur, how they were selected, who or what organization is conducting the research, and the importance of the research. Box 7.2 illustrates the letter used by the United States Census Bureau prior to conducting interviews for the Community Population Survey.

After the initial distribution of self-administered surveys, the majority of responses for mail questionnaires will be returned within 10 to 14 days, but within a couple of days for e-mail and Web surveys. As a reminder, researchers send out follow-up letters or postcards to everyone where anonymity exists or to the nonrespondents 1 to 2 weeks after the initial distribution of the survey (see Box 7.3). If the reminder does not yield more responses, then researchers sometimes send out the entire survey again.

Another strategy to improve response rates is to include an incentive. A monetary incentive is an amount of money paid to respondents and is included in the survey or promised upon the return of a completed survey. Other forms of compensation exist, such as coupons, drawings for a big-ticket item such as a television or MP3 player, a $100 bill, or extra credit for the psychology class. The incentive acts as a sign of gratitude—the researcher showing appreciation for the respondent's involvement—but its underlying purpose is to encourage participation.

**BOX 7.2   PRENOTIFICATION LETTER FROM THE
UNITED STATES BUREAU OF THE CENSUS**

**FROM THE DIRECTOR
BUREAU OF THE CENSUS**[13]

You may have read in the newspaper—or heard on the radio or television—
that official Government figures on total employment and unemployment are issued each month. The Census Bureau obtains these figures, as
well as information about persons not in the labor force, from the Current
Population Survey (CPS). This information, which we collect for the Bureau
of Labor Statistics, provides vital up-to-date estimates of the number of persons working, the number who are unemployed, and many other related
facts. Occasionally, we ask additional questions on education, health, family
income, housing, and other important subjects.

A Census Bureau representative, who will show an official identification
card, will call on you during the week in which the 19th of the month falls. The
representative will ask questions concerning the ages, employment status, and
occupations of the members of your household, as well as other related information. By law, Census Bureau employees hold all information you give in strict
confidence. Your answers will be used only for statistical purposes in a manner
in which no information about you as an individual can be identified.

We have selected your address and about 48,000 others throughout the
United States for this survey. Because this is a sample survey, your answers
represent not only yourself and your household, but also hundreds of other
households like yours. For this reason, your participation in this voluntary
survey is extremely important to ensure the completeness and accuracy of the
final results. Although there are no penalties for failure to answer any questions, each unanswered question lessens the accuracy of the final data. Your
cooperation will be a distinct service to our country.

Thank you for your cooperation.

Sincerely,

The Bureau of the Census

The incentive provided to respondents should reflect the amount of time necessary to complete the survey. That is, where the subject matter is of little interest
to the respondent and the survey takes 10 minutes to complete, an incentive of a
dollar would suffice. However, if the survey takes more of the respondent's time,
a larger incentive might be necessary. Incentives are most useful for sit-down,
lengthy, face-to-face interviews but help improve response rates for all types of
surveys. Some researchers compensate participants $10 to $20 for an hour-long (or

BOX 7.3 EXAMPLE OF A FOLLOW-UP POSTCARD FROM THE UNITED STATES CENSUS BUREAU[14]

UNITED STATES DEPARTMENT OF COMMERCE
Economics and Statistics Administration
U.S. Census Bureau
Washington, DC 20233-0001
OFFICE OF THE DIRECTOR

Dear Resident:

A few days ago, you should have received an American Community Survey questionnaire. If you have already mailed it back, thank you. If you have not, please send it soon.

Local and national leaders use the information from this survey for planning schools, hospitals, roads, and other community needs.

If you need help filling out the questionnaire or have questions, please call our toll-free number (1-800-354-7271).

Sincerely,

Charles Louis Kincannon
Director, U.S. Census Bureau

ACS-20S (1-2003)

longer) sit-down, face-to-face interview; respondents have to be compensated for their time, and the longer the interview, the larger the incentive ought to be.

The incentive also depends on the occupation, particularly income levels, of the target population. For example, if the target population consists of medical doctors, then an incentive larger than a dollar might be necessary to compensate and encourage them to participate in a survey that takes 15 minutes to complete. On the other hand, a dollar might be incentive enough for a target population comprising college students.

The incentive should not be too large, though, to compromise the data; the respondent should remain impartial (not change answers) regardless of the amount offered. The validity and reliability of the study run the risk of increased threats where compensation is viewed as buying answers. For example, suppose a company with which you are familiar and from which you purchase products offers you $50 to participate in their 10-minute consumer satisfaction survey. Would you be as impartial as if they had offered you no incentive? Questions would surely arise about the quality of the data received where large incentives were included.

Overall, incentives as small as a dollar and included in the initial mailing have been shown to significantly improve response rates or do a better job at improving response rates than nearly everything else listed previously. In addition, incentives help defray data collection costs, particularly the costs associated with mail surveys. By including a dollar in the initial mailing, researchers might improve response rates beyond what follow-up reminders could produce. However, the promise of an incentive (for example, being entered in a drawing or sending a dollar or two upon the receipt of the completed survey) does not increase response rates.

Finally, questionnaires from familiar organizations or about known topics such as a citizen or customer satisfaction survey—those most often conducted in public and nonprofit administration—are more likely to have higher response rates without incentives because of the familiarity with the organization or genuine interest on the part of the respondent. Accordingly, there is little reason to provide an incentive with such a questionnaire.

7.7 Summary

The sampling process uses either a probability or nonprobability technique and includes defining the target population and sampling frame. If the purpose of the research is to explore and not generalize, then a nonprobability sample is acceptable; when researchers plan to describe and generalize to a larger population, probability sampling is required. However, probability sampling is not perfect and has shortcomings; for example, researchers cannot reach everyone, participation is voluntary, or too few people participate. Nevertheless, researchers employ a variety of techniques to increase the response rates. For example, The Pew Research Center for the People and the Press call the same phone number as many as 10 times when conducting phone interviews.[15]

Overall, researchers use a combination of techniques, such as drawing samples from both phone and mail surveys, to improve the validity and reliability of the results. For example, the Census Bureau uses phone interviews and face-to-face interviews to collect information from a sample of 50,000 people. Box 7.4 presents their sampling approach.

In the end, time and money are the final determinants of the sampling process, which is why researchers with limited resources typically use self-administered surveys and smaller sample sizes.

BOX 7.4   SAMPLING METHODS FOR THE UNITED STATES CENSUS BUREAU[16]

Estimates from the CPS [Community Population Survey] are based upon a probability sample of about 50,000 housing units. Each month, interviewers contact the sampled units to obtain basic demographic information about all persons residing at the address and detailed labor force information for all persons aged 15 or over.

To improve the reliability of estimates of month-to-month and year-to-year change, 8 panels are used to rotate the sample each month. A sample unit is interviewed for four consecutive months, and then, after an 8-month rest period, for the same four months a year later. Each month a new panel of addresses, or one-eighth of the total sample, is introduced. Thus, in a particular month, one panel is being interviewed for the first time, one panel for the second, . . . , and one panel for the eighth and final time.

Interviewers use lap-top computers to administer the interview, asking questions as they appear on the screen and directly entering the responses obtained. The first and the fifth month-in-sample interviews are almost always conducted by an interviewer who visits the sample unit. Over 90 percent of month-in-sample 2 through 4 and 6 through 8 interviews are conducted by telephone, either by the same interviewer or by an interviewer working at one of 3 centralized telephone interviewing centers.

Completed interviews are electronically transmitted to a central processor where the responses are edited for consistency, imputations are made for missing data, and various codes are added. Based on the probability of selection, a weight is added to each household and person record so that estimates of the population by state, race, age, sex, and Hispanic origin match the population projections made by the Bureau of the Census each month.

To improve estimates of month-to-month change, a composite estimator is used that incorporates data from prior months. Many of the summary labor force estimates are also seasonally adjusted to facilitate month-to-month comparisons.

Key Terms

Accuracy	Parameters	Selection bias
Confidence level	Probability sampling	Simple random sample
Convenience sample	Random numbers	Social desirability
Cluster sample	Response rates	Statistics
Elements	Rosenthal effect	Stratified random sample
Hawthorne effect	Sample size	Systematic sample
Nonprobability sampling	Sampling error	Target population
Nonsampling error	Sampling frame	Validity

Exercises

1. What are some potential sampling errors associated with onsite interviews, which were discussed in Chapter 6?
2. What can be said about the generalizability and causality of research designs that use a nonprobability sampling technique? What about a probability sample? Consider placing each in the context of voluntary participation.
3. When would a nonprobability sample be used or be useful?
4. Do Internet pop-up surveys employ probability sampling techniques? What about phone-in or log-on surveys (such as *American Idol*, *Dancing with the Stars*, or local news stations asking about your opinion)? Explain.
5. Find a recent poll and its results conducted by any organization. Does the article explain the sampling process, sample size, and margin of error? In your opinion, can the results be generalized? Explain.
6. Design a sampling technique useful for your organization. Which type of sampling technique and formula, if any, would you use and why? Besides the number (the sample size), what other factors would you consider when designing your sampling technique?

Recommended Reading

Dillman, Don A. (2006). *Mail and Internet Surveys: The Tailored Design Method*. New York: John Wiley.

Dillman, Don A. (1978). *Mail and Telephone Surveys*. New York: John Wiley.

Sudman, S. and Bradburn, N. M. (1974). *Response Effects in Surveys: A Review and Synthesis*. Chicago: Aldine Publishing.

Sudman, S. and Bradburn, N. M. (1988). *Polls and Surveys: Understanding What They Tell Us*. San Francisco: Jossey-Bass.

Sudman, S., Bradburn, N. M., and Schwarz, N. (1996). *Thinking about Answers: The Application of Cognitive Processes to Survey Methodology*. San Francisco: Jossey-Bass.

Appendix 7.1

Generating Random Numbers in Microsoft Excel: An Illustration

We can select the appropriate number of units using the random number formula in Excel. In our example discussed earlier in the chapter, we wanted to select seven elements from the following sampling frame:

01. Abby	05. Elaine	09. Irene	13. Mike	17. Quentin
02. Bill	06. Fred	10. Jerry	14. Nicky	18. Robert
03. Carl	07. George	11. Kim	15. Oliver	19. Sophie
04. Donna	08. Hope	12. Lynn	16. Pam	20. Tony

The random number formula is as follows:

$$=RANDBETWEEN(a,b)$$

where a is the lowest number in the sampling frame, and b is the highest number. To accomplish this in Excel 2003 or 2007, follow these instructions:

For the simple random sample, we would substitute 1 for a and 20 for b, for example,

After typing the formula, hit the enter key, and a number will appear. Remember: in Excel formulas, always begin with an equal sign.

This formula generates only one random number at a time, but we need seven for our sample. To yield more numbers, copy the information from cell A1 to the cells in the following Excel sheet until the desired sample size is achieved.

	A	B	C
1	13		
2	6		
3	12		
4	7		
5	7		
6	12		
7	9		
8			
9			

If the same number appears twice, as it does in the preceding cells, place the cursor in an open cell and hit the delete key. A new list of seven randomly generated numbers appears; do this until all seven numbers are different, as in the following:

	A	B	C
1	1		
2	8		
3	11		
4	10		
5	9		
6	7		
7	5		
8			
9			

Using this approach and these numbers, we select the following subjects from the sample frame: Abby, Hope, Kim, Jerry, Irene, George, and Elaine.

Besides the formula, Excel provides a random number generator for any given type of distribution (e.g., uniform, normal, discrete, and so on), which is useful when sample sizes are large. The most useful distributions for practitioners are the discrete and uniform distributions. We begin by explaining the process for discrete distributions.

For generating a discrete number, first we have to enter each of the numbers represented in the sampling frame along with the probability of selection. When the sampling frame is large, this exercise can take some time, but it becomes easy with the copy/paste and fill tools provided by Excel. For our example, there are 20 units in our target population, and each unit has a 1-in-20 chance (or a 5% probability) of being selected. Therefore, we enter this information in columns A and B as illustrated to the right.

	A	B
1	Number	Probability
2	1	0.05
3	2	0.05
4	3	0.05
5	4	0.05
6	5	0.05
7	6	0.05
8	7	0.05
9	8	0.05
10	9	0.05
11	10	0.05
12	11	0.05
13	12	0.05
14	13	0.05
15	14	0.05
16	15	0.05
17	16	0.05
18	17	0.05
19	18	0.05
20	19	0.05
21	20	0.05

Next, the Data Analysis option is selected. In Excel 2003, this is located under the Tools option of the toolbar as illustrated to the right. In Excel 2007, Data Analysis will be located on the far right, top side, at the end of the tool boxes.

If your computer does not have the Data Analysis option, then it needs to be added now. To do this in Excel 2003, select Add-ins from the Tools menu. An Add-in box appears. In this box, check the Analysis ToolPak and Analysis ToolPak VBA options and then click OK. If done correctly, Data Analysis will appear at the bottom of the Tools menu, as shown below.

To add Data Analysis in Excel 2007, click the Microsoft Office button, and then click Excel Options. Next click Add-ins, and then, in the Manage Box that appears, choose Excel Add-ins and click Go. In the Add-ins box, select Analysis ToolPak and Analysis ToolPak VBA, then click OK. If done correctly, Data Analysis will appear at the far right end of the Data tab as shown below.

Upon selection of the Data Analysis option in either version, a Data Analysis dialog box appears, as shown in the following Excel illustration. A number of statistical procedures are listed, including Random Number Generation.

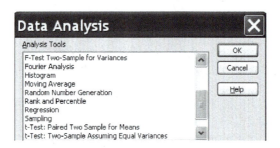

Click on the Random Number Generation option and select OK, and the box shown below appears. We have a number of distribution options to select from: we want seven discrete (whole) numbers to be generated, so we select Discrete distribution.

Next, we enter the requested information—one variable, seven random numbers, discrete distribution, the range (A2:B21) of the values and probabilities inserted earlier (note: do not include the title cells), and enter the location for the output; here, C2 is selected. Finally, select OK. This process is illustrated next.

	A	B	Random Number Generation ✕
1	Number	Probablity	
2	1	0.05	Number of Variables: [1] [OK]
3	2	0.05	Number of Random Numbers: [7] [Cancel]
4	3	0.05	Distribution: [Discrete ▾] [Help]
5	4	0.05	Parameters
6	5	0.05	Value and Probability Input Range:
7	6	0.05	[$A$2:$B$21]
8	7	0.05	
9	8	0.05	
10	9	0.05	
11	10	0.05	
12	11	0.05	
13	12	0.05	Random Seed: [ ]
14	13	0.05	Output options
15	14	0.05	⦿ Output Range: [$C$2]
16	15	0.05	◯ New Worksheet Ply: [ ]
17	16	0.05	◯ New Workbook
18	17	0.05	
19	18	0.05	
20	19	0.05	
21	20	0.05	

Excel generates the following numbers located in C2 through C8.

	A	B	C	D
1	Number	Probability	Select	
2	1	0.05	2	
3	2	0.05	3	
4	3	0.05	9	
5	4	0.05	17	
6	5	0.05	5	
7	6	0.05	14	
8	7	0.05	16	
9	8	0.05		
10	9	0.05		
11	10	0.05		
12	11	0.05		
13	12	0.05		
14	13	0.05		
15	14	0.05		
16	15	0.05		
17	16	0.05		
18	17	0.05		
19	18	0.05		
20	19	0.05		
21	20	0.05		

Using the generated numbers, the following are selected as the random sample: Bill, Carl, Quentin, Irene, Quentin, Elaine, Nicky, and Pam.

We can also use uniform distribution to generate a number. This method does not require us to enter the number of units and their respective probabilities, as with discrete distribution. However, it does not produce discrete numbers; rather, it produces continuous numbers (those with decimals). This is not a problem because Excel rounds off numbers with the click of a button. Uniform distribution generates as many numbers as needed, typically the sample size, in an equal fashion. This is particularly useful with large sampling frames. For example, if the sampling frame is 1000, uniform distribution generates approximately the same number of random numbers ranging from 1 to 100 as 101 to 200, 201 to 300, and so on. The procedure for generating a uniform distribution of random numbers is illustrated as follows.

To generate uniform numbers, select Uniform from the list of options in the Random Number Generation box. Then, enter the necessary information: one variable and seven random numbers, ranging from 1 to 20. Next, select a location for the output. Finally, select OK.

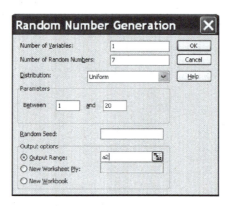

This process yields the following random numbers. Notice the decimal places. We can use the decrease decimal button to create whole numbers. This process is illustrated as follows.

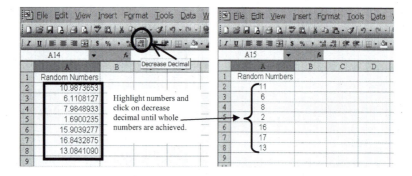

Using the generated numbers, the following are selected as the random sample: Kim, Fred, Hope, Bill, Pam, Quentin, and Mike.

Overall, each approach yields a random sample, summarized as follows:

Random number formula	Discrete distribution	Uniform distribution
Abby	Bill	Bill
Elaine	Carl	Fred
George	Elaine	Hope
Hope	Irene	Kim
Irene	Nicky	Mike
Jerry	Pam	Pam
Kim	Quentin	Quentin

Appendix 7.2

Sample Size for Small Populations (50,000 or Less) Using Proportionate Data and a 95% Confidence Level

Population Size	Margin of Error									
	1%	2%	3%	4%	5%	6%	7%	8%	9%	10%
1,000	906	707	517	376	278	211	165	131	107	88
2,000	1,656	1,092	697	462	323	236	179	140	112	92
3,000	2,287	1,334	788	501	341	246	185	143	115	94
4,000	2,825	1,501	843	523	351	251	187	145	116	94
5,000	3,289	1,623	880	537	357	254	189	146	116	95
6,000	3,694	1,715	907	546	362	256	190	147	117	95
7,000	4,050	1,788	927	553	365	258	191	147	117	95
8,000	4,365	1,847	942	559	367	259	192	148	117	95
9,000	4,647	1,896	955	563	369	260	192	148	118	96
10,000	4,900	1,937	965	567	370	260	193	148	118	96
11,000	5,128	1,971	973	570	372	261	193	149	118	96
12,000	5,335	2,001	981	572	373	261	193	149	118	96
13,000	5,524	2,027	987	574	374	262	194	149	118	96
14,000	5,697	2,050	992	576	374	262	194	149	118	96
15,000	5,856	2,070	997	578	375	263	194	149	118	96
16,000	6,002	2,088	1,001	579	376	263	194	149	118	96
17,000	6,138	2,104	1,005	580	376	263	194	149	118	96
18,000	6,263	2,119	1,008	581	377	263	194	149	118	96
19,000	6,380	2,132	1,011	582	377	264	195	149	118	96
20,000	6,489	2,144	1,014	583	377	264	195	149	118	96
21,000	6,591	2,155	1,016	584	378	264	195	150	118	96
22,000	6,686	2,165	1,018	585	378	264	195	150	118	96
23,000	6,776	2,175	1,020	586	378	264	195	150	118	96
24,000	6,860	2,183	1,022	586	379	264	195	150	118	96
25,000	6,939	2,191	1,024	587	379	264	195	150	119	96
26,000	7,014	2,199	1,026	587	379	265	195	150	119	96
27,000	7,085	2,205	1,027	588	379	265	195	150	119	96
28,000	7,152	2,212	1,028	588	379	265	195	150	119	96
29,000	7,215	2,218	1,030	589	380	265	195	150	119	96
30,000	7,276	2,224	1,031	589	380	265	195	150	119	96
31,000	7,333	2,229	1,032	589	380	265	195	150	119	96
32,000	7,388	2,234	1,033	590	380	265	195	150	119	96
33,000	7,440	2,239	1,034	590	380	265	195	150	119	96
34,000	7,489	2,243	1,035	590	380	265	195	150	119	96
35,000	7,537	2,247	1,036	591	380	265	195	150	119	96
36,000	7,582	2,251	1,037	591	381	265	195	150	119	96

(continued)

Population Size	Margin of Error									
	1%	2%	3%	4%	5%	6%	7%	8%	9%	10%
37,000	7,626	2,255	1,038	591	381	265	195	150	119	96
38,000	7,667	2,259	1,038	591	381	265	195	150	119	96
39,000	7,707	2,262	1,039	592	381	265	196	150	119	96
40,000	7,745	2,266	1,040	592	381	266	196	150	119	96
41,000	7,782	2,269	1,041	592	381	266	196	150	119	96
42,000	7,817	2,272	1,041	592	381	266	196	150	119	96
43,000	7,851	2,275	1,042	592	381	266	196	150	119	96
44,000	7,884	2,277	1,042	593	381	266	196	150	119	96
45,000	7,915	2,280	1,043	593	381	266	196	150	119	96
46,000	7,946	2,282	1,043	593	381	266	196	150	119	96
47,000	7,975	2,285	1,044	593	382	266	196	150	119	96
48,000	8,003	2,287	1,044	593	382	266	196	150	119	96
49,000	8,031	2,289	1,045	593	382	266	196	150	119	96
50,000	8,057	2,292	1,045	594	382	266	196	150	119	96
1,000,000	9,513	2,396	1,066	600	385	267	196	151	119	97
5,000,000	9,586	2,400	1,067	601	385	267	196	151	119	97

Appendix 7.3
Sample Size for Small Populations (50,000 or Less) Using Proportionate Data and a 99% Confidence Level

Population Size	Margin of Error									
	1%	2%	3%	4%	5%	6%	7%	8%	9%	10%
1,000	944	806	649	510	399	316	253	206	171	143
2,000	1,785	1,350	960	683	499	375	290	230	186	154
3,000	2,541	1,741	1,142	771	544	400	305	239	192	158
4,000	3,223	2,036	1,262	824	569	414	312	244	195	160
5,000	3,842	2,267	1,347	859	586	422	317	247	197	161
6,000	4,406	2,452	1,410	884	598	428	321	249	198	162
7,000	4,922	2,604	1,459	903	606	433	323	250	199	162
8,000	5,397	2,731	1,498	918	613	436	325	251	200	163
9,000	5,834	2,838	1,530	930	618	439	327	252	201	163
10,000	6,238	2,931	1,556	939	622	441	328	253	201	164
11,000	6,613	3,011	1,578	947	626	442	329	254	201	164
12,000	6,962	3,081	1,597	954	629	444	330	254	202	164
13,000	7,287	3,143	1,614	960	631	445	330	254	202	164

Population Size	Margin of Error									
	1%	2%	3%	4%	5%	6%	7%	8%	9%	10%
14,000	7,591	3,198	1,628	965	634	446	331	255	202	164
15,000	7,875	3,248	1,641	970	636	447	331	255	202	164
16,000	8,142	3,292	1,652	974	637	448	332	255	203	165
17,000	8,394	3,333	1,662	977	639	449	332	256	203	165
18,000	8,630	3,369	1,671	980	640	449	333	256	203	165
19,000	8,854	3,403	1,680	983	641	450	333	256	203	165
20,000	9,065	3,433	1,687	986	642	451	333	256	203	165
21,000	9,265	3,462	1,694	988	643	451	333	256	203	165
22,000	9,454	3,488	1,700	990	644	452	334	257	203	165
23,000	9,634	3,512	1,706	992	645	452	334	257	203	165
24,000	9,805	3,535	1,711	994	646	452	334	257	203	165
25,000	9,968	3,555	1,716	995	646	453	334	257	203	165
26,000	10,123	3,575	1,721	997	647	453	334	257	204	165
27,000	10,272	3,593	1,725	998	648	453	335	257	204	165
28,000	10,413	3,610	1,729	1,000	648	454	335	257	204	165
29,000	10,548	3,627	1,732	1,001	649	454	335	257	204	165
30,000	10,678	3,642	1,736	1,002	649	454	335	257	204	165
31,000	10,802	3,656	1,739	1,003	650	454	335	257	204	165
32,000	10,921	3,670	1,742	1,004	650	454	335	257	204	165
33,000	11,035	3,682	1,745	1,005	651	455	335	257	204	165
34,000	11,144	3,695	1,748	1,006	651	455	335	258	204	165
35,000	11,250	3,706	1,750	1,007	651	455	336	258	204	165
36,000	11,351	3,717	1,753	1,008	652	455	336	258	204	166
37,000	11,448	3,727	1,755	1,008	652	455	336	258	204	166
38,000	11,542	3,737	1,757	1,009	652	455	336	258	204	166
39,000	11,633	3,747	1,759	1,010	652	456	336	258	204	166
40,000	11,720	3,756	1,761	1,010	653	456	336	258	204	166
41,000	11,805	3,764	1,763	1,011	653	456	336	258	204	166
42,000	11,886	3,773	1,765	1,012	653	456	336	258	204	166
43,000	11,965	3,780	1,767	1,012	654	456	336	258	204	166
44,000	12,041	3,788	1,768	1,013	654	456	336	258	204	166
45,000	12,115	3,795	1,770	1,013	654	456	336	258	204	166
46,000	12,186	3,802	1,771	1,014	654	456	336	258	204	166
47,000	12,255	3,809	1,773	1,014	654	457	336	258	204	166
48,000	12,322	3,815	1,774	1,015	655	457	336	258	204	166
49,000	12,387	3,822	1,776	1,015	655	457	336	258	204	166
50,000	12,450	3,828	1,777	1,016	655	457	337	258	204	166
1,000,000	16,307	4,128	1,839	1,035	663	461	339	259	205	166
5,000,000	16,522	4,141	1,842	1,036	663	461	339	259	205	166

Endnotes

1. U.S. Department of Commerce (2002). *Measuring America: The Decennial Censuses from 1790–2000*. Appendix A. Accessed from http://www.census.gov/prod/2002pubs/pol02-ma.pdf.

2. U.S. Census Bureau, http://www.census.gov/acsd/www/history.html.

3. Newport, F. and Carroll, J. (2007, August 29). Most say that presidential candidates should refuse lobbyist money: Majority says that Hillary Clinton should refuse. Gallup Poll News Service. http://www.galluppoll.com/content/default.aspx?ci=28543.

4. U.S. Census Bureau, *American FactFinder*. http://factfinder.census.gov/servlet/QTTable?_bm=y&-geo_id=01000US&-qr_name=DEC_2000_SF1_U_QTP1&-ds_name=DEC_2000_SF1_U.

5. Washington Post–Kaiser Foundation–Harvard University (2007). Survey of Political Independents. http://www.washingtonpost.com/wp-srv/politics/interactives/independents/post-kaiser-harvard-topline.pdf.

6. American Treasure Exhibit, Library of Congress. http://www.loc.gov/exhibits/treasures/trm145.htm/

7. Bureau of Labor Statistics. *Frequently Asked Questions*. http://www.bls.gov/cpi/cpifaq.htm. Accessed November 19, 2007.

8. Bryson, M.C. (1976). The Literary Digest poll: Making of a statistical myth. *The American Statistician, 30*, 184–185.

9. Hobbs, F. and Stoops, N. (2002). Demographic trends in the 20th Century. Washington, D.C.: United States Bureau of the Census, pp. 17, 19. http://www.census.gov/prod/2002pubs/censr-4.pdf.

10. The Pew Center for Research (2004). Study experiment shows: Polls face growing resistance but still representative. Washington, D.C.: The Pew Center for Research for the People and the Press, pp. 9–10.

11. Tucker, C., Brink, J. M., and Meekins, B. (2007). Household telephone service and usage patterns in the United States in 2004: Implications for telephone surveys. *Public Opinion Quarterly, 71*, 3–22.

12. Rochford, L. and Venable, C.F. (1995). Surveying a targeted population segment: The effects of endorsement on mail questionnaire response rates. *Journal of Marketing, Theory and Practice* (Spring), 86–97. This article summarizes the literature on improving response rates.

13. United States Bureau of the Census (2002). Current Population Survey Technical Paper 63RV Design and Methodology. Figure 7-1, p. 62. http://www.census.gov/prod/2002pubs/tp63rv.pdf.

14. United States Census Bureau (2006). Design and methodology: American Community Survey, p. B-76. Available at http://www.census.gov/acs/www/Downloads/tp67.pdf.

15. Visit http://people-press.org/reports/methodology.php3 to review the sampling methods used by The Pew Research Center for the People and the Press.

16. United States Bureau of the Census. http://www.bls.census.gov/cps/bmethovr.htm. See the Census Bureau's Technical Paper 63RV available at http://www.census.gov/prod/2002pubs/tp63rv.pdf for a more detailed presentation of the sampling methodology.

Chapter 8

Questionnaire Construction

8.1 Introduction

Questionnaires—or surveys, as they are sometimes called—are the tools researchers use to measure the variables of interest; they measure what we want to know. Questionnaires ask people to answer questions or reply to statements based on:

1. What people are—their characteristics such as age, gender, ethnicity
2. How people think—their beliefs and attitudes
3. How people act—their behaviors
4. What people know—their knowledge

Suppose, for example, a township clerk is interested in knowing some information about the township's residents. In addition, she wants to use a variety of questions designed specifically to maintain validity and reliability. How does she construct a survey to accomplish this? Should she just create and administer a list of questions? No, she should not create the questionnaire without first developing a plan. If she does develop the survey without a plan, the survey might look similar to the one shown in Box 8.1. Although the survey might appear valid and likely to produce reliable data, the clerk violated a number of questionnaire development rules.

Researchers need to understand that the steps in the research process are not mutually exclusive. When we ask, "How are we going to measure what we want to

BOX 8.1 TOWNSHIP SURVEY

Township Community Survey

Did you know we have a Web site? Yes_____ No_____

Have you used it? Yes_____ No_____

Is the Township Office open enough hours for you to: Pay taxes, purchase dog licenses, purchase building permits, pay sewer bills, register to vote, notarize papers, or just get needed information? Yes_____ No_____

If no, what hours would you suggest?_____

Have you used the Township Park located on Main St.? Yes_____ No_____

What did you like or dislike about the park?_____

_____

How well do you feel our 1.45 extra voted mileage for road maintenance is doing to keep up the repairs on our roads?

   Good_____ Fair_____ Poor_____ Not Sure_____

Would you support our township funding maintenance of border roads currently under the jurisdiction of the neighboring county? Yes_____ No_____

How important is the Community Policing Service we contract with the county's sheriff's department at a cost of $14,000 for 8 hours per week to you?

Very important_____ Somewhat important_____ Not important_____

Not sure_____

Do you feel our zoning ordinance is effective? Yes_____ No_____

Do you feel it is being enforced fairly? Yes_____ No_____

Do you see areas in the Township that need to be improved?

   Yes_____ No_____

If yes, please specify_____

_____

Do you feel we have enough information in our Township Newsletter?

   Yes_____ No_____

If no, what other items of information would you like us to include?_____

_____

Cemeteries: Did you know we have 3—MacDonald, Little Falls, Benedict?

Have you been to one of our cemeteries within the last year?

   Yes_____ No_____

If yes, which one and how was it maintained?_____

   Good_____ Fair_____ Poor_____

Do you plan to be buried in one of our cemeteries? Yes_____ No_____

Overall do you feel that the Township is a good community to live in?

Yes_____ No_____

Additional comments may be added to the back of this survey.

Please drop off to the Township Office or mail to PO Box 123, Anytown, USA

know?" we not only need to know the rules that apply to measurements and questionnaire construction, we also need to be familiar with sampling techniques and data analysis procedures. We need a good design, a representative sample, valid and reliable measures, and proper data analysis to obtain information about the target population, draw conclusions, and make recommendations. Therefore, the administrator needs to map out a plan from start to finish. Designing a survey without a plan most likely will result in invalid research and unreliable findings, and a survey that resembles the one in Box 8.1.

This chapter presents a comprehensive overview of creating surveys by discussing the rules that apply to question writing, question selection, response options, questionnaire layout, and cover letters. Although the focus is on self-administered surveys, the logic, particularly question wording and response formats, applies to all types of surveys.

8.2 Question Wording

Writing valid and reliable questions appears easy; however, one of the biggest mistakes you can make when writing the survey questions is to assume that the question makes sense to everyone because it makes sense to you. The question makes sense because you wrote it. Valid and reliable information is collected from questions that maintain certain criteria. They must be simple, clear, unbiased; avoid future intentions, past recollections, negative language, and assumption making; and ask one question at a time about one concept. In addition, the question should be interpreted the same way by all respondents. Questions violating these rules yield unreliable data. This section presents illustrations where questions violate these rules, and offers suggestions to improve each.

8.2.1 Simplicity

Survey questions and statements need to use simple language. When writing questionnaires, researchers should avoid words that are large, uncommon, complex, or have multiple meanings. For example, rather than saying "exhausted," use "tired"; replace "priority" with "most important," or use "nearly" rather than "virtually."[1] Moreover, the questions or statements should be complete sentences, not fragments, as illustrated here.

Fragments	Complete sentences
Age _____	What is your age? _____
Gender _____	What is your gender? _____
Annual income $_____	What is your annual income? $_____

8.2.2 Clarity

Survey question clarity is achieved through well-defined concepts that are written into the questions such that all respondents understand what is being measured. Consider the following questions a group of students used to measure alcohol consumption and study habits of undergraduate students. The concepts are consumption and studying. Are the questions clear enough so that respondents will interpret each the same way?

1. How many times do you drink by yourself?_____
2. How many times have you had an alcoholic beverage in the last 30 days? _____
3. When did you first start drinking alcohol?_____
4. About how much do you usually drink?
   ☐ 0–4 drinks
   ☐ 5–9 drinks
   ☐ 10–14 drinks
   ☐ 15 or more drinks

Does each question measure quantity of drinking? Will the interpretation be the same for all respondents? Each seems clear but all four questions are vague. In the first and last questions, there are no indications of what is meant by drinking. Moreover, there is no defined time frame. By using an open response format (in questions one through three) where respondents are free to write out the answer, a variety of answers are possible. For example, in the first question one respondent might answer "all the time," whereas another participant might answer "10." In addition, some subjects might want to be funny, or what they think is being funny, and answer "10,000" or "1 million." For the third question, respondents might say, "in 2002" or "when I was 18." Finally, each question depends on memory recall and assumes each drink is of equal weight or strength—a pint of beer versus a shot of whiskey.

In these examples, the questions are not clear; they are too vague. Therefore, researchers need to better define their concepts, such as the type of alcohol, how often each is consumed, and what "often" means. In addition, researchers should provide situations or settings; for example, at the bar, at home, alone, or with friends.

8.2.3 Unbiased

Biased and leading questions are those that provide information to respondents that cause the respondents to alter their response. Consider the following example:

> We have estimated that you pay some 35 to 40% of your earnings each year in taxes. Do you believe this level of taxation is too high, too low, or about right?

How might you respond to this question now knowing that perhaps 40% of your income goes to the government? You might respond, "too high." These types of questions are typical with advocacy organizations trying to promote their agendas through research findings gathered in surveys. To create an unbiased question, we can convert the question into separate questions—measuring knowledge and opinion:

1. Do you know the income tax rate for the state of Michigan?
   ☐ No (Skip to question 4.)
   ☐ Yes
2. If so, please tell us what the rate is. _____

3. Do you believe that the rate listed above is too high, too low, or about right?
   ☐ Too high
   ☐ Too low
   ☐ About right

4. What is your zip code? _____

This approach accomplishes a couple of objectives. First, it holds the respondents responsible for telling the truth; that is, if the respondent really knows the rates, then he has to define them. Therefore, the first two questions take knowledge to another level. People can say they know something, but when asked for proof of their knowledge, those who do not know are now more likely to check "no." Second, given their knowledge, we can interpret their beliefs about the tax rates. Even if a respondent's answer to question two is incorrect, the answer to the third question still reveals information about her beliefs. For example, if a respondent says the tax rate is 3% (which is incorrect) and believes that rate is too high or about right, then we know that the correct rate of 4.8% would be too high. However, if the respondent claimed the 3% rate to be too low, then the information for that particular person is inconclusive.

Loaded questions also are biased and should be rewritten. Questions that include certain adjectives such as "prestigious" or "respected," or verbs like "forbid," "prohibit," or "allow" are considered loaded. Consider the question below. How might most participants answer the question knowing the organization is prestigious, respected, and unbiased?

> Do you support the efforts made by our prestigious organization, through our respected Research Center, to provide clear, unbiased analysis?

By dropping the strong, subjective, and leading language, the question is improved and shortened to, "Do you support our research efforts?" Organizations associated with advocacy research—liberal, conservative, or otherwise—typically use loaded questions. The findings linked to these questions should always be questioned. This is another reason why we evaluate secondary sources of information prior to using them in our studies.

Sometimes questions are not intentionally written to be biased, but the presence of certain words creates different interpretations. Consider the following questions:

> Do you think the United States should forbid public speeches against democracy?
> Do you think that the United States should allow public speeches against democracy?[2]

Although both questions are about a well-defined concept—free speech—and seem clear, the validity and reliability of the questions are threatened. Why? More than half of the respondents in the study from which the questions were drawn, answered positively (said "yes") to the first question, whereas three-quarters answered negatively (said "no") to the second question.[3] Given the substantial differences between the answers, something must be wrong with the wording. Could the word "forbid" be so strong that people felt to forbid speech would violate the First Amendment and be un-American? What about language in the second question? Allowing speeches against democracy? Respondents might think, How much more unpatriotic can a person be to allow such heresy? Which word is most appropriate? Does it depend on what the researcher is trying to prove? The moral here is that one word that is seemingly unthreatening, unbiased, or otherwise, could result in respondents misconstruing the meaning. The only way to know the power of the language is to test the survey prior to administering it.

8.2.4   Realistic Time Frames

Sometimes researchers are interested in the past as well as the future. For example, polling organizations ask respondents whom they voted for in the last presidential election or whom they intend to vote for in the next presidential race. Questions about major events such as a presidential election are easier to remember than those about monotonous activities, like hours surfing the Web or about unplanned intentions. Consider the following examples, the first about future intentions and the second on past behavior.

1. Do you plan to purchase a more fuel-efficient vehicle in the next 5 years?
2. How many hours did you surf the Web last year?

People are not sure when they are going to buy a new car. If Bob's car works fine and is relatively new, he would not know the answer to the first question. And Bonnie most likely cannot recall every time she surfed the Web. But we do not know how many people are similar to Bob or Bonnie. Respondents are not likely to accurately predict the future or recall the frequency of past occurrences. As a result, they estimate frequencies, likelihoods, and behaviors. Both questions are improved by using a more realistic time frame; for example, "In the typical day, how many hours do you surf the Web?"

8.2.5   *Specificity without Assumption Making*

Often, researchers make assumptions about respondents' behaviors or knowledge level. Not only do the two questions in the previous section ask about future intentions or memory recall, they also make assumptions about the respondent. The first assumes the respondent does not own a fuel-efficient car and the second assumes the respondent has a computer with Internet access. Below are some additional examples of questions based on false premises:

1. Do you drive to work? _____
2. When did you graduate from college? _____
3. What is your annual income after taxes? _____

Each of the above questions is based on a false premise; each makes certain assumptions about the respondent. The first question assumes that the respondent works and owns a vehicle; the second assumes the respondent went to college, and the third assumes the participant has an annual income. We improve each question by adding appropriate response formats that allow for screening and follow-up questions. (We discuss response options and contingency questions in more detail later in this chapter.) For example, the first two questions are improved by building in a response option to offset the assumption:

1. When traveling to work, what is your most frequent mode of transportation? (Please select only one option.)
   - ☐ I am currently unemployed
   - ☐ A vehicle (my own or someone else's car)
   - ☐ Public transportation
   - ☐ Taxi
   - ☐ Bicycle
   - ☐ Walk

2. What is your highest educational degree achieved to date?
   - ☐ Did not graduate from high school
   - ☐ High school diploma or equivalent
   - ☐ Associate's degree
   - ☐ Bachelor's degree
   - ☐ Master's degree
   - ☐ Doctorate degree
   - ☐ Other, please specify _____

The assumptions have been removed by adding predefined responses. The questions and response sets should reflect the concepts being measured and the target population being studied. In addition, researchers should take into consideration respondent perceptions and classifications when creating the list of responses. For example, if the respondents in the sample are undergraduate students, then the second question about highest level of education is mostly irrelevant; all those in the sample have a high school diploma (unless a high school student is enrolled in the class), and some may have an associate's degree.

8.2.6 *Negatives without Nots and Double Nots*

Questions or statements should avoid negatives or double negatives; that is, the word "not" should not be used in survey questions and statements. Consider the following statements and questions:

1. I do not ride the bus.
2. I do not support the program that bans nuclear weapons.
3. Do you oppose a program that does not support senior citizens?
4. Do you not support a program that does not make public transportation more accessible?

Respondents will overlook the word "not" or will be confused by what the question is asking, particularly when double negatives are present. If respondents do not fully understand the question but respond anyway, the responses are not reliable and the aggregate data are questionable at best. When negative questions or statements cannot be avoided, they should be worded differently to avoid the word "not"; for example:

1. I never ride the bus.
2. I oppose a program banning nuclear weapons.

Although both statements are negatives, by rewriting each statement we remove the "not," making the statement clearer. However, the better approach is to combine the positive with the negative aspects in the question or statement. For example:

1. Do you support or oppose a program banning nuclear weapons.
   ☐ Support   ☐ Oppose

Overall, researchers should avoid negatives and double negatives, but where negatives are necessary, the question should not include the word "not."

8.2.7 *One Concept, One Question*

Each survey question or statement should ask only one question; if the word "and" appears, then the question most likely asks two or more questions. These are called double-barreled questions. Consider the following questions:

1. When tuition increases, are you more likely to drop out of school and look for a job?
   ☐ Yes   ☐ No

2. Do you support an increase in sales taxes to pay for police and fire services?
   ☐ Yes   ☐ No

3. In your trip to the city, are you likely to carpool or use public transportation to reduce traffic congestion and pollution?
   ☐ Yes   ☐ No

The first two examples ask two questions each. How are respondents to answer? And how do researchers interpret the responses? A "yes" response to the first question means they drop out and look for a job, but a "no" response has multiple meanings. Respondents might not drop out, but look for a job; continue with school, but look for a job; or neither drop out nor look for a job. The same is true in the second example. A "no" response may mean the respondent is opposed to an increase in the sales tax, but in favor of funding police and fire services. Or the response may imply that the respondent is in favor of an increase in the sales tax, but opposed to additional funding for police and fire services. The third example makes assumptions while asking four different questions at once:

1. Do you carpool to reduce traffic congestion?
2. Do you carpool to reduce pollution?
3. Do you use public transportation to reduce traffic congestion?
4. Do you use public transportation to reduce pollution?

If the words "and" and "or" appear, then the question is most likely double-barreled and should be rewritten by either separating the question into multiple questions or adding an exhaustive list of responses. We can rewrite the first three questions from above to ask one question about one idea:

1. When tuition increases, are you more likely to drop out of school?
   ☐ Yes   ☐ No

2. When tuition increases, are you more likely to look for a job?
   ☐ Yes   ☐ No

3. Do you support an increase in the sales tax that would be used to pay for police and fire services?
   ☐ I do not support an increase in the sales tax.

   ☐ I support an increase in the sales tax, but only to fund police services.

   ☐ I support an increase in the sales tax, but only to fund fire services.

   ☐ I support an increase in the sales tax as long as it goes to both police and fire services.

8.2.8   Recap

To maintain validity and reliability, survey questions and statements should be complete sentences and should be clear and unbiased. In addition, the questions or statements

Table 8.1 Examples of Question Wording to Avoid

Questions should not be ...	Examples
Ambiguous	How many times do you drink by yourself?
Leading or biased	It has been estimated that Americans pay some 35 to 40% of their earnings each year in federal taxes. Do you believe this level of taxation is too high, too low, or about right?
Based on memory recall	How many hours did you surf the Web last year?
About distant future intentions	Do you plan to purchase a more fuel efficient vehicle in the next 5 years?
Presumptions	Do you drive to work?
Double negatives	Do you oppose a program that does not support senior citizens?
Double-barreled	When tuition increases are you more likely to drop out of school and look for a job?

should not be loaded, based on assumptions, or leading. Moreover, question wording should avoid the words "and" and "not." Finally, the researcher should define a reasonable time frame when asking about future intentions or past experiences. Keeping with these rules will produce questions that are interpreted the same way by all (or mostly all) the respondents. Table 8.1 lists the items to avoid when writing questions.

8.3   Question Structure

Questions take on one of three structures—open-ended, closed, or partially closed. Which question format should the researcher use? The answer depends on what is being measured, how it is being measured, the type of survey used, characteristics of the sample, and the data analysis procedures.

8.3.1   Open-Ended Questions

Open-ended questions are those where respondents write an answer to the question or statement; there are no constraints or forced answers to impact responses and the information gathered are qualitative or quantitative data. The qualitative open-ended questions are useful when the researcher wishes to probe for deeper meaning. Quantitative open-ended questions collect specific and precise ratio level data; however, the answers are dependent on the respondents' interpretation of the question. Consider the following open-ended questions:

1. When did you graduate from college? _____
2. How old are you? _____

3. What is your annual income?_____
4. Why do you think poverty exists?_____

_____

For each question, the list of potential answers is lengthy (i.e., you would not want to list out all possible years, ages, or incomes) so an open-ended response is most useful. However, the first and third questions are not structured well; they leave room for a large variation in the responses because they are based on assumptions (attending and/or graduating from college, and being employed) and are vague (what does "when" mean; what does "income" mean). How would you answer the first question? Some potential responses are: "When I was 21." "In 1994." "Ten years ago." The point here is that when a question is open-ended, there is no room for wording error; therefore, researchers define the concept in the statements and questions, and wording of the statement and questions must maintain the principles from the previous section. We could change the first question to read: "If you attended and graduated from college with a bachelor's degree, in what year did you graduate with this degree?_____"

Although this question is not perfect, it avoids many of the previous problems. Overall, open-ended questions yield many benefits, but they have their share of problems, such as reducing response rates as well as difficulty in coding responses, deciphering handwriting, and interpreting the meaning of explanations. For example, open-ended questions requiring a short response are normal and acceptable; however, the presence of many open-ended questions that involve lengthy explanations typically reduce response rates in self-administered questionnaires—the more time-consuming the questionnaire, the lower the response rates.

Short-answer, open-ended questions, particularly those requesting quantitative information, are easy to code; however, an open-ended question that requires a long response (a sentence or more) is sometimes difficult to interpret and code. For example, respondents may not be able to articulate effectively their opinions or beliefs, or may have horrible handwriting; in both cases, the interpretation and response coding is left to the researcher. How is the researcher supposed to know what a respondent meant to say? This threatens the validity and reliability of the data. Moreover, qualitative responses make statistical analyses and generalizations virtually impossible. Consequently, open-ended questions gathering lengthy responses are more appropriate where deeper probing is required, as with face-to-face interviews and focus groups—those methods that are most common in exploratory research.

8.3.2 Closed and Partially Closed Questions

Rather than allowing respondents to write in their answers, researchers can force participants to select a response from a predefined list of nominal or ordinal responses. The list is either closed or partially closed as shown below.

1. What is your age?
   ☐ <20   ☐ 20–29   ☐ 30–49   ☐ 50–64   ☐ 65+
2. How would you rate the mayor's overall job performance?
   ☐ Very Good   ☐ Good   ☐ Average   ☐ Poor   ☐ Very Poor
3. What is your major?
   ☐ Undeclared/Undecided
   ☐ Business
   ☐ Education
   ☐ Psychology
   ☐ Other, please specify_____

The first two questions are closed questions, whereas the third question is partially closed. Partially closed questions are those where the list of responses includes an "other" option, because listing every option for some questions is inefficient. For example, if we were interested in the college major of survey respondents, we would want to list the general and most popular categories, and add the "other" option to capture the rest of the majors.

However, because these options are housed in the "other" option, this approach results in underreported alternatives.[4] Furthermore, certain conjectures about the data cannot be made. We cannot say that the psychology major is four times more popular than the public administration major because public administration was not on the original list. To make such comparisons, the partially closed question is changed to a closed question by dropping the "other" option and all of the options to be compared in the analysis are listed.[5]

The closed, and partially closed, question formats require little skill and effort on the part of the respondents, which is likely to improve response rates. In addition, closed questions are more advantageous than open-ended questions because closed questions are uniform, more reliable, and have responses that are easier to interpret, code, and analyze.

Although the benefits associated with forced responses are plentiful, particularly for self-administered surveys, selecting the appropriate response format for the survey question can be a difficult task. Both the question and response set must measure the concept, and the question and responses must match. For example, questions about opinion should list responses reflective of opinion; those asking about frequency should list responses that summarize occurrences. Consider the following example that asks about activities but offers opinion-based responses:

1. I have made a purchase over the Internet.
   ☐ Strongly Agree
   ☐ Agree
   ☐ Neutral
   ☐ Disagree
   ☐ Strongly Disagree

This is an inappropriate response set for the statement. The responses should be "yes" and "no," not those listed. Therefore, the response depends on the survey question and the type of measurement, which, in turn, depends on the type of analysis to be performed. In addition, we have to decide to use "other," "don't know," or "no opinion," and how to display and order the responses in our response set. The next section discusses each of these issues, as well as the different types of response formats and their respective strengths and weaknesses.

8.4 Response Formats for Closed Questions

Closed and partially closed questions use a list of responses to obtain quantifiable qualitative data. These lists contain options that maintain the characteristics of measurement rules discussed in Chapter 3. The list must be mutually exclusive and exhaustive, and categorical or continuous. In addition, the list must be balanced when using ordinal level measures.

Here is a quick review of Chapter 3. Consider the following examples.

1. What is your age?
   ☐ <18   ☐ 18–25   ☐ 26–33   ☐ 34–41   ☐ 42–49   ☐ 50+

2. How would you rate the mayor's overall job performance?
   ☐ Very good   ☐ Good   ☐ Average   ☐ Poor   ☐ Very poor   ☐ No opinion

Both response sets are nonoverlapping (mutually exclusive), where respondents will choose only one option. A participant cannot fall into more than one option in the first example; this is impossible. In addition, both questions are exhaustive where all possible responses are listed. In the second question, we might argue that some options are missing, such as an option between good and average, or average and poor. However, the response list should not be too long or too short, but should capture common perceptions or opinions.

Finally, the categories are balanced. With the exception of the first and last option in the age response set, each range is the same—8 years separates the low and high boundaries. The first and last options are different to capture those respondents who are different from the sampling frame. For example, if we are interested in undergraduate students who are traditionally between the ages of 18 and 24, we would want to add options to represent nontraditional undergraduates—those younger than 18 and older than 24. The response set that measures the mayor's performance is balanced; equal numbers of good and poor surround a midpoint.

Beyond the measurement rules reviewed above, other factors influence the ability to gather valid and reliable data from closed questions. For example, as we construct the list of responses, we have to consider the following: the levels of measurement; the use of options such as "don't know," "undecided," or "unsure," "no opinion" or "neutral," and "check all that apply"; and the layout and the order of the items in the list. We discuss each in turn.

8.4.1 Measurement Levels

We can use any level of measurement to determine frequencies, preferences, behavior, characteristics, opinions, and knowledge. Recall the different levels of measurement discussed in Chapter 5. When measuring frequencies, nominal and ordinal responses typically sacrifice the precision (the actual number of occurrences) found in ratio level measures because we cannot always count on respondents' memory recall to provide accurate answers in open-ended quantitative questions. Typically, higher levels of data are gathered in open-ended questions, whereas forced-answer questions are useful to gather nominal and ordinal measures where a response list is easy to create and contains typical responses. Consider the following questions and statements:

1. John Smith is the current mayor.
   ☐ True   ☐ False

2. Are you a registered voter?
   ☐ Yes   ☐ No

3. How do you get to work most days?
   ☐ Drive   ☐ Ride the bus   ☐ Take a taxi   ☐ Ride a bike

4. How often do you drive to work?
   ☐ Every day   ☐ Most days   ☐ Some days   ☐ Never

5. I ride the bus
   ☐ frequently.   ☐ occasionally.   ☐ never.

6. On average, about how many times do you ride the bus in a typical week?
   ☐ 0 times   ☐ 1–4 times   ☐ 5–9 times   ☐ 10 or more times

All six examples measure something different in both the wording and the responses; but in each, the question or statement matches its respective response set; for example, knowledge (true/false), behavior (traveling to work or riding the bus), and frequency (how often one drives or rides the bus). The responses for the first three questions are nominal level responses, whereas the last three are ordinal. Which one is more useful? The answer depends on what the administrator wants to know, how accurate the data should be, and how the data will be analyzed.

The first two questions provide binary, nominal responses. Both are easy to understand and interpret. "True" means John Smith is the mayor, while "false" suggests someone else is the mayor. A "yes" response to being a registered voter implies the respondent is, in fact, a registered voter, but "no" means he is not a registered voter. However, some questions that use true/false or yes/no responses threaten the reliability of the data. For example, if respondents are asked if they always ride the bus for all transportation needs, a "true" or "yes" response is easy to understand and interpret: yes, the respondent always rides the bus. A "false" or "no" response, however, is misleading because it takes on multiple meanings; it could mean the respondent either never rides the bus or sometimes rides the bus.

Fixing the problem by rewording the question to "I sometimes ride the bus" creates even more problems. An affirmative response could mean some days, most days, or even every day; a negative response could also mean every day or most days, since these frequencies are different from "sometimes," as well as implying that the respondents might never ride the bus. The interpretation of the responses in both questions—always or sometimes riding the bus—falls to the respondent and the researcher. Respondents have no way of knowing what is meant by "sometimes" or "always," and the researcher has no idea how the respondent interpreted the meaning of those terms. When the question includes a subjective measure of frequency in the wording, the binary responses take on multiple meanings.

The last three examples use ordinal responses to measure the frequency of some phenomenon; however, examples 4 and 5 are too vague. What does "every day" mean when the number of days worked varies among respondents; for example, some respondents might work 3 days a week and drive every time. In this instance, the respondent would probably select "every day" because every time she travels to work, she drives. In the fifth example, the definitions "frequently" and "occasionally" are unknown because there is no established time frame.

The last example improves the ambiguity found in examples four and five. "Per week" is added to the question to establish a time frame, and the ordinal response set is changed from the vague responses to scale increments or number ranges. The question still leaves room for the participants to estimate ridership, but overall this example provides greater precision than the others do. However, the scale in the last question is unbalanced, so how would the administrator know what scale and increments to use?

Constructing a numerical scale requires mathematical skills, assumption making, and intuition. The scale establishes a midpoint using the average or typical behavior. In addition, the scale includes the polar extremes, listing something similar to never or always. From these three points, the scale increments are established. Let us use the sixth example from above for illustration purposes. The fewest number of times someone rides the bus is one time and those most dependent probably ride the bus at least 10 times per week—two times a day, to and from work, 5 or 6 days a week. We can start the scale with one and end with a number somewhere around 10. The increments representing the values between the polar ends of the scale should reflect low, medium, and high levels of ridership. Therefore, increments should replicate the normal patterns of occurrences for the concepts being studied and include the extremes to capture the fringe.

Developing the increments for the scales can be tricky, though. For example, one study compared two groups of students using the two different scale increments illustrated below.[6]

Scale A Low response scale	Scale B High response scale
30 min or less	2.5 h or less
30 min to 1 h	2.5 to 3 h
1 to 1.5 h	3 to 3.5 h
1.5 to 2 h	4 to 4.5 h
2 to 2.5 h	4.5 h or more
2.5 h or more	

Both scales use 30-minute increments. The first scale begins with 30 minutes or less and ends with 2.5 hours or more, whereas the second scale starts with 2.5 hours or less and ends with 4.5 hours or more. The researchers asked each group of students the same two questions: How many hours do you study per day? And how many hours of television do you watch per day? The first group used Scale A to answer these questions, and the second group used Scale B. Overall, the findings suggest that the scales influenced the responses, and the two groups had significantly different studying and television-viewing habits. In fact, 23% of the respondents using Scale A compared to 69% of the respondents using Scale B reported studying 2.5 or more hours per day. As for watching television, two times as many respondents using Scale B reported watching 2.5 or more hours of television per day than those using Scale A.[7]

This research shows that the scale increments can influence respondents' answers. This is particularly true of questions that ask about activities, behaviors, actions, or beliefs that are viewed as socially desirable, undesirable, or mundane. In these cases, estimation replaces calculated thought, and respondents either overstate or underestimate their behaviors. For example, a respondent exposed to Scale A may think that watching 3 hours of television a day is socially unacceptable because it is included in the last option, so he chooses a different option. The same interpretation might occur for Scale B when measuring studying habits. A participant may think her 30 minutes of studying a day will be viewed as undesirable because the scale begins and ends with much larger numbers; therefore, she selects a different option.

At least two options exist to improve the scale to reduce the effect of social desirability. Researchers can combine both scales to have one large scale with 30-minutes nonoverlapping increments, beginning with 30 minutes or less and ending with 4.5 or more hours. Or, they can ask an open-ended question where respondents write in the number of minutes or hours they study and watch television.

Another response option available to researchers is a nonnumerical ordinal scale, which is used to measure opinions, beliefs, and behaviors. Sometimes these scales are binary using agree or disagree, support or oppose, for the choices. For example,

The facilities at the park are clean.   ☐ Agree   ☐ Disagree

However, some respondents prefer not to pick from just two options. They favor variation, particularly with vague questions. Respondents may find ascribing to a definite position impossible when a vague question with a binary response set is asked. For example:

Do you support or oppose tax cuts?   ☐ Support   ☐ Oppose

How might the subject respond? If she supports tax cuts for all taxpayers then "support" is an easy choice, and the same is true for opposing all tax cuts. However, suppose she supports tax cuts for all income levels except the wealthiest taxpayers? Which option should she select? To capture these differences, the researcher could change the question by adding questions with generic classifications or precise income levels. For example:

Example of basic tax cut questions	*Support*	*Oppose*
1. Do you support or oppose tax cuts for the poor?	☐	☐
2. Do you support or oppose tax cuts for the middle class?	☐	☐
3. Do you support or oppose tax cuts for the wealthy?	☐	☐

Example of more specific tax cut questions (with possible responses)	*Support*	*Oppose*
1. Do you support or oppose tax cuts for individuals who make less than $24,999?	☒	☐
2. Do you support or oppose tax cuts for individuals who make between $25,000 and $49,999?	☒	☐
3. Do you support or oppose tax cuts for individuals who make between $50,000 and $74,999?	☒	☐
4. Do you support or oppose tax cuts for individuals who make between $75,000 and $99,999?	☐ ☓	☐
5. Do you support tax cuts for individuals who make $100,000 or more?	☒	☒

These examples are better than the vague question about supporting or opposing tax cuts in general, but the first set of questions leaves much to be desired. Poor, middle-class, and wealthy are too vague; what is poor to one person might be middle-class or wealthy to another. The second set of questions provides more clarity; however, the response set

Table 8.2   Balanced, Nonoverlapping Ordinal Response Lists

Agreement	Quality	Frequency	Importance
Strongly agree	Very good	Always	Important
Agree	Good	Frequently	Somewhat important
Somewhat agree	Average	Occasionally	Not at all important
Somewhat disagree	Poor	Never	
Disagree	Very poor		
Strongly disagree			

does not provide enough distinction between the two options. Some respondents still prefer more variation, such as adding "strongly" and "somewhat" to the "agrees" and "disagrees." This will be apparent in the returned surveys when both boxes are checked for the same question (like question 5) or an X in the middle of "support" and "oppose" (like question 4). Such responses are invalid and have to be discarded. These problems are associated with self-administered paper-and-pen surveys because Web and e-mail surveys can be created to force respondents to check only one box.

Where researchers want additional information, the binary list of responses is expanded into a nonnumerical scale. Such scales offer a balanced number of options, which are exhaustive and nonoverlapping. The list is balanced if equal numbers of positive and negative responses are provided and these responses are different (nonoverlapping). Table 8.2 provides four examples of balanced, nonoverlapping ordinal lists.

Adding "outstanding" and "excellent" to the list for quality creates an unbalanced and overlapping scale. The scale is unbalanced because there would be two more positive ratings than negative ones, and it is overlapping because "outstanding," "excellent," and "very good" are all close in meaning. None of the lists in Table 8.2 is exhaustive, however. None of them includes an option for respondents who have no opinion, don't know, or who are undecided. We discuss the inclusion of these options in a few moments.

These scales, and other comparable ones, are also used to rate some phenomenon of interest. Suppose the city manager wanted to ask citizens to rate the quality of certain services. He creates a survey and asks respondents to rate each service using a provided scale. For example:

Using a scale of 1 to 5, where 1 is very poor and 5 is very good, please rate each of the following city services:

_____ Recycling services

_____ Street maintenance

_____ Street lighting

_____ Street sweeping

_____ Trash collection

Notice the scale. The manager decided to assign numbers to a nonnumerical scale to represent each category; the higher the number, the better the rating. Researchers usually use higher numbers to code positive feedback with positive questions—a "very good" or "strongly agree" receives a five. Some respondents, however, may reverse the meaning of the scale, thinking a number one rating means very good because the number one is generally associated with things like first place, first in show, or "number one dad." Another problem associated with the above set-up is that some respondents may interpret rating as rank order, as illustrated below.

Using a scale of 1 to 5, where 1 is very poor and 5 is very good, please rate each of the following city services:

   1   Recycling services
   5   Street maintenance
   3   Street lighting
   4   Street sweeping
   2   Trash collection

The manager wonders if this really is the rating or if the respondent ranked the items. A matrix, as shown below, is useful to avoid reversing the scale, ranking rather than rating, and other potential misunderstandings:

Using a scale provided below, please check the box that best represents the quality of each of the following city services. Select only one box per service.

	Very Good	Good	Average	Poor	Very Poor
Recycling	☐	☐	☐	☐	☐
Street maintenance	☐	☐	☐	☐	☐
Street lighting	☐	☐	☐	☐	☐
Street sweeping	☐	☐	☐	☐	☐
Trash collection	☐	☐	☐	☐	☐

Here, the city manager does not assign numbers and lists each service with its respective quality rating. This approach eliminates the confusion posed by the preassigned numbers. Of course, other potential problems may occur; for example, respondents checking more than one box per service or checking in between two boxes. These problems can be minimized with interviews or Web or e-mail surveys.

In sum, the response lists for nonnumerical and numerical scales should be balanced, exhaustive, and nonoverlapping. An unbalanced and overlapping list like "excellent," "great," "very good," "good," "average," and "poor," produces biased and unreliable information. In addition, the number of options included in the response list, regardless of measurement level, depends on the question wording, the target population, and the phenomenon of interest. This is particularly true when using ordinal scales; the scale should fit the question, specifically where numerical scales are used.

8.4.2 Ranking Responses

We can use scaled responses such as "best" to "worst" to rank options by translating the rank into a numerical scale. Rank order is useful when we are interested in respondents' most favorite or least favorite activities, political candidates, and public services, to list a few. For example:

> Using a scale of 1 to 5, where 1 is most favorite and 5 is least favorite, please rank the following Democratic presidential candidates.
>
> _____ Hillary Clinton
> _____ John Edwards
> _____ Dennis Kucinich
> _____ Barack Obama
> _____ Bill Richardson

For this particular scale, the small number represents the most favorite rating, and the highest number depicts the least favorite rating. In addition, the range of numbers (one to five) corresponds to the number of items (five presidential candidates) in the list. Rank order questions are not without problems, however. Some respondents may use one number more than once because they have not decided on their most favorite candidate or are otherwise undecided between two or more candidates. Researchers add instructions such as "Please use each number once" to reduce such occurrences. No matter how perfect the question and its responses, a handful of respondents always seem to misinterpret the question and/or responses, they do not follow instructions, or they simply do not understand what is being asked of them.

8.4.3 Don't Know or Undecided

Question wording and response sets are interrelated; therefore, the list of options should not only fit but also include special response options, for instance, "don't know," "undecided," "have no knowledge of topic," "have not used," or "other, please specify," when appropriate. For example, there is nothing wrong with asking respondents to rate the quality of the public transit system—very good, good, average, poor, very poor—however, some respondents may not use public transportation. By not providing additional choices, respondents are forced to either answer, providing inaccurate information, or skip the question altogether. Either way, such cases create unreliable data. Rather than forcing them to choose a rating, researchers provide additional options similar to "don't know" or "haven't used public transit." A "don't know" response suggests that those respondents who have no knowledge of public transportation do not know about its quality because they have never used it.

However, even the "don't know" and "have no knowledge of" options cause problems. For example, say respondents are asked to rate the job performance of the mayor. However, some respondents do not know who the mayor is and others do not know what the mayor does. In turn, these respondents may not want to admit that they do not know (another social-desirability issue), so rather than saying or checking "don't know" they select an option that claims they have an opinion or some knowledge of the topic. Such behaviors are more common with interviews, but do exist in self-administered surveys and create unreliable data in both instances. The better, less precarious option is to include "undecided" or "unsure" among the choices, whichever one is most fitting to the question.

Both "don't know" and "undecided" are useful options in their own right. The "undecided" choice is more appropriate when asking respondents about opinions— the mayor's job performance—whereas the "don't know" option is more practical when asking about experiences, topics, or issues with which respondents are unfamiliar. Finally, both options should be located at the end of the list of options. For example,

1. Academic advising is valued in the tenure and promotion review process.
   ☐ Strongly agree ☐ Agree ☐ Disagree ☐ Strongly disagree ☐ Undecided

2. Please rate the quality of the city's recycling program.
   ☐ Very good ☐ Good ☐ Average ☐ Poor ☐ Very poor ☐ Don't know

3. The university should provide opportunities for the recognition and reward of outstanding faculty academic advising.
   ☐ Strongly agree
   ☐ Agree
   ☐ Disagree
   ☐ Strongly disagree
   ☐ Undecided

8.4.4 No Opinion or Neutral

The "no opinion," and "neutral" are also useful in certain instances, particularly when surveying opinions. The meanings or definitions of "neutral" and "no opinion" are not different. If a respondent has no opinion, then she neither agrees nor disagrees; she is neutral. However, the placement of each option leads the respondent to different interpretations. Both options are appropriate at the end of the list of options, but only "neutral" is sometimes appropriate in the middle of the list. (Other language can be substituted for "neutral" when it is located in the middle;

for example, "neither agree nor disagree.") Finally, response options using neutral and/or no opinion should provide "undecided" or "don't know" as choices, as well. Although some respondents may have absolutely no opinion, others may still be undecided or not know enough about the topic to form an opinion; therefore, researchers include both in some fashion as illustrated below.

1. The university should provide opportunities for the recognition and reward of outstanding faculty academic advising.
   ☐ Strongly agree
   ☐ Agree
   ☐ Neutral
   ☐ Disagree
   ☐ Strongly disagree
   ☐ Undecided

2. Academic advising is valued in the tenure and promotion review process.
   ☐ Strongly Agree
   ☐ Agree
   ☐ Neither agree nor disagree
   ☐ Disagree
   ☐ Strongly Disagree
   ☐ Don't know

3. The university should provide more instruction to its faculty on the interpersonal aspects of academic advising.
   ☐ Strongly agree
   ☐ Agree
   ☐ Disagree
   ☐ Strongly disagree
   ☐ No opinion
   ☐ Undecided

If the survey has an entire section devoted to one particular topic, filter questions are useful to weed out those who have no knowledge of the topic. Rather than providing the "no opinion" or "don't know" options over and over again, survey writers add one or two questions at the beginning of the section asking respondents if they are familiar with the topic or concept of interest. If the respondents are familiar, then they answer "yes" and continue with the section; if they answer "no," that they are unfamiliar with the topic, they skip the section altogether. For example:

> The following section asks questions about your usage of the local public transportation system. Have you ever used this system?
> ☐ Yes (please continue to answer the questions in this section)
> ☐ No (please skip to the next section)

Studies have shown, however, that although some respondents do not know or have no opinion, many participants would rather answer the question than admit to an absence of knowledge or opinion. For example, in one research study, large numbers of respondents formed an opinion about fictitious issues. Why? The study's authors suggest that some respondents feel that they should know or have some opinion on an issue because the question is being asked.[8]

8.4.5   One versus All

Often, researchers are interested in understanding behaviors, characteristics, or knowledge of a series of items. For example:

1. How do you usually get to work?
   - ☐ Drive a vehicle   ☐ Public transportation
   - ☐ Taxi   ☐ Bicycle
   - ☐ Walk   ☐ Other
2. When traveling to work, what is your most frequent mode of transportation? (Please select only one option.)
   - ☐ I am currently unemployed
   - ☐ Drive a vehicle (your own or someone else's car)
   - ☐ Public transportation
   - ☐ Taxi
   - ☐ Bicycle
   - ☐ Walk
3. In the past year, have you felt that you were discriminated against for any of the following reasons? (Check all that apply.) [9]
   - ☐ Race or ethnicity   ☐ Sex/gender   ☐ Age
   - ☐ Disability   ☐ Religion   ☐ Sexual orientation
   - ☐ Appearance   ☐ Economic status   ☐ Other
4. In the past year, have you felt that you were or were not discriminated against for any of the following reasons?

Race or ethnicity	☐ Yes	☐ No
Sex/Gender	☐ Yes	☐ No
Age	☐ Yes	☐ No
Disability	☐ Yes	☐ No
Religion	☐ Yes	☐ No
Sexual orientation	☐ Yes	☐ No
Appearance	☐ Yes	☐ No
Economic status	☐ Yes	☐ No

When the survey provides nominal lists of items within a question, directions such as "Check all that apply" or "Check only one option" should be provided. Without directives, as illustrated in the first example, some respondents might check all that apply, rather than selecting just one option. Rewording the questions might solve these types of problems. For example, the second example adds a directive and language to make "usually" more clear—the most frequent mode of transportation. Finally, when researchers are interested in all the items in the response list, "Check all that apply" is added, as shown in third example.

The "check all" phrase is a common format among self-administered surveys, whereas a forced choice format, illustrated in the fourth example, is preferred in telephone surveys because of its user friendliness. For example, the "check all" on self-administered surveys is user friendly because it takes up less room, which makes the survey look shorter and less intimidating. The yes/no format creates greater efficiency for phone interviewers as they can read off each option and check the appropriate box as the respondent answers yes or no to each option. However, both methods are conducive in self-administered surveys.[4]

For example, the "check all" option is useful when researchers want respondents to compare all items collectively, and then select all options that apply, such as most used, most favorite, and so on. However, problems exist when the lists are long. Respondents might not compare each item equally or they might speed through the list, overlooking options. In fact, research studies find that when lists are long, respondents are more likely to check the first few items provided.[10] Another problem with the "check all" approach is the interpretation of an unchecked box; an unchecked box does not indicate an explicit "no." Perhaps an unchecked box indicates that the option does not apply to the respondent or that the respondent is unsure or neutral about the option.[4] When researchers want participants to consider each item separately, without regard to the other options, each item should be listed separately, as illustrated above in example 4. With this method, no additional interpretation of the responses is needed; the meanings of yes and no are explicit. However, forced choice questions have an increased potential for response set bias, where respondents check the same option repeatedly as illustrated in Box 8.2.

Regardless of the benefits of each, research suggests that respondents overlook more options in the check-all approach than the forced-choice method and, as a result, respondents selected significantly more options under the forced-choice layout than the check-all approach.[11] One study reveals that in both Web and mail surveys, respondents took more time answering the questions with forced-choice options than the questions with check-all that apply directives suggesting that respondents were more methodical about each option when forced to respond to each separately.[12] This same study finds that the problems of response set bias and item nonresponse are insignificant. There are so few people who answer this way that we need not worry about the impact on the validity and reliability of the aggregated data.

These findings should not stop survey writers from using the "check all that apply" setup. To make a lengthy survey more time efficient, the check-all format is the better option. In fact, researchers suggest that these research results do not imply that forced-choice questions are more accurate than the check-all questions;

**BOX 8.2   EXAMPLE OF QUESTION SEQUENCE USING A
MATRIX LAYOUT THAT IS THREATENED
BY RESPONSE SET BIAS**

Instructions: For each of the following city services, please place an X in the box that best represents the quality of that service. Mark only one box per statement.

	Very Good	Good	Average	Poor	Very Poor
1. Police			X		
2. Fire			X		
3. Streets			X		
4. Garbage collection			X		
5. Recycling			X		
6. Water			X		
7. Sewer			X		
8. Park maintenance			X		
9. Library			X		
10. Street lighting			X		
11. Recreation			X		
12. City's Web site			X		
13. Leaf pickup			X		
14. Transportation			X		
15. Sewer			X		

---

rather, the forced choice reveals an explicit "no" and allows respondents to consider each item separately.

8.4.6 Recap

Question are open-ended, closed, or partially closed. Poorly worded open-ended questions have the potential to create unreliable answers, whereas a list of options helps clarify what the question is asking. When closed questions are used, the response choices must be mutually exclusive, nonoverlapping lists that are exhaustive and balanced. Researchers add to the list of options don't know, undecided, no opinion, or neutral to achieve exhaustiveness. Finally, directions are necessary to instruct the selection of one or all that apply and to clarify ranking and rating. The next section discusses the layout of the questionnaire, which builds on the topics of question wording and response formats.

8.5 Questionnaire Layout

The layout of a questionnaire depends on the type of survey. However, regardless of the type of survey, the layout is structured so it is easy to complete. The interview questionnaires are set up for the convenience of the interviewer, whereas self-administered surveys are arranged for respondent expediency. Moreover, with self-administered surveys, the layout should accomplish three goals: improve response rates, reduce the number of skipped questions, and generate reliable and valid data. Many factors affect all three goals, some individually, others collectively. This section discusses the overall appearance and length of the survey, including question-and-response sequence and placement. In addition, this section presents some of the typical and sometimes unavoidable problems that affect the three goals.

8.5.1 Length and Appearance

The key to increased response rates is respondent motivation and interest. When respondents are not interested in the survey, or when they lose interest because the survey is too long or too difficult, their motivation to participate decreases. Moreover, where respondents continue to participate but lose interest in the questions, the quality (i.e., reliability) of data deteriorates. Therefore, the overall length and layout of the survey affects response rates; the shorter and more user friendly the survey, the higher the response rates.

The quality of data would drastically improve by simply using shorter surveys. A study conducted on the participation in the 1990 United States census found that of those who did not respond to the survey, 37% never opened the envelope, 27% opened the envelope but did not proceed further, 12% started to fill out the survey, but stopped, and 23.5% completed the survey but never returned it.[13] In an attempt to improve response rates in upcoming censuses, a group of researchers concluded that short, user-friendly surveys improve response rates.[14]

As for the appearance of the questionnaire, survey questions should be numbered and printed on high quality white or pastel-colored paper; dark-colored paper with white print should be avoided. Similar to much of the literature on survey construction, no consensus exists on the impact of the color of paper on response rates. Studies have found that pastel colors like green, blue, yellow, and pink do improve response rates, but not significantly.[15] Others say colored paper is sometimes associated with fliers[16] and response rates are higher for white paper, but again the differences are not significant.[17]

If the survey is longer than a page, a booklet presentation adds style and simplicity. For example, a four-page survey can be copied onto one piece of paper that is 11 inches by 17 inches. The paper is folded in half where the first page becomes the front cover, pages two and three are on the inside of the booklet, next to one another, and the last page is on the back. This size of paper also is useful when there are two or three pages of questions. The first page or cover can be used to present the cover letter. Moreover, where a two-page survey is used, the back page is useful for returning the survey. The respondents fold the survey in half, from top to bottom, so that the preprinted return address and postage is displayed, tape the ends shut, and place the survey in the mail. This saves time and money; researchers do not have to purchase return envelopes.

The font of the questionnaire should be large enough to read with ample spacing between questions and response sets. Arial font is easier to read than Times New Roman, but either suffices. Small fonts and font sizes and/or too many questions per page create clutter, and a cluttered survey reduces response rates because it looks too complex and is too difficult to read.

Moreover, the space for open-ended questions should be large enough to accommodate the appropriate length of response. The literature suggests providing lines for short answers as illustrated below, but the research on the allowable space for lengthy responses is inconsistent.

> If you attended and graduated from college with a bachelor's degree, in what year did you graduate with this degree? _____

Some researchers argue that lines add clutter and reduce the quality and length of responses.[18] Others, however, suggest that the length of responses do not change; rather, respondents alter their explanations by using fragments rather than complete sentences and abbreviations rather than whole words.[19] In any event, the space allowed dictates how much will be written; the larger the space, the longer the response.[19] When lines are used, the space between the lines should be large enough to accommodate large handwriting.

Researchers write questions and statements using complete sentences and provide the necessary instructions both at the beginning of the survey and throughout the questionnaire. In the beginning, the directions tell respondents the following:

- The overall importance of the survey
- To read each question or statement carefully
- To answer each question or statement as honestly as possible
- Assure the respondent it is acceptable to select don't know, undecided, or unsure when answers are unknown or no opinion exists
- When and where to return the survey

An "over" directive at the bottom of the page is useful to instruct the respondent when additional questions are listed on the back of the survey. Beyond the instructions at the beginning, specific directions throughout the survey are necessary, particularly when sections or response scales change, or skip or contingency patterns are used. Questionnaires should not be guessing games for respondents. Increased time and effort on the part of the respondent will reduce individual question response rates as well as overall participation rates. Box 8.3 illustrates how directions should guide respondents through a survey. In this example, different sets of instructions provide different information. One set provides readers with the scale, while others

BOX 8.3   EXAMPLES OF DIRECTIONS FROM A DIVERSITY SURVEY[20]

PART 1: BACKGROUND INFORMATION
Instructions: Please complete the following questions by filling in the appropriate circle completely or filling in the blank spaces for each question. Use either a Number 2 pencil or a pen with black or blue ink. Provide only one response unless prompted otherwise. Do not skip any questions unless instructed to do so. PLEASE ANSWER ALL QUESTIONS IN THIS SURVEY WITH RESPECT TO THE CAMPUS COMMUNITY IDENTIFIED IN QUESTION #1.

PART 2: CAMPUS EXPERIENCES WITH DIVERSITY
Instructions: Below you will find a set of statements about experiences with diversity that you may have had on your campus. Please provide a response to each statement.Use the following rating guide for your responses to questions #10 through #12.

　N = Never
　R = Rarely, i.e., once or twice a year, on average
　O = Occasionally, i.e., 3 to 5 times a year, on average
　V = Very often, i.e., 6 to 9 times a year, on average
　F = Frequently, i.e., 10 or more times a year, on average

PART 4: IMPROVING THE CAMPUS ENVIRONMENT TOWARDS DIVERSITY
Use the following rating guide to respond to questions #36 through #39, according to how much you believe that each one would affect the climate for diversity on this campus.

　IC = Improve climate considerably
　IS = Improve climate somewhat
　WS = Worsen climate somewhat
　WC = Worsen climate considerably
　NC = No change in climate

Instructions: Answer questions #42 and #43 ONLY IF YOU ARE A PERSON OF COLOR. If you are White/Caucasian, please proceed to question #44.

Instructions: Answer questions #44 through 46 ONLY IF YOU ARE A GAY, LESBIAN OR BISEXUAL PERSON. If you are not part of one of these groups, proceed to question #47.

Instructions: Answer questions #47 through #49 ONLY IF YOU ARE A PERSON WITH A DISABILITY. If you are not a person with a disability, do not answer any of the remaining questions in this survey.

THANK YOU FOR COMPLETING THIS SURVEY.
YOUR TIME AND EFFORT ARE GREATLY APPRECIATED.

direct specific respondents to answer certain questions; the remaining respondents are told to skip the question and go to the next question.

Professional-looking surveys have a title at the top of the first page of the survey and extend a "thank you" to respondents at the beginning, both in the cover letter or instructions where no cover letter is used, and again at the end of the survey. Along with the thank you at the end, researchers often reiterate the return process—where and when to return the survey—in case respondents misplace the cover letter or return envelope.

In some instances, researchers do not want certain people to participate in the survey or answer certain questions. When this is necessary, researchers rely on filter and contingency questions. For example, suppose the city manager defines the target population as city residents who are register voters and homeowners. He writes the following three questions and provides directions for the participants:

1. Are you a registered voter? ☐ Yes ☐ No
2. Are you a resident of the city? ☐ Yes ☐ No
3. Are you a homeowner? ☐ Yes ☐ No

If you answered yes to all three questions, please continue, completing the rest of the survey. If you answered no to any one of the three questions, your participation is not necessary; however, please return the survey using the envelope provided. Thank you.

Those who meet the requirements continue, whereas those who answer at least one "no" are asked not to continue with the survey. Regardless of participation, all are asked to return the survey.

Contingency questions are appropriate when additional information is needed, particularly when the question is based on assumptions, preexisting knowledge, behaviors, characteristics, and perceptions. As the example below illustrates, when we ask, "Do you drive to work?" or "When did you graduate from college?" we are making assumptions about current employment, ownership of a vehicle, and college attendance. The addition of follow-up questions controls for the assumption making and the arrows direct the respondents through the contingencies.

1. Are you currently employed?
   ☐ No (please skip to question 2)
   ☐ Yes
   └─────► If yes, how do you get to work?
                  ☐ Own, personal vehicle
                  ☐ Public transportation
                  ☐ Taxi
                  ☐ Bicycle
                  ☐ Walk
                  ☐ Other, please specify _____

2. Did you go to college for an undergraduate degree?
   ☐ No (please skip to question 3)
   ☐ Yes

   → If yes, did you graduate?
      ☐ No (please skip to question 3)
      ☐ Yes

      → If yes, in what year did you graduate from college? _____
3. What is your gender?
   ☐ Male
   ☐ Female

On occasion, respondents overlook contingency questions. Therefore, the best practice is to minimize them. To accomplish this, we rewrite the above questions and/or add responses to the list of options, as illustrated below.

1. When traveling to work, what is your most frequent mode of transportation? (Please select only one option.)
   ☐ I am currently unemployed
   ☐ Drive a vehicle (my own or someone else's car)
   ☐ Public transportation
   ☐ Taxi
   ☐ Bicycle
   ☐ Walk
2. What is your highest educational degree achieved to date?
   ☐ Less than a high school diploma
   ☐ High school diploma or equivalent
   ☐ Associate's degree
   ☐ Bachelor's degree
   ☐ Master's degree
   ☐ Other, please specify _____

The questions still measure the same concept—transportation to work and education—but avoid the contingency questions and the potential errors associated with skip patterns.

8.5.2 Question Placement and Sequence

We need respondents to gain confidence and trust in us as researchers; we accomplish this by producing a professional-looking survey and through proper placement of questions. Beyond trust and confidence, we need to motivate the respondents in the beginning to capture their interests so they will want to participate in, complete, and return the survey. As such, the first question or sets of questions at the beginning of the questionnaire should be simple, pleasant, interesting, and nonoffensive, and use forced-choice responses. The first question should not be one of these: Do you support abortion? How old are you? Are you against the death penalty? What is your race/ethnicity? Where were you born? If any of these were the first question on a survey, would you participate? These questions and other comparable ones are sensitive and personal, and decrease response rates when placed at the beginning of a survey. Therefore, researchers place sensitive questions toward the middle of the questionnaire.

Questionnaires that take a long time to complete cause survey fatigue, which diminishes the quality of the data. As a result, survey writers place open-ended questions that require more thought, particularly those requiring long responses toward the beginning to middle of the questionnaire. Open-ended questions at or near the end of the document will likely yield short, unusable responses or be skipped altogether.[21] And those questions requiring little brainpower, such as demographic and personal questions (i.e., race, gender, age, and income), are appropriate at the end of the survey.

The sequence of questions should be logical and organized into sections by topics; for example, keeping together questions about opinions, habits, experiences, knowledge, and demographics. This is particularly helpful when the survey is longer than one page. In addition, questions intended for a specific subset of the sample are grouped together with directions as shown in Box 8.3. In addition, those questions utilizing the same response set should be grouped together, as illustrated in Box 8.2. In Box 8.2, all questions use the same nonnumerical scale, which is located at the top and each question is listed vertically, on the left side of the matrix. Sequencing by topic and response set helps both the researcher and respondent. How? The matrix helps the researchers in the coding process and helps the respondent quickly move through the survey.

However, research shows that the order of the questions can manipulate responses, which threatens the validity and reliability of the data. For example, a question asked or information provided early on in the survey might influence the response to a later question or set of questions. In one research study, the same two questions were asked to two separate groups of individuals but in a different order as shown below.[22]

Group 1	*Group 2*
1. How happy are you with life in general?	1. How often do you normally go out on a date?
2. How often do you normally go out on a date?	2. How happy are you with life in general?

The researchers found no difference between the two questions for the first group; whereas, the second group's answers were highly correlated. The authors of this study argue that when related questions are asked where one is specific (dating) and the other is general (happiness), the general question "may be affected by its position while the more specific question is not."[23] Therefore, they suggest asking the general question first, followed by the more specific questions as illustrated in Group 1 in the above example.

Questionnaire writers evaluate the threats of question sequence by testing the survey prior to its final distribution. Researchers compare the responses of two versions of the same survey—one with the influential question first and the other version with the influential question later. If a question creates biased responses, then the results from the comparison will reveal these differences and the questions should be reordered.

8.5.3 Response Order and Layout

The layout of responses should be convenient for the respondent but the layout should not influence responses. Researchers can list the responses horizontally but only if all the options fit on the same line. If this is not possible, then the options are listed vertically. In either list—horizontal or vertical—equidistant spacing is used. Moreover, all responses should be listed under the question, slightly indented, and together on the same page; the responses should never be separated or listed on two separate pages. Consider the following examples.

1. What is your current relationship status?
   ____Single, but not dating ____Dating one partner exclusively
   ____Single dating various partners
   ____Dating one partner regularly but also seeing other people
   ____Engaged to be married ____Married ____Separated
   ____Divorced ____Living with partner but not married

2. What is your current relationship status?
   ____Single, but not dating   ____Dating one partner exclusively
   ____Single dating various partners   ____Engaged to be married
   ____Married   ____Separated
   ____Divorced   ____Living with partner but not married
   ____Dating one partner regularly but also seeing other people

3. What is your current relationship status?
   ____Single, but not dating
   ____Dating one partner exclusively
   ____Single dating various partners
   ____Dating one partner regularly but also seeing other people
   ____Engaged to be married
   ____Married
   ____Separated
   ____Divorced
   ____Living with partner but not married

4. What is your marital status?

____Single ____Married   ____Divorced

5. What is your marital status?

____Single ____Married ____Divorced

6. What is your marital status?

____Single   ____Married ____Divorced

____Widow/er ____Separated

For our purposes in this section, let us look beyond the overlapping and nonexhaustive issues in the above examples. In the first example, the responses are not spaced well. Can you imagine a survey set up this way with 30 questions? Respondents might overlook some options or be disoriented and skip the question or stop participating altogether. To improve the possibility of skipping a response or the question because its response options look confusing, we add more space between the items as illustrated in the second example. However, the layout is still not perfect.

When respondents are asked to select one item from a list of options and these items cannot all fit on the same horizontal line, responses are listed vertically, as shown in the third example. This takes up more room but reduces the propensity to overlook some of the options particularly if the spacing in the horizontal list is not equidistant, as shown in the fourth example. In this instance, respondents are likely to overlook the divorced option. We eliminate this problem in the fifth example where the spacing is the same between options; all three items are listed horizontally because they all fit on one line. The final question lists five items in a nonlinear fashion. Research studies find that similar presentations result in more respondents choosing items from the top line rather than from the second line of responses.[19] In the end, the third and fifth examples are best.

The list of responses should follow order when ordinal scales are used. For example, the list should look like those in the first column, not like those in the second column:

Proper ordering	*Improper ordering*
☐ Strongly disagree	☐ Strongly disagree
☐ Disagree	☐ Strongly agree
☐ Agree	☐ Disagree
☐ Strongly agree	☐ Agree
☐ Unsure	☐ Unsure

When the list is comprised of nominal responses, order does not necessarily matter, but alphabetical listings improve response time as they allow respondents to quickly locate the response. However, where lists are long, respondents typically select the items listed first, because reading through the entire list takes too much time.[24]

Sometimes researchers use the same response set for multiple questions, as displayed in the following example. The first four questions begin the same way and each uses and lists the same nonnumerical scale—strongly agree to strongly disagree. This approach is inefficient in both time and space. To improve the layout, a matrix form or table is used where the questions are listed in the left column, and each response option is assigned a column as illustrated in the fifth question below.

1. Do you feel the municipality is competing to attract private investment with a nearby local government?

   [1] Strongly agree   [2]Agree   [3]Disagree   [4]Strongly disagree   [5]Unsure

2. Do you feel the municipality is competing to attract private investment with other local governments within the state?

   [1] Strongly agree   [2]Agree   [3]Disagree   [4]Strongly disagree   [5]Unsure

3. Do you feel the municipality is competing to attract private investment with other states?

   [1] Strongly agree   [2]Agree   [3]Disagree   [4]Strongly disagree   [5]Unsure

4. Do you feel the municipality is competing to attract private investment with foreign countries?

   [1] Strongly agree   [2]Agree   [3]Disagree   [4]Strongly disagree   [5]Unsure

5. Do you feel the municipality is competing to attract private investment with any of the following? Please check the most appropriate response for each question.

	Strongly agree	Agree	Disagree	Strongly disagree	Unsure
1. A nearby local government	☐	☐	☐	☐	☐
2. Other local governments within the state	☐	☐	☐	☐	☐
3. Other states	☐	☐	☐	☐	☐
4. Foreign countries	☐	☐	☐	☐	☐

Although using a matrix saves time and space, problems still exist. When there are many questions or statements listed that use the same response set format, the potential for response-set bias increases. Response set bias is where respondents simply select the same option over and over again (i.e., all unsures) without really reading the questions or statements. Box 8.2 illustrates response-set bias. In these instances, the researcher wonders if response set bias has occurred or if the respondent is truly neutral on all issues. Response set bias occurs most often when fatigue or lack of interest sets in, typically an issue with longer surveys. Shorter surveys help reduce the potential for response set bias, but where surveys are longer, the matrix should be placed toward the beginning or middle of the survey.[25]

Finally, some researchers prefer to use numbers rather than boxes or circles for the responses in self-administered surveys as illustrated in the following example. That is, researchers precode the survey prior to its distribution. Although this approach is more efficient for data entry (discussed in the next chapter), studies suggest that precoded answers influence responses. In the illustrations that follow, the scale used in the first example assigns a number 1 to strongly agree and a 4 to strongly disagree. In the second example, the same questions and nonnumerical scale are used; however, the numbers assigned range from 2 to –2.

1. Please circle the number that best represents your opinion for each of the following statements.

	Strongly agree	Agree	Disagree	Strongly disagree	Unsure
1. The park bathrooms are clean.	1	2	3	4	5
2. The park's grounds are well maintained.	1	2	3	4	5
3. The park has enough picnic tables.	1	2	3	4	5

2. Please circle the number that best represents your opinion for each of the following statements.

	Strongly Agree	Agree	Unsure	Disagree	Strongly Disagree
1. The park bathrooms are clean.	2	1	0	–1	–2
2. The park's grounds are well maintained.	2	1	0	–1	–2
3. The park has enough picnic tables.	2	1	0	–1	–2

Respondents are more likely to associate the value of the number to the meaning of the word. For example, when the scale used negative and positive numbers, respondents were less likely to select the negative numbers.[26] Given the potential bias and confusion created by pre-coding, the best practice is to avoid pre-coding altogether and use boxes or circles to be checked by the respondent, as illustrated below.

Please check the box that best represents your opinion for each of the following statements.

	Strongly Agree	Agree	Disagree	Strongly Disagree	Unsure
1. The park bathrooms are clean.	☐	☐	☐	☐	☐
2. The park's grounds are well maintained.	☐	☐	☐	☐	☐
3. The park has enough picnic tables.	☐	☐	☐	☐	☐

8.5.4 Recap

Although most of the literature regarding response rates and data quality for self-administered surveys is inconclusive or at odds with one another, the consensus suggests that, overall, the physical appearance for self-administered surveys must be attractive and professional looking, as well as easy to use, follow, and read. Finally, the key to improving participation and keeping the respondent's interest is to keep the survey or interview short.

8.6 Cover Letters

A cover letter is a letter that researchers include with a survey that introduces the researcher and the research project to the respondent. In addition, the letter provides instructions to the respondent on how to complete the survey, the sampling selection process, and where and when to return the survey. The presence of a cover letter along with a personal salutation and a written rather than a stamped signature creates authenticity and significantly improves responses rates.[27] Moreover, to improve the legitimacy of the survey, researchers seek sponsors and/or endorsers of the project.

Beyond the project, the cover letter communicates the protections extended to the human subjects by federal law. The federal government's regulation code (45CFR46) lists eight basic elements to include in cover letters:[28]

1. A statement of the study, its purpose, the amount of time the subject can expect to be involved, a description of the procedures, and identification of any experimental procedures
2. A description of risks
3. A description of the benefits
4. A disclosure statement of alternative treatments that may be more beneficial to the subject
5. An explanation of how confidentiality will be maintained
6. Where more than minimal risk is involved, details should be provided about compensation and available medical treatments should injury occur
7. Contact information on whom subjects can call to find out more about the research and subjects' rights
8. A narrative explaining that participation is voluntary and no consequences exist for not participating[29]

Researchers must never assume respondents are familiar with their rights. Protection must be ensured and following the above guidelines protects the rights of the research subjects. Overall, researchers must obtain consent through a signed consent form and do so in a noncoercive manner.

When using surveys that pose no risk to the participants, informed consent forms are not used. In this case, the respondent's action connotes informed consent; the subject either fills out and returns the survey—representing consent—or does not fill out the survey and tosses the survey in the trash. Most of the research conducted by practitioners poses no physical, mental, or financial risk to human subjects. However, this does not mean that the eight basic elements are ignored; rather, they are conveyed in the cover letter.

Overall, a cover letter gives respondents the first impression about the survey; therefore, participation depends on the presence of a professional-looking document. Moreover, a respondent's confidence and trust in the project is increased when the cover letter communicates the purpose of the study, communicates the respondents' rights and ensures their protection, and provides instructions on how to complete the survey. Box 8.4 presents an example of a cover letter from the School Survey on Crime and Safety.

BOX 8.4   SAMPLE COVER LETTER FROM THE SCHOOL SURVEY ON CRIME AND SAFETY[30]

Dear Principal/School Administrator:

The School Survey on Crime and Safety (SSOCS) is being administered to a nationally representative sample of public elementary and secondary schools. Your participation is important. Below are answers to some general questions.

WHAT IS THE PURPOSE OF THIS SURVEY?

The SSOCS is the primary source of school-level data on crime and safety for the U.S. Department of Education. It provides nationwide estimates of crime, discipline, disorder, programs, and policies in public schools. Data on crime, violence, and disorder in our nation's schools are collected so that policymakers, parents, and educators will have the information necessary to identify emerging problems and gauge the safety of American schools.

WHO IS CONDUCTING THIS SURVEY?

The U.S. Census Bureau is conducting this survey on behalf of the National Center for Education Statistics (NCES) of the U.S. Department of Education.

WHY SHOULD I PARTICIPATE IN THIS SURVEY?

Policymakers and educational leaders rely on data from this survey to make informed decisions concerning school programs and policies to reduce crime in public schools. Because the SSOCS is a sample survey, your responses represent the responses of many schools that serve similar student populations. Higher responses rates give us confidence that the findings are accurate. Your cooperation is essential to make the results of this survey comprehensive, accurate, and timely.

WILL MY RESPONSES BE KEPT CONFIDENTIAL?

Your responses are protected from disclosure by federal statute (P.L. 107-279, Title I, Part E, Sec. 183). All responses that related to or describe identifiable

---

**BOX 8.4   SAMPLE COVER LETTER FROM THE SCHOOL
SURVEY ON CRIME AND SAFETY (Continued)**

characteristics of individuals may be used only for statistical purposes and may not be discloses, or used, in identifiable form for any other purposes, unless otherwise compelled by law.

HOW WILL MY INFORMATION BE REPORTED?
The information you provide will be combined with the information provided by others in statistical reports. No data that discloses the identities of either you, your school, or your district will be included in the statistical reports.

WHERE SHOULD I RETURN MY COMPLETED QUESTIONNAIRE?
Please return your completed questionnaire in the enclosed postage-paid envelope or mail it to:

U.S. CENSUS BUREAU
ATTN: SPB 64 C
1201 E. 10TH STREET
JEFFERSONVILLE, IN 47132-0001

We hope you will participate in this voluntary survey.

Sincerely,

Commissioner
National Center for Education Statistics

8.7   Final Stages

The final stages of developing the survey include proofreading, testing, retesting, and sending out prenotification letters. When proofreading the survey, ask yourself the following about the wording of each question:

- Is the question unnecessary or not useful?
- Is the question biased or loaded?
- Is the question using leading/emotional language?
- Is the question double barreled?
- Is the question based on memory recall?
- Is the question based on assumptions?
- Is the question about future intentions?
- Does the question use negatives or double negatives?
- Does the question use jargon, slang, or abbreviations?

If the answer to any one of these questions is yes, then rewrite the question. If the answer to every question is no, then ask yourself the following about the responses where forced choice questions are used:

- Are the responses equally balanced?
- Are the responses nonoverlapping?
- Are the responses exhaustive?
- Are the responses understandable?
- Do the responses match the question?

If the answer to any one of these questions is no, then rewrite the responses. If the answer to every question is yes, then ask yourself the following about the overall appearance of the survey:

- Are all the questions numbered?
- Where skip patterns are used, do they flow properly?
- Is the survey organized by subject and response set?
- Are instructions provided on how to complete and return the survey?
- Is there enough space between questions, between responses, and for open questions?
- Is the space equidistant for the responses?

If the answer to any one of these question is no, then alter the layout. If the answer to every question is yes, then make sure the cover letter incorporates all the necessary information communicated earlier in this chapter. After asking and answering each question and making the necessary changes, the survey is ready to be tested.

All questionnaires must be tested prior to distributing them to the sample. Testing the survey helps researchers establish reliability and validity by revealing uncertainties and ambiguities that were not apparent in the construction phase. A number of testing options are available and some were discussed in Chapter 3, such as the test–retest, parallel forms, and interrater reliability methods. Others include giving a draft questionnaire to colleagues, friends, and relatives, or to a small sample (i.e., focus groups) that mirrors the target population. The group of friends and relatives are helpful editors—editing grammar, punctuation, and flow of skip and contingency patterns. The focus group is useful to evaluate each question at great pains. Researchers ask the members of the group what each question means—how they interpret each—and how they would respond. This is helpful with open and closed questions to expose wording and response set issues.

Upon the completion of the test, researchers make the necessary changes. Someone or a group of people other than the researcher should conduct one final edit of the survey. The outside reader should make sure the numbering is in order, the sections are properly labeled and numbered, and where skip patterns are used, that the proper sequence is maintained.

Before administering the survey, researchers sometimes send out a prenotification letter to the sample. Similar to the cover letter, the prenotification is a bit shorter, telling the subjects about the researcher and the project, saying that they can expect a survey to arrive shortly, and suggesting how important their participation is to the project. Prenotification letters have been shown to improve the response rates of self-administered surveys, particularly e-mail surveys.[31] When using e-mail and Web surveys, the prenotification is sent via e-mail rather than using the postal service. Given the immediate receipt of e-mail, the prenotification for e-mail and Web surveys can be sent a few days before sending the survey. Prenotification for mail surveys, on the other hand, should be sent out a week or two before the survey. See Chapter 7 for an example of a prenotification letter.

The next step is to distribute the survey. Mail surveys should include an addressed postage-paid envelope to assist with the return process, and e-mail surveys should include the return e-mail address. Most of the completed surveys will be returned within the first few days for e-mail surveys and within the first 10 days for mail surveys. To improve response rates, follow-up contact should be made after two weeks for mail surveys, and a week for e-mail surveys. See Chapter 7 for examples.

8.8   Summary

The questionnaire construction process requires time, common sense, as well as an understanding of research designs, measurement theory, data analysis, and the target population. A good survey is one that covers the scope and purpose of the research, asks valid and reliable questions, uses appropriate response formats, and is professional looking. However, even the best survey question suffers from uncontrollable factors that affect response rates and the quality of the data. Table 8.3 summarizes these factors.

Other factors affect the quality of the data and responses rates; for example, length and complexity are well within the control of the researcher. Long surveys create fatigue that results in response set bias, skipping open-ended questions, and avoiding contingency questions, all of which affect the quality of the data. An understanding all of these factors helps researchers create surveys that yield high response rates, and valid and reliable data.

Table 8.3 Factors Affecting Self-Administered Surveys

Affects Overall Response Rates	Affects Number of Nonresponses to Individual Questions	Affects Validity and Reliability of Data
Survey length	Open-ended questions	Social desirability/truth
Color of paper	Threatening questions	telling
User friendliness/	Objectionable questions	Knowledge
booklet form	Sensitive questions	Comprehension
Open-ended questions	Nonlinear lists of	Mode
Personal salutation	responses	Layout of responses
Signature	Directions	Don't know/undecided
Paid postage	Skip patterns	options
Anonymity/	Spacing	Neutral/no opinion
confidentiality	Complex design	options
Prenotifications	Mode: mail, e-mail, Web,	Directions
Follow ups	phone	Check all
Cover letters		Question sequence
Endorsements/sponsors		
Incentives		
Mode: mail, e-mail, Web,		
phone		
Motivation/interest		

Key Terms

Balanced	Informed consent	Prenotification
Closed questions	Mutually exclusive	Ranking
Contingency questions	Nominal responses	Rating
Cover letters	Open-ended questions	Reliability
Double-barreled	Ordinal responses	Response set bias
Forced choice responses	Partially closed questions	Scaled responses
Exhaustive	Participant fatigue	Validity

Exercises

1. Identify the problems with the survey provided in Box 8.1. Then rewrite the questions, assuming it is a self-administered survey, so that the errors are eliminated.
2. Write a cover letter that would accompany the above survey.

3. Create a questionnaire that measures what you and your workers do with their work time. Ask about formal and informal job responsibilities. How could you test for reliability?

4. Search the journal *Political Opinion Quarterly* for the most up-to-date information on questionnaire construction. Find three articles on one of the major topics discussed in this chapter and write a summary of their findings as they relate to questionnaire construction and distribution.

Recommended Reading

DeVellis, R. F. (2003). *Scale Development: Theory and Applications*. Second edition. Thousand Oaks, CA: Sage Publications.

Dillman, D. A. (2006). *Mail and Internet Surveys: The Tailored Design Method*. New York: Wiley.

Dillman, D. A. (1978). *Mail and Telephone Surveys*. New York: Wiley.

Fink, A. (2006). *How to Conduct Surveys: A Step-By-Step Guide*. Thousand Oaks, CA: Sage.

Fowler, F. J. (1995). *Improving Survey Questions: Design and Evaluation*. Thousand Oaks, CA: Sage.

Groves, R. M. (2004). *Survey Errors and Survey Costs*. New York: Wiley.

Sudman, S. and Bradburn, N. M. (1974). *Response Effects in Surveys: A Review and Synthesis*. Chicago: Aldine Publishing Company.

Sudman, S. and Bradburn, N.M. (1982). *Asking Questions: A Practical Guide to Questionnaire Design*. San Francisco: Jossey-Bass

Sudman, S. and Bradburn, N. M. (1988). *Polls and Surveys: Understanding What They Tell Us*. San Francisco: Jossey-Bass.

Sudman, S., Bradburn, N. M., and Schwarz, N. (1996). *Thinking about Answers: The Application of Cognitive Processes to Survey Methodology*. San Francisco: Jossey-Bass.

Endnotes

1. Dillman, D. A. (1978). *Mail and Telephone Surveys: The Total Design Method*. New York: John Wiley & Sons, p. 97.

2. Bertrand, M. and Mullainathan, S. (2001). Do people mean what they say? Implications for subjective survey data. *American Economic Review, 91* (2), 67–72. Papers and Proceedings of the 113th Annual Meeting of the American Economic Association.

3. Bertrand, M. and Mullainathan, S. (2001), pp. 67–68.

4. Sudman, S. and Bradburn, N. M. (1982). *Asking Questions: A Practical Guide to Questionnaire Design*. San Francisco: Jossey-Bass, p. 21.

5. Dillman, D. A. (2007). *Mail and Internet Surveys: The Tailored Design Method,* second edition. Hoboken, NJ: John Wiley & Sons, p. 47.

6. Rockwood, T. H., Sangster, R. L., and Dillman, D. A. (1997). The effect of response categories on survey questionnaires: Context and mode effects. *Sociological Methods and Research, 26*, 125.

7. Ibid, p. 128.

8. Bertrand, M. and Mullainathan, S. (2001). p. 69

9. *Greater Grand Rapids 2007 Community Report Card* Survey administered by the Johnson Center for Philanthropy.

10. Sudman, S. and Bradburn, N. M. (1982); Bertrand, M. and Mullainathan, S. (2001); Krosnick, J. A. (1999). Survey research. *Annual Review of Psychology, 50*, 537–567. Smyth, J. D., Dillman, D. A., Christian, L. M., and Stern, M. J. (2006). Comparing check-all and forced-choice question formats in web surveys. *Public Opinion Quarterly, 70*(1), 66–77.

11. Rasinski, K. A., Mingay, D., and Bradburn, N. M. (1994). Do respondents really mark all that apply on self-administered questions? *Public Opinion Quarterly, 58*, 400–408.

12. Smyth, J. D., Dillman, D. A., Christian, L. M., and Stern, M. J. (2006).

13. Study conducted by Kulka, R. A., Holt, N. A., Carter, W., and Dowd, K. L. (1991). Self-reports of time pressures, concerns for privacy and participation in the 1990 mail census. In *Proceedings of the Bureaus of the Census 1991 Annual Research Conference*, pp. 33–54. Washington, DC: Department of Commerce. Cited in Dillman, D. A., Sinclair, M., and Clark, J. R. (1993). Effects of questionnaire length, respondent-friendly design, and a difficult question on response rates for occupant addressed census mail surveys. *Public Opinion Quarterly, 57*, 289–304.

14. Dillman, D. A., Sinclair, M., and Clark, J. R. (1993).

15. Fox, R. J., Crask, M. R., and Kim, J. (1988). Mail survey response rate: A meta-analysis of selected techniques for inducing response. *Public Opinion Quarterly, 52*, 467–491. Gullahorn, J. E. and Gullahorn J. T. (1963). An investigation of the effects of three factors on response to mail questionnaires. *Public Opinion Quarterly, 52*, 294–296. Jobber, D. and Sanderson, S. (1983). The effects of a prior letter and colored questionnaires paper on mail survey response rates. *Journal of the Market Research Society, 25*, 339–349. Crittenden, W., Crittenden, V., and Hawes, J. (1985). Examining the effects of questionnaire color and print font on mail survey response rates. *Akron Business and Economic Review, 16* (4), 51–56. Matteson, M. (1974). Type of transmittal letter and questionnaire color as two variables influencing response rates in a mail survey. *Journal of Applied Psychology, 59*, 535–536.

16. Dias de Rada, V. (2005). Influence of questionnaire design on response to mail surveys. *International Journal Social Research Methodology, 8*, 61–78.

17. Pressley, M. M. and Tuller, W. L. (1997). A factor interactive investigation of mail survey response rates from a commercial population. *Journal of Marketing Research, 14*, 108–111.

18. Sudman, S. and Bradburn, N. M. (1982). p. 244.

19. Christian, L. M and Dillman, D. A. (2004). The influence of graphical and symbolic language manipulations on responses to self-administered questions. *Public Opinion Quarterly, 68*, 57–80.

20. Portions from The Campus Diversity Study sponsored by the Regional Consortium for Multicultural Education. The entire survey can be found at www.marywood.edu/instresearch/camdiv.htm.

21. Johnson, W. R., Sieveking, N. A., and Clanton, E. S. (1974). Effects of alternative positioning of open-ended questions in multiple choice questionnaires. *Journal of Applied Psychology, 59*, 776–778.

22. Bertrand, M. and Mullainathan, S. (2001), p. 67.

23. Sudman, S. and Bradburn, N. M. (1982), p. 143.

24. Bertrand, M. and Mullainathan, S. (2001), p. 68.

25. Herzog, A. R. and Bachman, J. G. (1981). Effects of questionnaire length on response quality. *Public Opinion Quarterly, 45*, 549–559.

26. Schwarz, N., Knauper, B., Hippler, H. J., Noelle-Neumann, E., and Clark, L. (1991). Rating scales: Numeric values may change the meaning of scale labels. *The Public Opinion Quarterly, 55*, 570–582.

27. Heerwegh, D. (2005). Effects of personal salutations in e-mail invitations to participate in a web survey. *Public Opinion Quarterly, 69*, 588–598.

28. The tip sheet can be found at http://www.hhs.gov/ohrp/humansubjects/guidance/ictips.htm.

29. Department of Health and Human Services. (2005, June 23). Code of Federal Regulations, Title 45 Public Welfare, Part 46 Protection of Human Subjects. www.hhs.gov/ohrp/humansubjects/guidance/45cfr46.htm. Accessed October 24, 2005.

30. Nolle, K. L., Guerino, P., and Dinkes, R. (2007). *Crime, Violence, Discipline, and Safety in U.S. Public Schools: Findings From the School Survey on Crime and Safety: 2005–06* (NCES 2007-361). National Center for Education Statistics, Institute of Education Sciences, U.S. Department of Education, Washington, DC.

31. Rochford, L. and Venable, C. F. (1995). Surveying a targeted population segment: The effects of endorsement on mail questionnaire response rates. *Journal of Marketing, Theory and Practice* (Spring), 86–97. Mehta, R. and Sivadas, E. (1995). Comparing response rates and response content in mail versus electronic mail surveys. *Journal of the Market Research Society, 7*, 29–33. Schaefer, D. R. and Dillman, D. A. (1998). Development of a standard e-mail methodology: Results of an experiment. *Public Opinion Quarterly, 62*, 378–397.

Chapter 9

Coding and Managing Data

9.1 Introduction

Up to this point, we have discussed data in the context of measurements, data sources, and questionnaire construction. Concepts become variables, and the variables are measured through a variety of methods, including the use of survey questions as illustrated in Box 9.1. When respondents complete and return the survey, the answers to the questions yield observations which are coded into numbers, and the aggregation of the observations begets data. Prior to coding each survey, researchers create a codebook, similar to the one shown in Box 9.2. The codebook is an expansion of the survey, where the level of data (nominal, ordinal, or ratio), numerical codes, and their definitions are added. The database, presented in Box 9.3, is where the researcher enters the information from each survey by placing the variables in the columns, and the observations in the rows. This chapter demonstrates how to create both the codebook and database.

9.2 The Codebook

To understand coding and data entry, we begin with a brief discussion of the codebook, explaining its purpose and contents using Box 9.2 as an illustration. The codebook, sometimes called the a data dictionary, guides data recording by

---

BOX 9.1 ILLUSTRATION OF SURVEY USED TO CREATE A CODEBOOK AND DATABASE

1. During the 2003–2004 school year, was it a practice of your school to do the following? (If your school changed its practices during the school year, please answer regarding your most recent practice. Check one response for each line.)

	Yes	No
a. Require visitors to sign or check in	☐	☐
b. Control access to school buildings during school hours	☐	☐
c. Control access to school grounds during school hours	☐	☐

2. Does your school have a written plan that describes procedures to be performed in the following crises? If yes, has your school drilled students on the use of this plan this school year? (In each row, please check whether you have a written plan. For every "Yes" answer, check whether your school has drilled students on the plan this year.)

	Have a written plan?		If "Yes," has your school drilled students on the plan this year?	
	Yes	No	Yes	No
a. Shootings	☐	☐	☐	☐
b. Natural disasters (e.g., earthquakes, tornados)	☐	☐	☐	☐
c. Hostages	☐	☐	☐	☐

3. What is your best estimate of the percentage of students who had at least one parent or guardian participating in the following events during the 2003–2004 school year? (Check one response on each line.)

	0–25%	26–50%	51–75%	76–100%	School does not offer
a. Open-house or back-to-school night	☐	☐	☐	☐	☐
b. Regularly scheduled parent–teacher conferences	☐	☐	☐	☐	☐

4. How many of the following types of sworn law enforcement officers, security guards, or security personnel did you regularly have present in your school? (If an officer works full-time across various schools in the district, please count this as "part-time" for this school.)

When you have no such officer or guard, please record zero [0]

	Number of full-time at your school	Number of part-time at your school
a. Security guard or security personnel	_____	_____
b. School resource officers	_____	_____

Source: Adapted from the U.S. Department of Education, *School Survey on Crime and Safety 2003–2004.*[1]

BOX 9.2 ILLUSTRATION OF A CODEBOOK USING THE SCHOOL SURVEY ON CRIME AND SAFETY

Variable Label	Question Number	Question	Level of Data	Coding
ID		Unique six-digit number assigned to each returned survey	Nominal	
q1a	1a	School practice requires visitor check in	Nominal	1 = yes 2 = yes −1 = blank
q1b	1b	Access controlled locked/ monitored doors	Nominal	1 = yes 2 = yes −1 = blank
q1c	1c	Grounds have locked/ monitored gates	Nominal	1 = yes 2 = yes −1 = blank
q2a1	2a	Have a written plan for shootings	Nominal	1 = yes 2 = yes −1 = blank
q2a2	2a	Drilled students on plan for shootings	Nominal	1 = yes 2 = yes −1 = blank
q2b1	2b	Have a written plan for natural disasters	Nominal	1 = yes 2 = yes −1 = blank
q2b2	2b	Drilled students on plan for natural disasters	Nominal	1 = yes 2 = yes −1 = blank
q2c1	2c	Have a written plan for hostages	Nominal	1 = yes 2 = yes −1 = blank
q2c2	2c	Drilled students on plan for hostages	Nominal	1 = yes 2 = yes −1 = blank
q3a	3a	Parent participates in open house or back-to-school night	Ordinal	1 = 0–25% 2 = 26–50% 3 = 51–75% 4 = 76–100% 9 = does not offer
q3b	3b	Parent participates in parent–teacher conference	Ordinal	1 = 0–25% 2 = 26–50% 3 = 51–75% 4 = 76–100% 9 = does not offer
q4a1	4a	# of full-time security guards	Ratio	−1 = blank
q4a2	4a	# of part-time security guards	Ratio	−1 = blank
q4b1	4b	# of full-time Resource Officers	Ratio	−1 = blank
q4b2	4b	# of part-time Resource Officers	Ratio	−1 = blank

BOX 9.3 ILLUSTRATION OF AN EXCEL SPREADSHEET[2]

	A	B	C	D	E	F	G	H	I	J	K	L	M	N	O	P
1	ID	q1a	q1b	q1c	q2a1	q2a2	q2b1	q2b2	q2c1	q2c2	q3a	q3b	q4a1	q4a2	q4b1	q4b2
2	100001	1	1	1	1	1	1	1	1	1	1	3	0	0	2	0
3	100002	1	1	2	1	1	1	1	1	1	4	4	0	0	1	2
4	100003	1	1	2	1	1	1	1	1	1	4	3	-1	-1	-1	-1
5	100004	1	2	2	1	2	1	1	1	2	1	1	0	0	0	1
6	100005	1	1	1	1	2	1	1	1	2	2	1	0	0	0	0
7	100006	1	1	2	1	1	1	1	1	1	1	1	-1	-1	-1	-1
8	100007	1	1	2	1	1	1	1	1	1	2	1	0	0	1	0
9	100008	1	1	2	1	2	1	1	1	2	4	4	-1	-1	-1	-1
10	100009	1	1	1	1	1	1	1	1	1	3	2	-1	-1	-1	-1
11	100010	1	1	2	1	1	1	1	1	1	4	3	-1	-1	-1	-1
12	100011	1	1	1	1	1	1	2	1	1	2	1	0	0	0	0
13	100012	1	1	2	1	1	1	1	1	2	1	3	0	1	0	1
14	100013	1	1	2	1	1	1	1	1	1	2	2	0	0	0	1
15	100014	1	1	2	1	1	1	1	1	1	4	4	0	0	0	1
16	100015	1	1	1	1	1	1	1	1	1	4	4	-1	-1	-1	-1
17	100016	1	1	1	1	1	1	1	2	-1	2	2	0	0	1	0
18	100017	1	1	2	1	1	1	1	1	1	4	4	0	0	0	1
19	100018	1	1	2	1	1	1	1	1	1	2	2	0	0	1	0
20	100019	1	1	1	1	1	1	1	1	1	2	1	0	0	0	0
21	100020	1	1	2	2	1	2	2	2	2	2	2	0	2	0	1
22	100021	1	1	2	2	1	2	2	2	2	5	1	1	1	0	-1
23	100022	1	2	2	2	1	2	2	2	2	2	2	-1	-1	-1	0
24	100023	1	1	1	2	1	1	1	1	1	2	2	0	0	1	1
25	100024	1	1	1	1	1	1	1	1	1	4	4	0	0	0	0
26	100025	1	1	2	2	1	1	1	2	2	2	2	-1	-1	-1	-1
27	100026	1	1	2	2	1	1	1	2	2	4	2	0	0	0	0
28	100027															

crime

standardizing responses and maintaining consistency such that all those responsible for handling the data are able to code and enter the data the same way. The
codebook for a questionnaire provides the following information:

- Variable label
- Question number from the questionnaire
- Question definition or shorter version of the question
- Level of measurement for question responses
- Appropriate codes for each response

Codebooks are constructed for the convenience of the researcher using a word pro-
cessing program or a spreadsheet; as such, they do not all look alike, and codebooks
are not just for questionnaires. Some data dictionaries define secondary data. For
example, the codebook shown in Box 9.2 is much different from the one depicted
in Box 9.4. The codebook in Box 9.4 is from the *State Politics and Policy Quarterly*
(SPPQ) published by the Institute of Legislative Studies at the University of Illinois–
Springfield and the Institute of Government and Public Affairs at the University of
Illinois–Urbana–Champaign. SPPQ provides state information—a codebook and
dataset—based on preexisting data from the FBI, the Census Bureau, and the Statistical Abstract, as well as many other sources.[3] This particular codebook provides
the variable label, its definition, and the source of the secondary data. Regardless of
its setup, all codebooks achieve the same goal: to label and define the variables and
data used by the researcher.

Box 9.2 provides an illustration of a codebook based on the survey shown in
Box 9.1. The survey is grouped into four questions; however, each grouping asks at
least two questions, and some ask follow-up questions. In the end, the questionnaire
asks 15 different questions; therefore, the codebook defines all 15 items. Finally, as
each questionnaire is returned, researchers write an identification number on the
top of the survey and enter the ID into the database. This serves a mechanism to
keep track of the surveys as they are returned. This is usually the first item listed in
the codebook, as well as the first entry in the database.

Let us turn our attention to the contents of the codebook. The purpose of the
variable label is to have a short (i.e., eight or fewer characters), unique identifier for
each variable. The easiest approach is to label the variable as its corresponding question number. Using the survey in Box 9.1, each question can be label to correspond
to its sequence; for example, q1a, q1b, q2a1, q2a2, and so forth. We know q1a refers
to the first part of question one and q2a2 is the label for the follow-up question to
first part of question two. Another label option is to truncate the question into a
label; for instance, VISITCK could be assigned as the label for the first question—
requiring visitors to check in. Researchers use this approach to keep the variable
straight; that is, they would recognize what VISITCK represents faster than knowing what q1a denotes. Moreover, questions about age, gender, and income could be

BOX 9.4 ILLUSTRATION OF A CODEBOOK BASED ON SECONDARY DATA[4]

STATE DATA CODE BOOK

This file provides variable descriptions for the complete data set. Sources are listed for each variable, although complete citations are not given because they frequently involve multiple years and/or multiple publications. Variable descriptors indicate when data are cross-sectional, or not available for all years. Both the complete state data set and the separate divisions of the data set all contain the ID and YEAR variables. ID is a numerical state identification number running from 1 to 50 and identifying the states in alphabetical order (1 is Alabama and 50 is Wyoming). No data set includes Washington, DC. The YEAR variable indicates the year the data are associated with. All data sets are stacked by state by year.

POPULATION AND VITAL STATISTICS

ABREV — State abbreviation

POP — Population in 1000s. *The Statistical Abstract of the United States*

AREA — Land area in square miles (excludes water). *Statistical Abstract of the United States*

POPDENS — Population per square mile. Calculated from POP and AREA

BLACKPOP — Black population in 1000s. Bureau of the Census. *Current Population Reports/Statistical Abstract of the United States.* These data are not available for every year

ESTBKPOP — Estimated black population in 1000s. BLACKPOP used in a regression analysis to estimate black population in 1000s for all years

DIVORCE — Divorce rate per 1000 population. *Vital Statistics of the United States*

CHRISTAD — Percent of population that are Christian adherents. *Statistical Abstract of the United States.* This is 1990 and 2000 data

ABORT — Abortion rate per 1,000 women aged 15–44. For an explanation of why data is problematic after 2000/2001; see source: The Allan Guttmacher Institute

RESMOB — Percent of population residing in state for less than 5 years. Bureau of the Census *Current Population Reports/Statistical Abstract of the United States.* Data not available for every year

ESTMOB — Estimated yearly residential mobility (i.e., estimated percentage of population residing in state for less than 5 years based on regression analysis using RESMOB)

MURDER — Murders per 100,000 population. *Uniform Crime Reports,* FBI

RAPE — Rapes per 100,000 population. *Uniform Crime Reports,* FBI

ROBBERY — Robberies per 100,000 population. *Uniform Crime Reports,* FBI

ASSAULT — Aggravated assaults per 100,000 population. *Uniform Crime Reports,* FBI

BURGLARY — Burglaries per 100,000 population. *Uniform Crime Reports,* FBI

LARCENY — Larcenies and thefts per 100,000 population. *Uniform Crime Reports,* FBI

labeled AGE, GENDER, and INCOME. In any case, the labels should make sense to the researcher.

The codebook lists the question number, variable definition or the question from the survey, and level of data gathered. In the survey illustrated in Box 9.1, the first two questions provide respondents with a yes/no response set, and in the codebook they are defined as nominal. The third question is ordinal because the ranges of percentages are grouped into categories, and increase from lowest to highest. The last question asks about the number of officers; therefore, it is ratio-level data.

Finally, we add numerical codes to their corresponding variables. The numbers serve as labels for nominal and ordinal level measures or as measurable, discrete, or continuous integers for ratio level information. Coding and data entry are easy when surveys ask closed questions with forced-choice options or open-ended questions requesting ratio-level data. Qualitative information, on the other hand, is more difficult, sometimes impossible, to code, especially where respondents are asked to provide lengthy comments.

9.3 Coding

Prior to entering the data, researchers define the codes used in the dataset, and these codes correspond to the rules of measurement. Because nominal and ordinal data are the lowest form of data, any number can be used to denote their responses because the numerical code represent labels and lack numerical meaning. However, the code for ratio data represents the actual numerical meaning.

Codes are logical and consistent. When two dichotomous categories are used (for example, Yes or No, Male or Female, Agree or Disagree), a researcher can code the two different options with any number—for instance a 5 and an 8—but this makes no sense. Instead, the codes generally begin with 1 and move to left or right on a whole number continuum. For example, the researcher could use 1 and 0 for the two categories, or 1 and 2. In the codebook illustration in Box 9.2, we assign a 1 to the Yes response and a 2 for the No response.

When the survey provides respondents with more than two nominal categories, the codes do not use 0 but begin with 1. For example, suppose we asked respondents about their current marital status using the following categories:

■ Currently Married
■ Widowed
■ Divorced
■ Separated
■ Never Married

The researcher could code these categories in any fashion, but the commonsensical approach is to assign a code in order of the appearance of each category. Therefore,

Currently Married receives a 1, Widowed a 2, a 3 is assigned to Divorced, a 4 represents Separated, and Never Married is coded with 5.

However, longer lists of nominal-level options lengthen the list of codes. For example, the questionnaire used for the 2000 Census asked respondents about their race and provided 15 different options; four of these options asked for further specific information (i.e., the principle tribe if American Indian, specific Asian background, Pacific Islander background, or other race not listed). Moreover, the survey allowed respondents to select more than one box. The options and potential codes are listed below.

1. White	2. Black	3. American Indian/Alaskan Native
4. Asian Indian	5. Chinese	6. Filipino
7. Japanese	8. Korean	9. Vietnamese
10. Other Asian	11. Native Hawaiian	12. Guamanian/Chamorro
13. Samoan	14. Other Pacific Islander	15. Other race

If the U.S. Census Bureau wanted to know and aggregate the 15 different options, then the codes listed above would be enough. However, the process is not that simple because the government wants to track all races. Therefore, the analysts define a new code and definition for each new other race as well as the different tribes for American Indians and Alaskan Natives, other Asians, and other Pacific Islanders. Moreover, they have to establish a coding procedure for those respondents selecting two or more categories. Data coders cannot use a 13 to code a White and American Indian respondent because 13 is the code for Samoan, and statistical programs do not recognize a 1,3 as an entry. The bureau tracks the additional races by adding more numerical codes and corresponding labels. For example, they can assign 16 to White/American Indian and continue adding numbers and new definitions to the list as needed.

In fact, the U.S. Census Bureau takes a more complex approach to coding these data; 11 different variables represent an individual's race. For one of the variables, labeled RACE1, the Bureau assigns codes 1 through 9 to represent the major race categories:

1 = White alone
2 = Black alone
3 = American Indian alone
4 = Alaska Native alone
5 = American Indian/Alaska native tribe specified alone
6 = Asian alone
7 = Native Hawaiian alone
8 = Other race alone
9 = Two or more races

Another variable, RACE2, has 65 codes where a 1 refers to White and 2 to Black, codes 3 through 30 represent different Indian tribes, 31 through 36 correspond to Alaska native tribes, different Asian backgrounds are coded using 37 through 55, and 56 through 65 denote different Native Hawaiian races.[5] This illustration demonstrates just how difficult the coding process can be, especially with a long list of choices where respondents are allowed to select more than one option.

Ordinal measures add ordering to the response options; for example, frequencies, levels of agreement, and rank order. Question 3 in Box 9.2 is ordinal, where percentages are grouped together and ranked from the lowest category (0 to 25%) to the highest category (76 to 100%).

Ordinal codes can begin and end anywhere, but the logical approach is to assign smaller numerical codes to the lower values and larger numerical codes to the higher values. For example, we can assign a 1 to the lowest percentage range in question 3 in Box 9, and code the highest range with a 4, as illustrated below:

1 = 0–25%
2 = 26–50%
3 = 51–75%
4 = 76–100%

Ordered numerical codes are assigned when frequency scales are present. Consider the following survey questions about behavior:

1. How often do you drive to work?
   ☐ Every day ☐ Most days ☐ Some days ☐ Never

2. I ride the bus
   ☐ Frequently ☐ Occasionally ☐ Never

3. On average, about how many times do you ride the bus in a typical week?
   ☐ 0 times ☐ 1–4 times ☐ 5–9 times ☐ 10 or more times

Applying the rule of assigning a high numbered code to the higher-level response, we code the responses as illustrated below in Table 9.1.

Table 9.1 Examples of Ordinal Coding for Frequency Scales

Question 1	Question 2	Question 3
4 = Every day	3 = Frequently	4 = 10 or more times
3 = Most days	2 = Occasionally	3 = 5–9 times
2 = Some days	1 = Never	2 = 1–4 times
1 = Never		1 = 0 times

Table 9.2   Examples of Ordinal Coding Using Zeroes

Question 1	Question 2	Question 3
3 = Every day	2 = Frequently	3 = 10 or more times
2 = Most days	1 = Occasionally	2 = 5–9 times
1 = Some days	0 = Never	1 = 1–4 times
0 = Never		0 = 0 times

Alternatively, we can alter the scale so that zero denotes Never or Zero times, as Table 9.2 shows. Either approach is acceptable.

Ordinal scales also measure quality and level of agreement. The following question uses a quality scale ranging from very good to very poor.

4. Using a scale provided below, please check the box that best represents the quality of each of the following city services. Select only one box per service.

Service	Very good	Good	Average	Poor	Very poor
Recycling	☐	☐	☐	☐	☐
Street maintenance	☐	☐	☐	☐	☐
Street lighting	☐	☐	☐	☐	☐
Street sweeping	☐	☐	☐	☐	☐
Trash collection	☐	☐	☐	☐	☐

Researchers can code this scale, similar to the frequency scales discussed above, using different approaches. For example, a 1 through 5 or –2 through 2 can be assigned, where the lowest number (1 or –2) denotes the lowest quality (very poor) and the highest number (5 or 2) represents the best quality (very good). Table 9.3 presents these coding options.

Table 9.3   Illustration of Coding Options for a Quality Scale

Quality Scale	Coding Options	
	A	B
Very good	5	2
Good	4	1
Average	3	0
Poor	2	–1
Very poor	1	–2

The following question uses a bipolar level of agreement scale with Strongly Agree and Strongly Disagree as its anchors.

5. The university should provide opportunities for the recognition and reward of outstanding faculty academic advising.
   ☐ Strongly Agree
   ☐ Agree
   ☐ Neutral
   ☐ Disagree
   ☐ Strongly Disagree
   ☐ Undecided/don't know

The level of agreement scales have at least three different coding schemes and are illustrated in Table 9.4. Besides the Undecided category, the highest numbered code denotes the highest level of agreement and the lowest numbered code is assigned to the lowest level of agreement.

Although the rule of thumb in questionnaire construction is to avoid asking negative questions or statements, researchers sometimes ask negative questions when building summated scales (see Chapter 3 for discussion on summated scaling). Consequently, the coding for negative questions will be the opposite of the coding for positive questions; that is, for negative questions, researchers assign a lower numbered code to the positive responses (agrees), and the higher-numbered code to the lower or negative responses (disagrees). To illustrate why this is important, let us consider the following set of statements as well as the respondent's answers regarding job satisfaction:

Statement	Strongly Agree	Agree	Neither Agree nor Disagree	Disagree	Strongly Disagree	Don't Know
1. I like my job.	☐	☒	☐	☐	☐	☐
2. I like my coworkers.	☐	☒	☐	☐	☐	☐
3. I like my boss.	☐	☐	☐	☒	☐	☐
4. I dislike the number of hours I work per week.	☐	☐	☐	☐	☒	☐

To create the job satisfaction scale, the values of the assigned codes are summed; the total becomes the scale's score. With coding Option A from Table 9.4 for the agreement scale, adding all potential scores from any respondent range from 4 (selecting

Table 9.4 Illustration of Coding Options for an Agreement Scale

Agreement scale	Coding options		
	A	B	C
Strongly agree	5	4	2
Agree	4	3	1
Neutral	3	0	0
Disagree	2	2	−1
Strongly disagree	1	1	−2
Undecided/don't know	0	5	9

all disagrees) to 20 (selecting all agrees). Furthermore, the groups within the range can be defined as Satisfied or Unsatisfied; for example:

Score Range	Classification
4–12	Unsatisfied
13–20	Satisfied

The respondent's answers above, Agree (4), Strongly Agree (4), Disagree (2), and Strongly Disagree (1) yield an individual score of 11 suggesting that the respondent is dissatisfied. But when we look more closely at the statements, the fourth one says, "I dislike the number of hours I work per week." This is a negative statement, therefore, its responses mean the opposite of those responses to the other questions—a Strongly Disagree to question 4 is the same as a Strongly Agree to questions 1–3. As a result, the coding for the fourth question needs to be reversed—Strongly Disagree is labeled a 5, Disagree is coded a 4, Agree labeled a 2, and Strongly Agree a one. With the new codes, we recalculate the scale yielding a new score of 15, moving the respondent from Unsatisfied to Satisfied.

Beyond the issues surrounding negative questions, other problems arise in scale creation. Missing data from skipped questions, neutral responses, and don't know answers impact the index score. For example, if a respondent skips a question or answers "Don't Know," the scale score is reduced. This reduction occurs because the code for missing data is not included in the calculation of the scale. If, for instance, the respondent skips the third question, but answers the others as Strongly Agree, Agree, and Disagree, then the scale score is 12, which implies the respondent is Unsatisfied. When we look closer at the individual responses, each suggests Satisfied, not Unsatisfied. The same is true for the Don't Know response; the codes are not included in the calculation of the scale, which in turn affects the interpretation of the score. To eliminate this problem, some researchers calculate the average score—dividing the total score by the number of responses. The person who skipped question 3 would have an average score of 4 (12 divided by 3), but the person who answered all the questions with a score of 15 would have an average of 3.75, suggesting the first person is more satisfied than the second person.

Another reason why researchers calculate averages for their summated scales is because of neutral responses. If a respondent selected Neither Agree nor Disagree to all four questions, the total score would be 12, suggesting dissatisfaction, but the respondent is neither satisfied nor dissatisfied; therefore, the scale score is misleading. This is true for any of the agreement coding options presented earlier in Table 9.4. Using the Option B coding plan, which codes neutral as zero, the index range changes to 0 to 16, but one or more neutral responses would reduce an individual's overall job satisfaction.

In the end, the useful option available to researchers to analyze these summated scales is to calculate an average score. As you will learn in the next chapter, averages of ordinal data are of little statistical value, though.

Any of the coding methods for the different scales (frequency, quality, and agreement) outlined above are acceptable, but choosing one depends on how the researchers code undecided answers and skipped questions. The undecided and don't know options can be coded in a variety of different ways; for example, subtracting one from the lowest code (Option A in Table 9.4), adding one to the highest code (Option B), or using a number that is much higher or lower than the rest (Option C).

Open-ended questions require respondents to fill in information that is either qualitative or quantitative. The quantitative information is ratio-level information—for example, annual income, years on the job, or miles traveled to work—require no preset coding. Question 4 in Box 9.1 is open-ended, asking respondents to enter a ratio-level number.

The qualitative data gathered from open-ended questions can be coded, but only in certain instances. Researchers code those answers that are short; for instance, occupation, undergraduate major, or favorite graduate class. The School Survey on Crime and Safety, which is distributed to administrators (e.g., principals, vice principals, superintendents) of the kindergarten through twelfth grade school systems, asks respondents, in an open-ended question, their job title/position. The answers are not coded until the respondents return the completed questionnaire. Every time a questionnaire arrives, a code for job title/position is defined. In the end, the open-ended question produces the following list of positions/titles:[6]

1 = Principal
2 = Vice principal or disciplinarian
3 = Counselor
4 = Administrative or secretarial staff
5 = Teacher or instructor
6 = Safe Schools staff
7 = Superintendent or district staff
8 = Security personnel
95 = Other
−9 = Not ascertained

Included in this list is Other, which is used to capture uncommon responses—those that appear only once or twice. Responses with limited repetition do not warrant an identity and code of their own, so they are lumped together with the other uncommon responses.

Qualitative questions can also produce lengthy responses, those that are longer than one or two words. Long responses are difficult to code. As a result, researchers do not attempt to code these answers, instead they enter the entire response into the database or a word-processing program. These qualitative responses provide researchers with anecdotal evidence, which is included in the final report for illustrative purposes.

9.4   Database Management

A database houses all the entered information collected from the individual survey. Although many programs exist, those that enable statistical procedures should be used; for example, SPSS, Excel, SAS, Minitab, and Stata. The one rule that applies to all databases is placement of variables and observations. Variables are placed in the columns, and the observations from the surveys are entered across in the rows; each respondent's answers occupy its own row. We focus on Excel, as it is the program most widely available to public and nonprofit administrators.

The total number of rows indicates the number of observations, such as the number of returned surveys, and the total number of columns reflects the number of variables, but not necessarily reflective of the total number of questions. For example, the survey shown in Box 9.1 asks four questions, but within each question is a series of questions; for example, question 2 uses a contingency question. If respondents answer Yes to having a plan for shootings, natural disasters, or hostages, then they answer the contingency questions about mock drills for such occurrences. If they answer No to the first question about plans, then they skip the contingency question. Overall, question 2 asks six questions, three about plans, and three follow-up questions on drilling. As a result, six columns are used to record the information for question 2 as shown in columns E through J in Box 9.3. Therefore, columns are added to the database when contingency questions (follow-up questions), rank order questions, and check all that apply questions are asked. In all, there are 15 columns in the database in Box 9.3, one for each of the questions asked in the survey.

Prior to entering the data, all variable labels are added to the database. Unless an identification number was assigned to each survey prior to the initial distribution, a unique code should be assigned to each survey as it is received. The researchers writes this code in an obvious place on each survey—for example, the upper right hand corner. These are used for data cleaning purposes; if an entry error occurs, the researcher uses the identification number in the spreadsheet and matches it to the corresponding survey to correct the mistake. Once variable labels and ID numbers are assigned, the analyst enters the information from the surveys, which is one of the easiest and fastest parts of the entire research process.

Data entry can transpire in a number of ways, but the responses from each survey are entered in one row of the database, from left to right, not top to bottom; that is, data from the first survey are entered in the first row, the second survey's information is recorded in the second row, and so forth. Researchers continue this process until they insert all the survey information in the database. Sometimes, analysts write the code in the left margin of the survey, prior to entering the data, as Box 9.5 illustrates.

By writing the codes in the margins, the researcher can quickly enter the codes in the database, rather than moving around from the survey, to the codebook, to the database. To eliminate this step altogether, some researchers precode the survey prior to its distribution. Some coding methods are demonstrated in the following examples:

1. Do you feel the municipality is competing to attract private investment with any of the following? Please circle the most appropriate response for each question.

Responses	Strongly agree	Agree	Disagree	Strongly disagree	Unsure
a. A nearby local government	4	3	2	1	9
b. Other local governments within the state	4	3	2	1	9
c. Other states	4	3	2	1	9
d. Foreign countries	4	3	2	1	9

2. The university should provide opportunities for the recognition and reward of outstanding faculty academic advising.
   ☐₄ Strongly agree
   ☐₃ Agree
   ☐₂ Disagree
   ☐₁ Strongly disagree
   ☐₉ Undecided

3. How do you usually get to work? Check the one that is most frequently used.
   (1) Drive a vehicle   (2) Public transportation   (3) Taxi
   (4) Bicycle   (5) Walk   (6) Other

As discussed in the previous chapter, precoding may influence a respondent's answer or confuse the respondent altogether. Studies find that respondents associate the value of the number to the meaning of the word. For example, when the scale ranged from negative and positive numbers, respondents were less likely to select the negative numbers.[7]

BOX 9.5 ILLUSTRATION OF COMPLETED SURVEY WITH IDENTIFICATION NUMBER AND CODES

ID=100004

1. During the 2003–2004 school year, was it a practice of your school to do the following? (If your school changed its practices during the school year, please answer regarding your most recent practice. Check one response for each line.)

		Yes	No
1 a.	Require visitors to sign or check in	☑	☐
1 b.	Control access to school buildings during school hours	☑	☐
2 c.	Control access to school grounds during school hours	☐	☑

2. Does your school have a written plan that describes procedures to be performed in the following crises? If yes, has your school drilled students on the use of this plan this school year? (In each row, please check whether you have a written plan. For every "Yes" answer, check whether your school has drilled students on the plan this year.)

		Have a written plan?		If "Yes," has your school drilled students on the plan this year?	
		Yes	No	Yes	No
1 2 a.	Shootings	☑	☐	☐	☑
1 1 b.	Natural disasters (e.g., earthquakes, tornados)	☑	☐	☑	☐
1 2 c.	Hostages	☑	☐	☐	☑

3. What is your best estimate of the percentage of students who had at least one parent or guardian participating in the following events during the 2003–2004 school year? (Check one response on each line.)

		0–25%	26–50%	51–75%	76–100%	School does not offer
1 a.	Open-house or back-to-school night	☑	☐	☐	☐	☐
1 b.	Regularly scheduled parent–teacher conferences	☑	☐	☐	☐	☐

4. How many of the following types of sworn law enforcement officers, security guards, or security personnel did you regularly have present in your school? (If an officer works full-time across various schools in the district, please count this as "part-time" for this school.)

When you have no such officer or guard, please record zero [0]

		Number of full-time at your school	Number of part-time at your school
0 0 a.	Security guard or security personnel	0	0
0 1 b.	School resource officers	0	1

Now we turn our attention to coding rank order and check all that apply formats. We discuss these here because they are better understood within the context of database management.

Researchers sometimes ask respondents to rank a set of objects as illustrated in the following example:

1. Using a scale of 1 to 5, where 1 is most favorite and 5 is least favorite, please rank the following democratic presidential candidates.

___Hillary Clinton

___John Edwards

___Dennis Kucinich

___Barack Obama

___Bill Richardson

As discussed in the last chapter, we use 1 as most favorite because people are most familiar with 1 as being the best or top ranked; although if necessary, we can recode them in the data entry process. Because each object in the list receives a number, we list each object separately in its own column in the database as illustrated in Figure 9.1.

	A	B	C	D	E	F
1	ID	Clinton	Edwards	Kucinich	Obama	Richardson
2	1001	1	2	4	3	5
3	1002	2	3	5	4	1
4	1003	3	4	5	1	2
5	1004	4	5	1	2	3
6	1005	5	4	1	2	3
7	1006	1	1	5	1	4
8	1007	4	2	5	1	2
9	1008	3	1	5	2	4
10	1009	2	5	4	3	1
11	1010	1	4	5	2	3
12	1011	1	3	4	2	5
13	1012	2	3	1	4	5
14	1013	3	1	5	2	4
15	1014	4	1	5	2	3
16	1015	5	2	4	1	3
17	1016	9	1	9	9	9
18	1017	4	5	1	2	3
19	1018	2	5	4	1	3
20	1019	1	2	5	3	4
21	1020	4	3	5	2	1
22	1021	5	3	4	2	1
23	1022	1	2	5	3	4
24	1023	2	4	5	3	1
25	1024	1	2	5	3	4

Figure 9.1   Database illustration for rank order question.

One respondent, #1019, ranks the candidates in the following order:

1	Hillary Clinton
2	John Edwards
5	Dennis Kucinich
3	Barack Obama
4	Bill Richardson

The codes 1, 2, 5, 3, and 4 are entered across the row for person #1019. Sometimes respondents are unable to decide who their most favorite or least favorite candidate is, or they do not follow directions. For example, person #1006 in the database ranks Clinton, Edwards, and Obama as her most favorite, whereas person #1016 has only one favorite, Edwards, so he leaves the remaining candidates unranked (coded as 9 to represent missing values). These responses, if included in the analysis, would alter the outcome, particularly where the person selected three candidates as most favorite—clearly, this respondent is undecided. What do we do? We can create a new code, for example a –1, to signify a respondent who does not follow directions. Rather than entering 1, 1, 5, 1, and 4 for respondent #1016, we would enter –1, –1, –1, –1, and –1. When the researcher presents the findings in the research paper, she provides a discussion about the missing values and the approach used to code the anomalies.

Similar to the rank order questions, the "check all that apply" questions use a similar approach. Consider the following example:

1. On any given day, how do you get to work? Please check all that apply.
   ☒ Drive a vehicle   ☒ Public transportation
   ☐ Taxi   ☒ Bicycle
   ☐ Walk   ☐ Other

Each of the items listed in the response set is assigned its own label, definition, code, and column in the database as shown in Figure 9.2. The variable label could coincide with the option that is listed, for example, DRIVE, TAXI, BIKE, and so on, or be as simple as 1A for drive a vehicle and 1B for taking a taxi, and so forth. A nominal code represents each item, where a 1 depicts a checked item and the number 2 or 0 denotes an unchecked option. The respondent in the above example, selects drive a vehicle, public transportation, and bicycle, so each is assigned a one and the other unselected options are coded as 0 as shown in in Figure 9.2. We use 0 in this instance to calculate the total number of ways traveled to work.

Before we can analyze the data, we need to clean the data. The purpose of the cleaning process is to locate missed entries or incorrectly coded information. The data are cleaned in a variety of different ways, but the simplest is an initial double

	A	B	C	D	E	F	G
1		1A	1B	1C	1D	1E	1F
2	ID	DRIVE	TAXI	WALK	PUBLIC	BIKE	OTHER
3	10001	1	0	0	1	1	0
4							

Figure 9.2   Illustration of "check all that apply."

check of the numbers upon entering each survey. Other ways include calculating frequency distributions for the nominal and ordinal variables (discussed in the next chapter). This approach catches those values that are outside of the range of codes; however, it will not reveal those errors where numbers within the range are entered incorrectly; for example, entering a 1 rather than a 2. When an error is discovered, the identification number in the database is used to locate the corresponding survey.

9.5   Summary

Once researchers conduct the interviews or respondents return the self-administered surveys, the next step for the researcher is to code the responses and enter them into a database. Some self-administered surveys have the coding structure built into the questionnaire to improve the efficiency of data entry; however, the configuration of the codes can influence the respondents' answers. Finally, although there is no set way to code nominal and ordinal responses, consistency among the codes is the best practice.

Key Terms

Codebook

Consistency

Database management

Nominal codes

Ordinal codes

Precoding

Summated scales

Exercises

1. Create a codebook using the reconstructed survey from the previous chapter in Box 8.1.
2. Find a survey, codebook, and database from a government organization. Is it consistent? Does the it make sense?

Recommended Reading

Berk, K. and Carey, P. (2004). *Data Analysis with Microsoft Excel*. Belmont, CA: Thomson.

Field, A. (2005). *Discovering Statistics Using SPSS*. London: Sage Publications.

Norusis, M. J. (2006). *SPSS 15.0 Guide to Data Analysis*. Upper Saddle River, NJ: Prentice Hall.

Endnotes

1. Adapted from the U.S. Department of Education, *School Survey on Crime and Safety 2003–2004*. Available at http://nces.ed.gov/surveys/ssocs/PDF/SSOCS_2004_Questionnaire.pdf.

2. Data are adapted from the Department of Education, *School Survey on Crime and Safety 2003–2004*. The entire database, codebook, and survey are available on the Internet at http://nces.ed.gov/surveys/ssocs/data_products.asp.

3. The codebook and dataset are found at http://www.ipsr.ku.edu/SPPQ/datasets/codes.pdf.

4. *State Politics and Policy Quarterly*, State Data, http://www.ipsr.ku.edu/SPPQ/datasets/codes.pdf.

5. The U.S. Census Bureau's data dictionary is available on the Internet at http://www.census.gov/prod/cen2000/doc/pums.pdf. Pages 6-44 through 6-48 provide the variables and codes for the race question.

6. U.S. Department of Education (2004). School Survey on Crime and Safety. Survey is found on the Internet at http://nces.ed.gov/surveys/ssocs/PDF/SSOCS_2004_Questionnaire.pdf. Codebook is found on the Internet at http://www.census.gov/prod/www/nshapc/datadocu/files2&3.pdf.

7. Schwarz, N., Knauper, B., Hippler, H.J., Noelle-Neumann, E., and Clark, L. (1991). Rating scales: Numeric values may change the meaning of scale labels. *The Public Opinion Quarterly, 55*, 570–582.

Chapter 10

Descriptive Data Analysis

10.1   Introduction

The purpose of the research (to explore, describe, or explain) and the type of data collected (nominal, ordinal, or ratio) dictate the data analysis process. Regardless of the purpose, researchers are interested in certain descriptors of each variable; for example, the central location and distribution of the data, as well as the presence of any anomalies. Measures of central tendency (e.g., an average), measures of dispersion (e.g., standard deviation), and graphics used to describe individual variables are called univariate (one variable) or descriptive statistics, and this chapter explains each in turn.

However, before discussing the different descriptors, let us take a few moments to recall the different levels of data. Nominal and ordinal data are categorical, and the numbers associated with these observations are labels; that is, they are not really numbers. On the other hand, ratio data depict real numbers with numerical meanings that are either discrete (e.g., number of children) or continuous (e.g., distance traveled). In order to analyze the data, researchers must have a general understanding of the different levels of data and their efficacies in the analysis process. That is, certain levels of data are conducive for one type of analysis, but not in others. Therefore, knowledge of what the data can and cannot provide is a precondition to development of the research purpose and focus, the questions or hypotheses, the measures and variables, and the data collection tool.

10.2 Central Tendency: Finding the Most, Middle, or Average

A measure of central tendency locates the middle, center, or central location of a group of observations. There are three measures of central tendency: the mode, median, and mean. The level of data and its distribution (discussed in the next section) determine which measure of central tendency is appropriate to convey in reports.

10.2.1 Mode

The mode represents the observation within a set of data that occurs most often—with the greatest frequency. The mode is an appropriate measure for all levels of data, but is most useful to understand central tendencies of nominal and ordinal data.

To calculate the mode, the data are ordered by category for nominal or from lowest to highest for ordinal and ratio data. The category or observation that occurs most often, the one with the greatest frequency, is the mode. Consider Example 10.1 below, where the observations represent educational attainment for a group of 20 people.

Example 10.1   Calculation of Mode

Variable labels	Education	Reordered	
1 = No high school diploma	1	1	
2 = High school diploma	2	1	
3 = Associate degree	1	1	4
4 = Bachelor's degree	2	1	
5 = Graduate degree	2	2	
	3	2	
	4	2	
	2	2	
	2	2	
	2	2	10
	2	2	
	1	2	
	2	2	
	1	2	
	4	3 → 1	
	2	4	
	5	4	3
	4	4	
	2	5	2
	5	5	

These data are ordinal, as the education level goes in order from no high school diploma to graduate degree. The observations listed in the education column are reordered in the next column by their respective categorical label. Each category's frequency is determined by counting the number of occurrences for the corresponding category. In doing so, category number two—high school diploma—appears most often (10 times) in comparison to the other attributes. Therefore, high school diploma is the mode.

The mode can be used with ratio level data, but it is most practical for discrete variables or where continuous data are bimodal—having two modes. Example 10.2 lists the ages of the graduate students in a research methods class. Once the ages are ordered from lowest to highest, we can see the students' ages are bimodal; there are two modes, 22 and 43 years old.

Example 10.2   Calculation of Mode

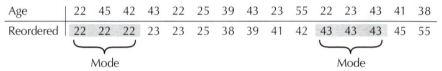

Age	22	45	42	43	22	25	39	43	23	55	22	23	43	41	38
Reordered	22	22	22	23	23	25	38	39	41	42	43	43	43	45	55

The analysis of nominal and ordinal data typically yields one or two modes, but can yield more than two modes (called multimodal) for ratio level variables, particularly continuous variables. When a variable has more than two modes and is ordinal or ratio, the mode is not suitable as a descriptor of the central location and researchers look to a different measure, such as the median or mean.

10.2.2   Median

The median is the exact middle location of the observations when the observations are listed in order from lowest to highest. Half of the values are below (smaller or lower than) the median, and the other half of the observations are above (larger or higher than) the median. Because some sort of ordering among the observations is present, analysts calculate medians for ordinal and ratio level data, but not for nominal data.

The middle location is determined by dividing the total number of observations in half. The result is the location of the median. If an even number of observations exist, no one middle point exists, so the median is the average of the two middle points. When an odd number of observations occur, the location of the median is the exact middle observation. In Example 10.3, there are 15 students and the location of the median is at the eighth data point. We determine the median by dividing the total number of observations, 15, by two. This yields 7.5, which we round to the next whole number, eight. The median age for the research methods course is 39 years old.

Example 10.3   Calculation of Median

Observation number	1	2	3	4	5	6	7	8	9	10	11	12	13	14	15
Age	22	22	22	23	23	25	38	39	41	42	43	43	43	45	55

Median

10.2.3 Mean

The final measure of central tendency is the mean. Researchers compute means for ratio level data. The mean, often referred to as the average, is the arithmetic average of all the observations, and is calculated by summing all of the values and dividing the result by the total number of observations. The formula for the mean is as follows:

$$\bar{x} = \frac{\sum x}{n} \tag{10.1}$$

where:

$\bar{x}$ (called x bar) is the sample mean

$\sum x$ is the summation of all the values in the data set

n is the number of observations

For example, to find the mean age of the graduate students in the research methods class, we add up all 15 values, ranging from 22 to 55. The sum, the $\sum x$ of the equation, totals 526. Next, 526 is divided by 15, the number of observations (n), which yields a mean ($\bar{x}$) of 35.07.

Sometimes weights are assigned to certain variables or values. For example, a grade point average (GPA) is the overall average of all the student's course grades. However, courses are worth different amounts of credit; for instance, a racquetball class may be worth one credit, whereas a calculus class might be worth four credits. The same may be true for individual classes where exams carry different weights than homework assignments. To calculate the weighted mean, each of the values is first multiplied by its respective weight, and then the new values are summed and divided by the sum of the weights, as illustrated mathematically in the following formula:

$$\bar{x} = \frac{\sum x * w}{\sum w} \tag{10.2}$$

where:

w is the weight

Table 10.1 Illustration of a Weighted Mean

Grade	Credits (Weight)	Grade × Weight
4.0	1	4
4.0	2	8
3.0	3	9
3.0	3	9
3.0	3	9
2.0	4	8
Total 19.0	16	47

For example, suppose a student takes six classes this semester; three classes are worth three credits, and the remaining courses are worth four credits, two credits, and one credit. Table 10.1 presents the student's grades at the end of the semester.

For each class, the number of credits (the weight) is multiplied by the grade to achieve the weighted grade. The weighted grades are added and then divided by the total value of the weights (47/16). The student's semester GPA is 2.94.

Overall, the level of data dictates the efficacy of the three different measures of central tendency. The mode is most beneficial to the researcher when analyzing nominal and ordinal data but useful with certain ratio level variables. The median helps describe ordinal and ratio level data, and the researcher calculates the mean when examining ratio level data. However, when studying ratio level data, researchers analyze all three measures in tandem with the variable's distribution.

10.3 Measures of Dispersion

Measures of central tendency are not the only descriptive statistics of interest when analyzing one variable; we also are concerned with their distributions and variations, referred to as measures of dispersion. We want to know the smallest value in the set of data, as well as the largest value, and the difference between them. In addition, we are interested in how the data are grouped, how far away each observation is from the measure of central tendency, and if anomalies among the observations exist. For instance, the mode, median, and mean for the students' ages in the research methods class are all different, and we want to know why. By looking at different measures of dispersion, we will be able to answer why the three measures are different, and determine which one of the three measures is most appropriate to use in reporting and in the decision-making process. This section presents the different measures of dispersion. Moreover, we discuss when and where the different measures are most useful.

10.3.1 Minimum, Maximum, and Range

When analyzing the data of one variable, researchers look at the minimum value—the lowest or smallest value—and the maximum value—the highest or largest value. Using the data in Example 10.3, we find the minimum value for the students' ages is 22 and the maximum value is 55. The range is the difference between the minimum and maximum values. The range for the students' ages is 33; the ages differ by 33 years. The range can be misleading, however, when extreme values are present. Let us look at the ages of students in two different graduate courses listed in Example 10.4.

Example 10.4   Data, Means, and Ranges for Student Ages

Age															
Class 1	22	22	22	23	23	25	38	39	41	42	43	43	43	45	55
Class 2	25	25	27	30	30	33	35	35	37	38	39	40	41	41	42

Mean	Class 1 = 35.1	Class 2 = 34.5
Range	Class 1 = 33	Class 2 = 17

The first class is the example with which we have been working throughout this chapter. The second class also has 15 students. The ages of the students are multimodal, and have a median of 35 and a mean of 34.5. The range for this dataset is 17 (42–25). Overall, the averages of the two datasets are similar, but the ranges are considerably different. In fact, the range for Class 1 is almost twice the size of the range for the second class. This example illustrates the sensitivity of the range; the range is influenced by extreme measures. In the first class, the presence of the 55-year-old increases the range by 13. Given the sensitivity, researchers resort to other methods, such as quartiles and percentiles, to better understand the distribution of the data.

10.3.2 Quartiles and Percentiles

Quartiles and percentiles, which are appropriate when the data are ratio level, separate the observations into equal parts, four parts for the quartiles and 100 parts for percentiles. The first quartile represents the 25th percentile, where 25% of the data are below the value and 75% are above it. The second quartile, or 50th percentile, is the median of the dataset, where exactly half of the observations are above and below the value. The third quartile or 75th percentile is where 25% of the values are above and 75% of the observations are below the value. Example 10.5 shows the different quartiles and selected percentiles for the two graduate courses. This table shows that 75% of the students in Class 1 are younger than 43.

The difference between the first and third quartiles (or 25th and 75th percentiles) is called the interquartile range. This range represents the variation between the

Example 10.5 Quartiles and Percentiles for Student Ages

Quartile	Percentile	Class 1	Class 2
1st	25th	23	30
2nd	50th	39	35
3rd	75th	43	40
	90th	44	41
	95th	48	41

majority of the values—the middle 50%—and is useful to compare one variable over time or two variables at one point in time; for example, the changes in income, or to evaluate two groups, for example, the ages of the two different graduate courses. The interquartile range for both classes is 10. That is, 50% of the graduate students in Class 1 are between 23 and 43 years old, and in Class 2, between 30 and 40 years.

10.3.3   *Frequency Distributions*

A frequency distribution is a tabular summary displaying frequencies and percents for any level of data. Table 10.2 displays a frequency distribution for the marital status of the U.S. population (a nominal level variable), and Example 10.6 summarizes the ages of the students (a ratio level variable), in the research methods class.

Table 10.2   Frequency Distribution Using Nominal Data

Marital status	Population	Percent
Now married	120,231,273	54.4
Never married	59,913,370	27.1
Divorced	21,560,308	9.7
Widowed	14,674,500	6.6
Separated	4,769,220	2.2
Total	221,148,671	100.0

Source: U.S. Census Bureau.

Example 10.6 Frequency Distributions for Student Ages

	Class 1		Class 2	
Age	*n*	*%*	*n*	*%*
20–29	6	40.0	3	20.0
30–39	2	13.3	8	53.3
40–49	6	40.0	4	26.7
50+	1	6.7	0	0.0
Total	15	100.0	15	100.0

The first column of the frequency distribution displays the attributes for nominal and ordinal data, or ranges of data, called classes, for ratio data. For example, Table 10.2 lists the five different attributes that characterize marital status (according to the U.S. Census), and Example 10.6 lists four classes that encompass the range of the observations. For frequency tables representing ratio data, each of the classes in Example 10.6 contains both a lower boundary and an upper boundary, with the exception of the first and last classes. The lower boundary of the third class is 40 and its upper boundary is 49. In addition, each of the classes, except the first and last, are balanced or equal in size; each has a class size of 10. Finally, the frequency tables present classes in ascending order.

The second column of the frequency table shows the frequency for its respective attribute or class. Here, each time the respective attribute or observation occurs within a class, it is counted, and the total is displayed in the frequency column. For example, 120.2 million people in the United States are currently married or two people in Class 1 are between 30 and 39 years old. Overall, the frequencies shed light on all those attributes or classes by indicating which ones occur more often than others do. However, researchers must put each frequency into context—that is, how it compares to the total number of observations.

When presenting frequencies and their distributions to readers and decision makers, percents are equally important in understanding the variable. Percents make the frequencies relative to the total number of observations, and are calculated by dividing the class or attribute frequency by the total frequency (i.e., the total number of observations for the variable). For example, in Class 1 six of the 15 students are younger than 30 years old; this is 40% of the class. The third column of Table 10.2 and the third and fifth columns in Example 10.6 present the percentages of the attributes.

Beyond numbers and percents, frequency distributions sometimes report cumulative frequencies and cumulative percentages as illustrated in Example 10.7. These are the accumulation of the frequencies and percents, from one class to the next.

Example 10.7 Frequency Distributions for Student Ages

Age	Frequency	Percentage	Cumulative frequency	Cumulative percentage
<30	6	40.0	6	40.0
30–39	2	13.3	8	53.3
40–49	6	40.0	14	93.3
50+	1	6.7	15	100.0
Total	15	100.0		

For example, six (40%) of the students are younger than 30, and in the following class, two students (13.3%) are between the ages of 30 and 39. Cumulatively, eight students (53.3%) are younger than 40 years old. However, cumulative frequencies and percents are not appropriate for nominal and certain ordinal level variables; for instance, presenting cumulative frequencies or percentages in Table 10.2 would not make sense.

Overall, frequency distributions, particularly those using scaled data, should have three or more classes, but fewer than 16 classes. The purpose of the frequency distribution is to illustrate the distribution of the data from the lowest values to the highest values. Using too few classes may conceal the distribution, as shown in Table 10.3, whereas providing too many classes may result in a scarce distribution for some of the classes as illustrated in Table 10.4. When either of these situations occurs, the distribution should be changed.

Frequency distributions are created using common sense and math. Researchers often group the data in a fashion that makes sense; for example, incomes might be grouped by tens of thousands of dollars or age classes might be clustered by decades—20s, 30s, 40s, and so forth—as illustrated in Example 10.6. However, the grouping—the class size—depends on the data. If, for example, the range of data for income is $20,000, then the class size should not be $10,000; rather, the groupings should be smaller to illustrate the distribution of the data. In addition, each class should be the same size (i.e., the distance between the lower and upper boundaries should be the same). However, the first and last classes generally are open (using only one boundary) to capture the values in the far ends of the lower and upper percentiles. Mathematically, the classes are built around the mean and the standard deviation (discussed later), whereas the class in the middle of the frequency distribution contains the mean. The distance for the remaining classes is separated by the standard deviation.

Table 10.3 Frequency Distribution with Too Few Classes

Income	Frequency	Percentage
≤20,000	403	85.0
20,001+	71	15.0
Total	474	100.0

Table 10.4   Frequency Distribution with Too Many Classes

Income	Frequency	Percentage
≤7000	17	3.6
7,001–9,000	71	15.0
9,001–11,000	120	25.3
11,001–13,000	102	21.5
13,001–15,000	47	9.9
15,001–17,000	27	5.7
17,001–19,000	14	3.0
19,001–21,000	10	2.1
21,001–23,000	15	3.2
23,001–25,000	12	2.5
25,001–27,000	9	1.9
27,001–29,000	9	1.9
29,001–31,000	4	0.8
31,001–33,000	6	1.3
33,001–35,000	2	0.4
35,001–37,000	3	0.6
37,001–39,000	1	0.2
39,001–41,000	1	0.2
41,001–43,000	2	0.4
43,001–45,000	1	0.2
45,001–47,000	0	0.0
47,001–49,000	0	0.0
49,001–51,000	0	0.0
51,001–53,000	0	0.0
53,001+	1	0.2
Total	**474**	**100.0**

10.3.4   Histograms

A histogram, shown in Figures 10.1 and 10.2, is a graphic of a ratio-level frequency distribution. The frequency or percentage is placed on the y-axis and the classes of the variable of interest are placed on the x-axis. The height of the bar represents the frequency or percentage. There is no space between the classes because of the continuity of the data (which is why histograms are appropriate only with ratio data). Overall, the histogram provides a picture of the distribution of the data.

The mean, median, and mode are located at the center or peak of a normal distribution, similar to the one in Figure 10.2. This means the histogram is symmetric, where half of the observations are to the right of the peak and the other half are to the left. Figure 10.1 is not normal and clearly illustrates the bimodal nature of the

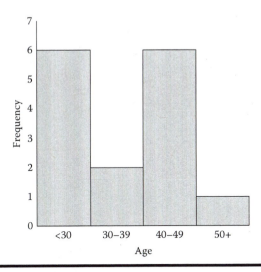

Figure 10.1   Histogram of student ages.

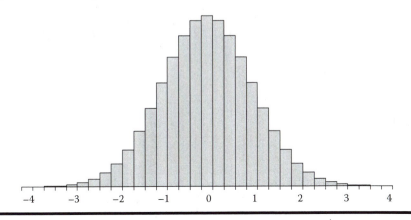

Figure 10.2   Illustration of a normal histogram.

students' ages (recall Class 1 has two modes, 22 and 43). The median age is 39 and the mean is 35. Because all three measures are not the same or even similar, and the histogram is not normal, we can say that the data for Class 1 are not normally distributed.

To assist in the determination of a normal distribution, researchers calculate the skewness and kurtosis. In a normal curve, skewness and kurtosis are absent and their values are zero. What does it mean to have skewed data or data with kurtosis? A skewed histogram can be positively skewed (as illustrated in Figure 10.3) or negatively skewed (as shown in Figure 10.4). A positively skewed histogram occurs when the data are concentrated to the left with a few larger values to the right. These larger values increase the mean such that it is no longer located in the peak. In fact, the mean will be larger than the median.

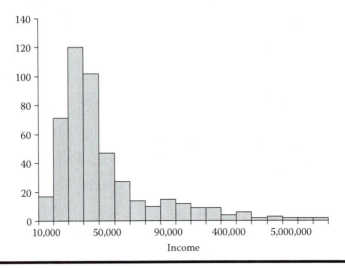

Figure 10.3 Illustration of a positively skewed histogram.

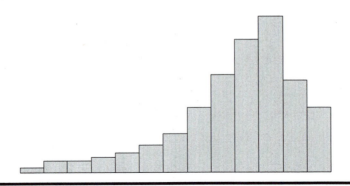

Figure 10.4 Illustration of a negatively skewed histogram.

Negatively skewed data occur when smaller values are less frequent than the larger values, as shown in Figure 10.4. Consequently, the mean will be smaller than the median. Overall, when the distribution is skewed, positively or negatively, the median or mode, not the mean, will best capture the central location.

Finally, the histogram illustrates the concentration of the data around the peak or mean. Data that are heavily concentrated about the mean are said to have positive kurtosis; these histograms will be steeper with a more defined peak than the normal curve. On the other hand, negative kurtosis occurs when the data congregate in the tails, away from the mean. Histograms with negative kurtosis will be flatter than the normal curve. Overall, a normal histogram is one where all three measures of central tendency are similar and the distribution is normal—where skewness and kurtosis are absent.

10.3.5   *Standard Deviation*

So far, we have discussed a variety of useful ways to analyze the distribution of the data; however, none of these different techniques incorporates a measure of central tendency until now. The standard deviation explains how the observations, on average, deviate from and concentrate around the mean. The standard deviation, labeled s, is calculated for ratio level data and is reported whenever the mean is reported. The value of the standard deviation is relative to the data. That is, it is in the same units as the data—for example, age, income, and so forth. Furthermore, the standard deviation reveals additional information about the histogram. As the size of the standard deviation increases, relative to its mean, the dispersion widens and the histogram becomes flatter. On the other hand, steeper curves are characterized by a smaller standard deviation. Therefore, the larger the standard deviation is relative to its mean, the larger the distribution of the data and the flatter the curve; the similar to the distribution shown in Figure 10.1. The formula for the standard deviation of a sample is as follows:

$$s = \sqrt{\frac{\sum (x_i - \bar{x})^2}{n-1}} \qquad (10.3)$$

where

s is the sample standard deviation
x_i is the observation
$\bar{x}$ is the mean
n is the total number of observations

The standard deviation for a variable is calculated by subtracting the mean (listed in the second column) from each observation (shown in the first column), to yield the difference, shown in the third column of Example 10.8. Each of these values is squared (presented in the fourth column) and then added together to yield a total (1697). Next, the total is divided by the number of observations, less one. This result is called the variance and the standard deviation is the positive square root of the variance.

The standard deviation for the ages of the first class is 11 years. Therefore, the average deviation from the mean age of 35 years old is 11 years. What is the standard deviation of the ages for the second class? If you said 5.9 years, you are correct. What do these numbers mean? The comparison between the two classes reveals that the distribution of ages in Class 1 is larger or more dispersed than the distribution of the ages in Class 2. We already knew this from the calculations of the range and interquartile range, but these ranges do not include all the data. The standard deviation includes all the data values not just the smallest and largest, or the middle 50%. Overall, when the standard deviation is large relative to the mean—similar to or larger than the mean—then the mean is not a good measure of central tendency,

Example 10.8 Calculation of Variance and Standard Deviation

Age	Mean	(Age – Mean)	(Age – Mean)^2
22	35	–13	171
22	35	–13	171
22	35	–13	171
23	35	–12	146
23	35	–12	146
25	35	–10	101
38	35	3	9
39	35	4	15
41	35	6	35
42	35	7	48
43	35	8	63
43	35	8	63
43	35	8	63
45	35	10	99
55	35	20	397

Total	1697
Number of observations	15
Variance	121.2
Standard deviation	11.0

but when the standard deviation is small, the smaller the distribution of the data, then the mean is the most appropriate measure.

Now we can determine the statistics to use for our age example. The frequency distribution and histogram in Class 1 reveal a bimodal distribution, and the range and standard deviation are large relative to the data. In addition, none of the central tendency measures is similar. Therefore, the mode seems to be most useful to identify the majority of student ages in Class 1. Which measure is the best for the second class? Clearly, the mode is inappropriate because the data have more than two modes, but either the median or mean (and standard deviation) are beneficial descriptors for the central location of the ages for Class 2.

10.4 Graphics

The statistics just discussed are often presented in reports as pictures using pies, bars, lines, or any other means of graphically describing what is happening. These quick and easy-to-read graphics are useful in communicating important research findings to a variety of decision-making groups, such as citizens, board members, council members, and legislators—people who generally do not understand much beyond descriptive statistics. This section illustrates the different types of basic graphics available to researchers.

10.4.1 Pie Charts

A pie chart is a circular graphic depicting each attribute's proportion of the total. That is, each occurrence of the attribute is counted, and its total frequency is divided by the total number of observations for the variable, which yields the percentage or proportion of the attribute. This graphic is best suited for nominal and ordinal level data as shown in Figures 10.5 and 10.6, respectively. Pie charts can also be used for discrete ratio level data (illustrated in Figure 10.7), or with continuous ratio level data that have been collapsed into classes (i.e., a frequency distribution).

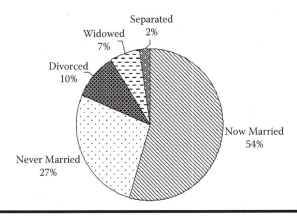

Figure 10.5   Marital status of the United States population, 2000. Source: U.S. Census Bureau.

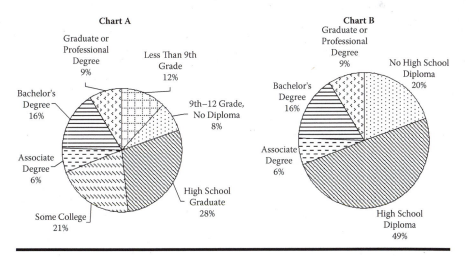

Figure 10.6   Educational attainment of the U.S. population, 2000. Source: U.S. Census Bureau.

The information provided in the pie chart typically begins at the top of the circle and moves counter-clockwise around the circle, unless changed by the graph maker. The order of slices can be presented from largest proportion of the pie to smallest proportion (depicted in Figure 10.5), in alphabetical order, or when ordinal data are used, in the order of the scale (as shown in Figure 10.6).

Finally, pie charts should be used where the number of attributes or categories is few rather than many. Where many attributes are present (more than seven), do not display all the categories separately, as shown in Chart A of Figure 10.8.

A better approach is to combine those slices with less than 6% and reproduce the graph as illustrated in Chart B of Figure 10.8. This also applies to variables with fewer

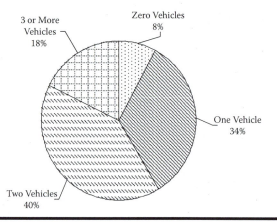

Figure 10.7   Percent of households with and without vehicles in the United States, 2000. Source: U.S. Census Bureau.

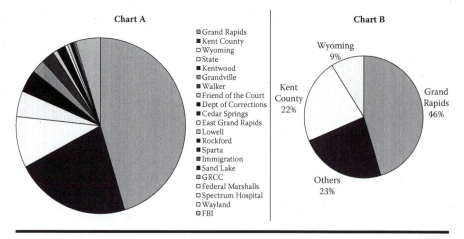

Figure 10.8   Arresting agency of inmates brought to county jail. Source: City of Grand Rapids Police Department Annual Report, 2006.

than eight attributes. If multiple slices of the pie are small (two or more attributes with less than 5 or 6%), consider combining them to make the chart easier to read. For example, in Chart A of Figure 10.6, although none of the slices are smaller than 5%, categories could be combined to display fewer slices. This is illustrated in Chart B where "less than 9th grade" and "9th grade to 12th grade, no diploma" are merged and so are "high school diploma" and "some college." With fewer slices, Chart B is not as complex as Chart A.

10.4.2 Bar Graphs

A bar graph is a graph with rectangular-shaped horizontal (see Figure 10.9) or vertical (see Figure 10.10) bars or stacks. Generally, bar graphs depict ordinal and nominal level data as shown in Figures 10.9 and 10.10, respectively. On occasion,

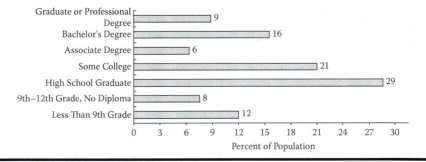

Figure 10.9   Levels of educational attainment (in Percent) of U.S. population, 2000. Source: U.S. Census Bureau.

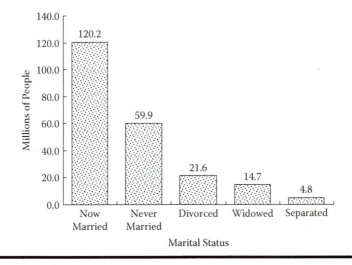

Figure 10.10   Frequency (in millions) of current marital status of the U.S. population, 2000. Source: U.S. Census Bureau.

however, discrete ratio level data, continuous annual data, and percent changes are depicted in bar graphs similar to those illustrated in Figures 10.11, 10.12, and 10.13, respectively.

Each bar in the graph represents the frequency of occurrence, or proportion, of the data. That is, each time an attribute occurs, it is counted, and the total number of occurrences is displayed by the height (in a vertical graph) or length (in a horizontal graph) of the bar. The graph has two axes: a horizontal axis, or x-axis, that presents the attributes, and a vertical axis, or y-axis, that displays the frequency (as shown in Figure 10.10) or percentage (as illustrated in Figure 10.9). In Figure 10.9, the axes are

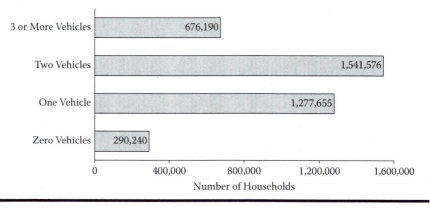

Figure 10.11   Number of households with and without vehicles in the United States, 2000.

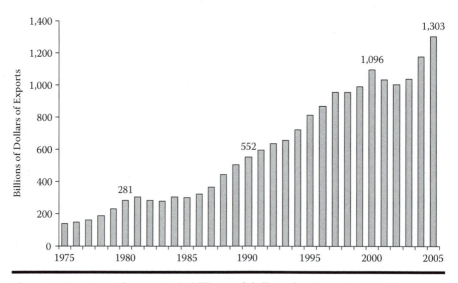

Figure 10.12   Annual exports (in billions of dollars) for the United States, 1975–2005.

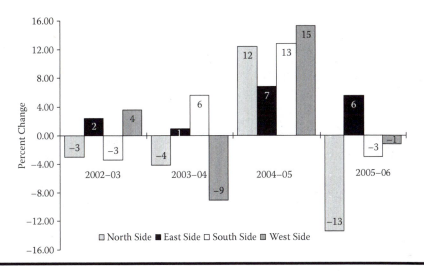

Figure 10.13   Annual change (percent) in crime by area, 2002–2006. Source: City of Grand Rapids Police Department Annual Report, 2006.

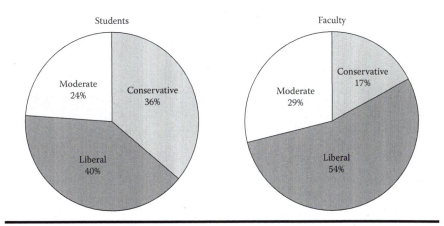

Figure 10.14   Political philosophy of students and faculty.

flipped so it looks as if the x-axis shows the percentage. This is not the case, however. The y-axis in a bar chart, regardless of the type, always displays the frequency or percentage. That is, a horizontal bar graphic is simply a transposed vertical bar chart.

Figures 10.9 and 10.10 show the same information as reported in Figures 10.6 and 10.5, respectively, but depicted differently, using bars rather than slices. The decision is up to the researcher as to what graphic to use.

Bar charts are useful to compare variables or groups. For example, rather than displaying information about two different groups in two different pie charts as illustrated in Figure 10.14, the information can be graphed in one bar chart as shown in all three charts in Figure 10.15. Chart A compares students and faculty for each

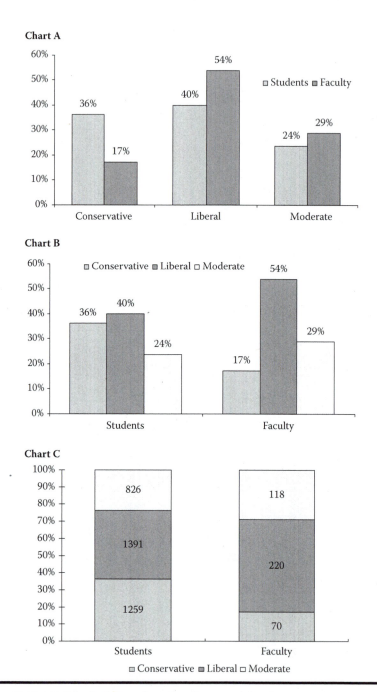

Figure 10.15 Political philosophy of students and faculty.

attribute of political philosophy—conservative, liberal, and moderate—whereas Chart B groups the political philosophies together by the type of person—student or faculty. In Chart C, the philosophies are stacked into one bar, one for the students and one for the faculty, and the percent is the y-axis. Although the number of observations per philosophy is displayed inside each bar, the presentation of this type of bar chart depends on the number of variables, but as more variables or groups are added, these charts will become more complex and difficult to read.

10.4.3 *Line Graphs*

A line graph displays ratio level data with three or more time periods. All line graphs place the period of time on the x-axis, and the frequency or percent on the y-axis. Figure 10.16 shows annual exports from 1975 to 2005. This graph is similar to Figure 10.12, but rather than using bars, the data points are connected by lines to easily observe trends.

Line graphs are also useful to depict trends for more than one variable or observe percent change in crime over time by area (see Figure 10.17). Figure 10.17 communicates the same information—percent change over time—as does Figure 10.13; however, as more variables are added, the graphic in Figure 10.17 becomes more difficult to read.

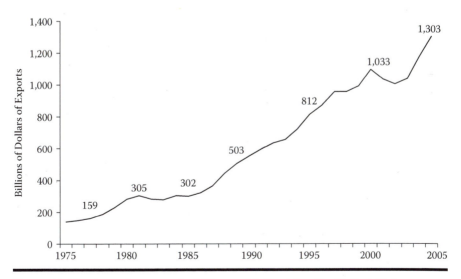

Figure 10.16 Annual exports (in billions of dollars) for the United States, 1975–2005. Source: Economic Report of the President, 2006.

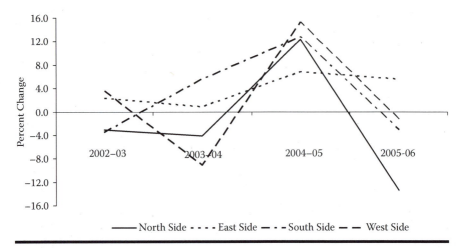

Figure 10.17   Annual percent change in crime by area, 2002–2006.

10.5   Calculating Descriptive Statistics and Creating the Graphics

All of the univariate statistics and graphics discussed in this chapter can be calculated or created using the functions, Data Analysis add-in, or chart wizard supplied by Microsoft Excel. However, to understand what follows, some familiarity with Excel is necessary. We begin with the calculation of descriptive statistics.

10.5.1   Descriptive Statistics

Excel provides a variety of prewritten formulas, called functions, that analysts use to calculate descriptive statistics. Some of the more useful statistical functions are presented in Table 10.5. However, the one rule to remember in Excel is that all functions begin with an equal sign. If at any time you want to know more about other functions performed in Excel, simply type statistical functions in the Help Bar, and a link to a list of options will appear.

Beyond the individual functions, Excel provides that add-in feature called Data Analysis. For directions to add this feature, see Appendix I of Chapter 7. The data analysis feature provides the analyst with a variety of statistical procedures, from creating frequency distributions to regression analysis: a few examples are found in Figure 10.18.

For the following illustrations, the age data from the two graduate courses are used. To calculate the univariate statistics for each class, Descriptive Statistics is selected from the list of options provided by the Data Analysis feature and a dialog box appears (see Figure 10.19). Filling out the information is relatively self-explanatory, but for the univariate statistics to appear, the "Summary Statistics" box must

Table 10.5   Some Useful Excel Formulas

Statistic	Formula
Count number of observations	=COUNT(range)
Kurtosis	=KURT(range)
Maximum value	=MAX(range)
Mean (or average)	=AVERAGE(range)
Median	=MEDIAN(range)
Minimum value	=MIN(range)
Mode	=MODE(range)
Percentile	=PERCENTILE(range,%)
Quartile	=QUARTILE(range,#)
Skewness	=SKEW(range)
Standard deviation	=STDEV(range)
Summation of cells	=SUM(range)

Note: All formulas must begin with an equal sign; % represents the percentile of interest (e.g., .10 for 10th percentile); # represents the number of the quartile (i.e., 1, 2, or 3).

be checked. Next, we enter the range of data in the input range location, and, if labels are used and included in the input range, as they are in Figure 10.19, then we select the "Labels in first row" option. Clicking OK instantly reveals a variety of univariate statistics for the selected variable; these are presented in Figure 10.20. Two disadvantages to Microsoft Excel's Data Analysis feature are that only one variable can be analyzed at a time and only one mode is displayed, even if more than one mode exists.

A frequency distribution is created in Microsoft Excel by selecting the Histogram option from the list in the Data Analysis box. Classes are created in one of two ways, either by Excel or by the analyst. However, in either case, only upper boundaries are used and listed in the output.

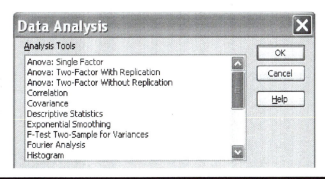

Figure 10.18   Data analysis tools.

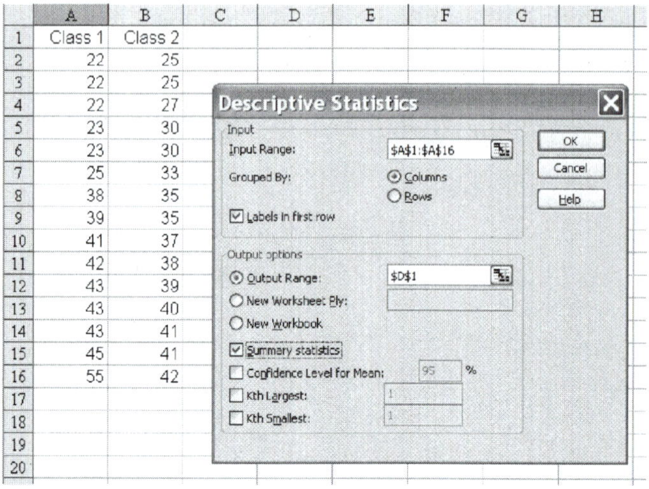

	A	B	C	D	E	F	G	H
1	Class 1	Class 2						
2	22	25						
3	22	25						
4	22	27						
5	23	30						
6	23	30						
7	25	33						
8	38	35						
9	39	35						
10	41	37						
11	42	38						
12	43	39						
13	43	40						
14	43	41						
15	45	41						
16	55	42						
17								
18								
19								
20								

Descriptive Statistics

Input
Input Range: $A$1:$A$16
Grouped By: ⊙ Columns ○ Rows
☑ Labels in first row

Output options
⊙ Output Range: $D$1
○ New Worksheet Ply:
○ New Workbook
☑ Summary statistics
☐ Confidence Level for Mean: 95 %
☐ Kth Largest: 1
☐ Kth Smallest: 1

OK Cancel Help

Figure 10.19   Descriptive statistics dialog box.

	A	B	C	D	E
1	Class 1	Class 2		*Class 1*	
2	22	25			
3	22	25		Mean	35 07
4	22	27		Standard Error	2 84
5	23	30		Median	39
6	23	30		Mode	22
7	25	33		Standard Deviation	11 01
8	38	35		Sample Variance	121 21
9	39	35		Kurtosis	-1 35
10	41	37		Skewness	-0 01
11	42	38		Range	33
12	43	39		Minimum	22
13	43	40		Maximum	55
14	43	41		Sum	526
15	45	41		Count	15
16	55	42			
17					

Figure 10.20   Descriptive statistics output.

Two illustrations are provided here: first, where Excel creates the classes, and second, where the researcher establishes the classes. In the Histogram dialog box, presented in Figure 10.21, the range of data (Excel refers to classes as bins) are entered, the Label box is checked because the variable label is included, the output range is entered, and the chart output option is selected (this will produce the histogram, whereas leaving it unselected produces only the frequency distribution).

Clicking OK yields a frequency table and histogram, both shown in Figure 10.22. The frequency table is missing some information; for example, there is no total, there are no lower boundaries (only upper boundaries are reported), and

	A	B	C	D	E	F	G	H
1	Class 1	Class 2						
2	22	25						
3	22	25						
4	22	27						
5	23	30						
6	23	30						
7	25	33						
8	38	35						
9	39	35						
10	41	37						
11	42	38						
12	43	39						
13	43	40						
14	43	41						
15	45	41						
16	55	42						
17								
18								
19								
20								

Histogram

Input
Input Range: $A$1:$A$16
Bin Range:
☑ Labels

Output options
◉ Output Range: $D$1
○ New Worksheet Ply:
○ New Workbook

☐ Pareto (sorted histogram)
☐ Cumulative Percentage
☑ Chart Output

OK
Cancel
Help

Figure 10.21   Histogram dialog box.

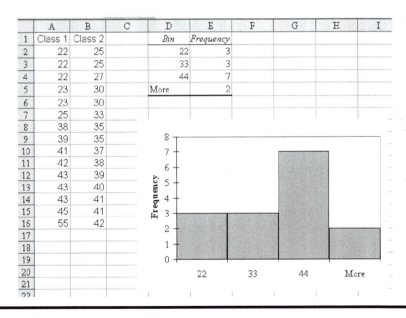

	A	B	C	D	E	F	G	H	I
1	Class 1	Class 2		Bin	Frequency				
2	22	25		22	3				
3	22	25		33	3				
4	22	27		44	7				
5	23	30		More	2				
6	23	30							
7	25	33							
8	38	35							
9	39	35							
10	41	37							
11	42	38							
12	43	39							
13	43	40							
14	43	41							
15	45	41							
16	55	42							
17									
18									
19									
20									
21									
22									

Figure 10.22   Histogram output.

there are no percentages. Never present a frequency table that looks similar to the one in Figure 10.22.

For researchers interested in generating their own classes, the bins or classes need to be created prior to engaging in the first step of the process outlined above.

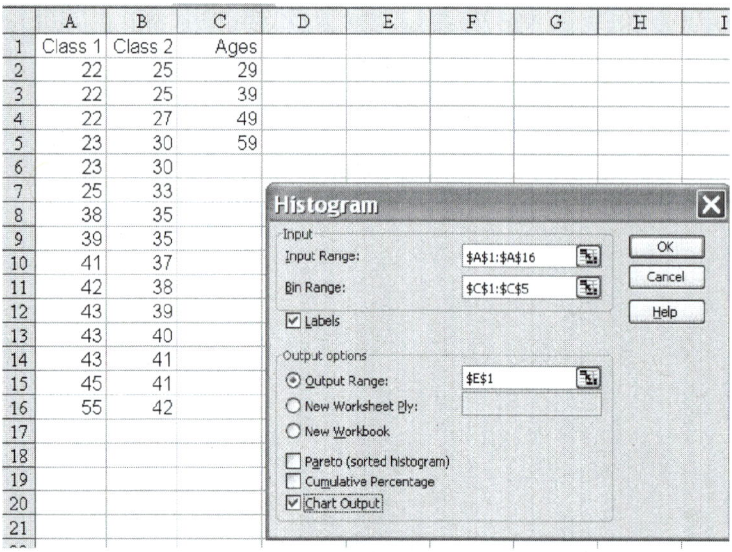

	A	B	C	D	E	F	G	H	I
1	Class 1	Class 2	Ages						
2	22	25	29						
3	22	25	39						
4	22	27	49						
5	23	30	59						
6	23	30							
7	25	33							
8	38	35							
9	39	35							
10	41	37							
11	42	38							
12	43	39							
13	43	40							
14	43	41							
15	45	41							
16	55	42							
17									
18									
19									
20									
21									

Histogram ☒

Input
Input Range: $A$1:$A$16
Bin Range: $C$1:$C$5
☑ Labels

Output options
⊙ Output Range: $E$1
○ New Worksheet Ply:
○ New Workbook

☐ Pareto (sorted histogram)
☐ Cumulative Percentage
☑ Chart Output

OK
Cancel
Help

Figure 10.23   Illustration of bins (classes).

This is accomplished by entering only the upper boundaries, one per cell, in the same worksheet as illustrated in Column C in Figure 10.23. After the classes are entered, select Histogram from the Data Analysis option and input the same information as above, but this time enter the range of cells (C1:C5 in the example) for the newly created classes in the "Bin Range."

Excel produces the same type of information—a frequency distribution and histogram—but the output, presented in Figure 10.24, is different from the output in Figure 10.22, because the researcher created the classes prior to running the data analysis procedure.

The frequency table is still unattractive and lacks the majority of information that is supposed to be provided in a frequency distribution. We improve the table by adding a title, proper class labels, a total, and percentages. The formulas and output for the new frequency table are illustrated in Figure 10.25.

Creating a frequency distribution using categorical data is no different from the above process. Rather than entering the upper boundaries for the classes or bins, the number for each attribute is listed. The best approach is to create the classes before running the data analysis procedure because Excel does not differentiate between categorical and continuous data, and most likely will not separate the attributes, so that each is listed individually.

10.5.2 Creating Graphics in Excel

Creating graphics in Excel is relatively simple and consists of four steps: selecting the type of graphic from a number of options, providing the data source, editing

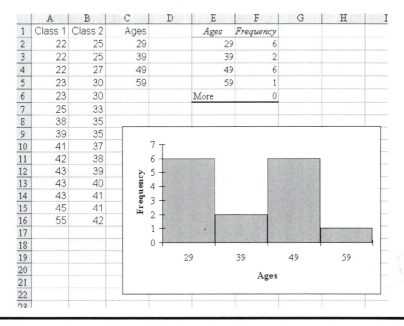

	A	B	C	D	E	F	G	H	I
1	Class 1	Class 2	Ages		*Ages*	*Frequency*			
2	22	25	29		29	6			
3	22	25	39		39	2			
4	22	27	49		49	6			
5	23	30	59		59	1			
6	23	30			More	0			
7	25	33							
8	38	35							
9	39	35							
10	41	37							
11	42	38							
12	43	39							
13	43	40							
14	43	41							
15	45	41							
16	55	42							
17									
18									
19									
20									
21									
22									
23									

Figure 10.24   Histogram output with predefined bins.

Formulas

E	F	G
Table 1. Ages of Graduate Students		
Ages	Frequency	Percent
<30	6	=F4/$F$8*100
30-39	2	=F5/$F$8*100
40-49	6	=F6/$F$8*100
50-59	1	=F7/$F$8*100
Total	=SUM(F4:F7)	=F8/$F$8*100

Output

E	F	G
Table 1. Ages of Graduate Students		
Ages	Frequency	Percent
<30	6	40.0
30-39	2	13.3
40-49	6	40.0
50-59	1	6.7
Total	15	100

Figure 10.25   Creating a better frequency table from histogram output.

the chart options, and determining the placement of the chart. Prior to creating a pie chart or bar chart for cross-sectional data, we first create a frequency table. (Excel cannot produce bar or pie charts from original data.) Next, we can highlight the data in the spreadsheet to be graphed, either at the beginning of the chart making process, or later on in the process. The directions that follow illustrate the creation of a line chart and assume we highlight the data prior to starting.

To begin to create a chart, select Insert on the Menu bar. From the list of options, we choose Chart, and the Chart Wizard dialog box shown in Figure 10.26, appears. The Chart Wizard follows four easy steps to produce a graphic. For the first step, we select the chart type from the list of options on the left side, and the chart subtype from the options listed on the right side of the dialog box. Once the appropriate chart is selected, we click Next.

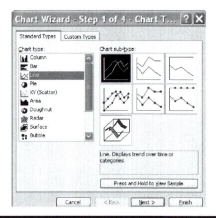

Figure 10.26   Chart dialog box.

In the second step, shown in Figure 10.27, a picture of the graphic appears only if the data are highlighted prior to the start of the Chart Wizard. If the data were not selected, then step 2 is where the data range is entered.

Notice the legend in Figure 10.27; Excel titles the labels for each line as Series 1, Series 2, and Series 3. We need to change the titles to reflect the labels of the variables. To assign a more appropriate title, click on the series tab at the top of the box and then click on one of the series; for example, Series 2. In the name box, located to the right, we enter the cell location of the label or type in the label name. We do this for each series and then click next.

In the third step, we can add chart options such as axis labels and figure titles, and we can change the position of the legend. Once we enter the desired information and options, we select next. The final box asks about placement of graphic. Excel will place the figure in the same worksheet or in its own worksheet. When placed in its own worksheet, the entire worksheet becomes the graphic, whereas a much smaller graphic appears when it is placed inside the current worksheet. After determining the chart's placement, we click finish and a chart appears. To edit the chart—the font, size, colors, axes, and so forth—we click as the area to edit and then right-mouse click. For example to edit the plot area, click within the plot area and small squares appear as illustrated below in Figure 10.28. Next, we right-mouse click and the formatting menu appears. The best way to learn all the different editing features is to experiment with the graphics.

10.6   Summary

The statistics and graphics presented in this chapter help us evaluate and describe single variables. Graphics are an alternative to tables and complementary to the prose of a research report. They provide the reader—the decision maker—with

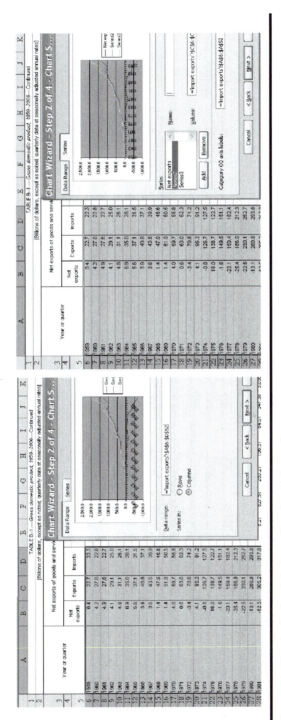

Figure 10.27 Assigning labels to the chart's legend.

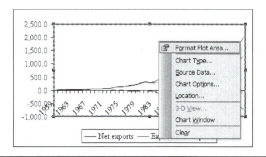

Figure 10.28   Illustration of formatting options.

a quick and easy illustration of what is happening. The three different measures of central tendency are all valuable measures, but their usefulness depends on the level of data, the values of each of the measures of central tendency, and the distribution of the data. Table 10.6 summarizes the univariate statistics discussed in this chapter.

Table 10.6   Definitions and Appropriate Levels of Data for Selected Univariate Statistics

Measure	Definition	Level of Data
Interquartile range	The difference between the first and third quartiles	Ratio
Mode	Observation occurring most often	All levels
Median	Observation in the middle	Ordinal, ratio
Mean	Arithmetic average of all values	Continuous, ratio
Percentiles	The division of data into 100 equal parts	Ratio
Quartiles	The division of data into four equal parts	Ratio
Range	The difference between the highest and lowest values in a set of observations	Ratio
Frequency distributions	Tabular summary of the observations	All levels
Histograms	Graphical summary of the frequency distribution	Ratio
Variance	The average squared deviation about the mean	Ratio
Standard deviation	The average deviation of values about the mean	Ratio

Overall, the mode is beneficial for all levels of data, but only when one or two modes are present. The median can be used with ordinal and ratio data, and the mean is appropriate only for ratio data. In addition, extremely large or small values influence the mean, but not the median; as such, the researcher considers the distribution of the data when deciding which measure of central location to present. In the end, the data dictate what you can and cannot do in the analysis process; do not ask what you can do with the data, rather ask what the data can do for you.

Key Terms

Bar charts	Mean	Pie chart
Interquartile range	Median	Quartiles
Frequency distribution	Minimum	Range
Histogram	Mode	Standard deviation
Line chart	Percentiles	Variance
Maximum		

Exercises

1. Explain when and why each of the measures of central tendency are appropriate for some statistical analyses but not for others.
2. Find census data on age, income, and race, and create a graph for each variable; in doing so, explain why you chose that particular graphic and not another.
3. Look inside any print newspaper or magazine and analyze its graphics. Is it using the appropriate graphic given its data; are the graphics easy to understand and self-explanatory? What, if anything, would you do differently to improve the graphic; explain.
4. Using the information below on annual income, calculate the all the necessary univariate statistics and determine which measure of central tendency best explains the data. Explain your answer (i.e., why the other measures are not appropriate).

66,878	37,170	32,745	50,703	41,825	53,371	104,863	47,868
25,559	41,932	68,940	79,959	91,536	99,305	49,188	39,899
28,819	42,494	30,662	71,642	81,912	93,328	40,928	36,905
72,555	77,376	31,588	97,973	45,346	40,744	63,474	56,106
40,467	44,145	47,887	83,566	35,802	22,832	40,863	33,627

5. The following data are from a survey question that asks respondents to rank five democratic presidential candidates from most favorite, labeled as a 1, to least favorite, coded as a 5. In Excel, enter the data and create a frequency distribution and chart of choice. In addition, write a brief summary of your findings.

ID	Clinton	Edwards	Kucinich	Obama	Richardson
1001	1	2	4	3	5
1002	2	3	5	4	1
1003	3	4	5	1	2
1004	4	5	1	2	3
1005	5	4	1	2	3
1006	1	1	5	1	4
1007	4	2	5	1	2
1008	3	1	5	2	4
1009	2	5	4	3	1
1010	1	4	5	2	3
1011	1	3	4	2	5
1012	2	3	1	4	5
1013	3	1	5	2	4
1014	4	1	5	2	3
1015	5	2	4	1	3
1016	9	1	9	9	9
1017	4	5	1	2	3
1018	2	5	4	1	3
1019	1	2	5	3	4
1020	4	3	5	2	1
1021	5	3	4	2	1
1022	1	2	5	3	4
1023	2	4	5	3	1
1024	1	2	5	3	4
1025	2	1	5	3	4
1026	3	2	4	1	5
1027	5	3	2	1	4
1028	4	1	3	2	4
1029	4	2	1	3	5
1030	1	3	5	2	4
1031	2	1	3	4	5
1032	5	4	3	1	2

Recommended Reading

Berk, K. and Carey, P. (2004). *Data Analysis with Microsoft Excel*. Belmont, CA: Thomson.

Field, A. (2005). *Discovering Statistics Using SPSS*. London: Sage Publications.

Norusis, M. J. (2006). *SPSS 15.0 Guide to Data Analysis*. Upper Saddle River, NJ: Prentice Hall.

Chapter 11

Bivariate Statistics

11.1   Introduction

Once researchers have described single variables using univariate statistics, they may delve deeper into additional analyses. That is, researchers may examine the relationship between two or more variables. When investigating the relationship between two variables, researchers are performing a bivariate analysis, whereas they are conducting a multivariate analysis when three or more variables are studied. This chapter focuses on bivariate analyses—studying two variables. Multivariate analyzes are more complex, and as such are beyond the scope of this book. In fact, the majority of the statistical techniques preferred by practitioners are simple univariate and bivariate analysis—those discussed in the previous chapter and presented in this chapter.

Similar to univariate statistics, the type of data drives the manner in which the two variables are analyzed; different types of analyses require different types of data. The purpose of this chapter is to illustrate four different, but very simple and popular, bivariate statistical procedures: cross tabulations, difference of means, analysis of variance, and correlations. Each of these procedures tests a supposition (i.e., hypothesis) by examining a relationship or an association between two variables, usually an independent and a dependent variable. Before discussing these different procedures, we briefly review the process of testing relationships.

11.2   Testing for Relationships

A researcher can look at the univariate statistics of two variables or their respective graphs and claim a relationship exists; however, they cannot say, beyond a reasonable doubt, that a relationship exists without testing for the statistical significance of a relationship. The statistical test is only one of the criteria researchers use to help support cause and effect. Beyond the statistical association between two variables, researchers need to establish time order, eliminate alternative explanations and spurious relationships, and randomize data collection or assignment; those factors that were discussed in Chapter 5.

Researchers propose two statements, one in the form of a null statement and the other as an alternative statement. Researchers try to prove the alternative statement true. After conducting the appropriate statistical test, researchers draw one of two conclusions: a significant relationship exists or a significant relationship does not exist. Let us evaluate the two different statements—the null and alternative—and the definition of significance as it is used in research.

A null statement, for any statistical test, states that there is nothing happening—no relationship or no difference—between the two variables. Administrators phrase the null statement a bit differently for each test, but its purpose is to claim that there is not enough evidence to suggest that the two variables being tested are related. Researchers phrase the alternative statement to support a relationship between the two variables. The alternative statement says something to the effect that one variable is significantly different from, related to, depends on, or causes change in another variable.

For every null statement, there is a corresponding alternative statement, and researchers test this set simultaneously. The results from the statistical test provide researchers with enough information to claim that the null is true (that there is no relationship between the two variables) or that the alternative is true (that there is a significant relationship between the two variables). The language used in statistics books and most scholarly research is different, however. The conclusions drawn about the statements (which they call hypotheses) revolve only around the null statement, and researchers either reject or do not reject the null hypothesis. A null hypothesis that is not rejected indicates that there is no relationship between the two variables, but one that is rejected suggests a statistically significant relationship exists. Although there are two statements being tested, researchers state only one in the research report, which is typically the alternative statement.

The decision to reject or not reject the null statement depends on the results from the statistical test. For every statistical test conducted, a test statistic and p-value are produced. Researchers compare the test statistic to the critical value, and the p-value to the alpha value. For the relationship to be significant (to reject the null hypothesis and accept the alternative hypothesis), the value of the test statistic must be larger

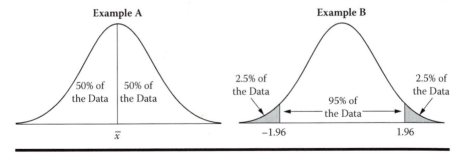

Figure 11.1   The normal distribution.

(in absolute terms) than the critical value, and the p-value must be smaller than the alpha value. But, what do these values mean?

The easiest way to understand these values is to understand the normal curve, which is illustrated in Example A of Figure 11.1. The normal curve is symmetric, where half of the values are located to the left of the peak (the location of the mean, median, and mode), and the other half of the values fall to right of the peak. In addition, the figure shows that much of the data fall underneath the curve with fewer observations located in the tails. For example, 95% of the data fall between ±1.96 standard deviations from the mean, and the remaining data, 5%, fall in the tails; 2.5% in each tail as shown in Example B of Figure 11.1. We consider the data in the tails to be significantly different from the rest of the data because the probability of their occurring by chance is less than 2.5% on either side; these data are not similar to the rest of the population.

Let us consider this using the age data from the graduate course discussed in Chapter 10. We have two classes, each with 15 students; Example 11.1 presents these data.

Example 11.1   Data, Means, and Standard Deviations for Student Ages

Age

Class 1	22	22	22	23	23	25	38	39	41	42	43	43	43	45	55
Class 2	25	25	27	30	30	33	35	35	37	38	39	40	41	41	42

	Mean	Standard Deviation
Class 1	35.1	11.0
Class 2	34.5	5.9

Class 1 has a mean age of 35.1 years old and a standard deviation of 11.0. Class 2 has an average age of 34.5, with a standard deviation of 5.9. Using the information from the second class, we know that 95% of the students are between the ages 22.9 and 46.1 years old, as shown in Figure 11.2.

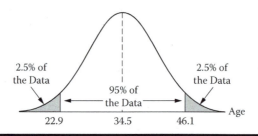

Figure 11.2 The distribution of ages.

We calculate these numbers by adding to and subtracting from the mean, the product of 1.96 and the standard deviation, as illustrated in the following steps:

$= \bar{x} \pm (1.96 * \text{standard deviation})$
$= 34.5 \pm (1.96 * 5.9)$
$= 34.5 \pm (11.56)$
$= 22.9 \text{ and } 46.1$

As stated earlier, 95% of the students fall between 23 and 46 years old, and those observations outside this range are considered different from the rest of the data. That is, the probability of a graduate student older than 46 being enrolled in the class is 2.5% or less; the same is true for a student younger than 23. In fact, no one in Class 2 falls in the tails.

This same logic applies to testing relationships between two variables. The values at the tails, such as the ±1.96, establish the critical regions and researchers do not reject the null statement when the results from the hypothesis test fall between the two critical values—the common area. None of the values falling in the common area is significant; that is, no relationship, significant or otherwise, is present between the two variables or groups being studied. Alternatively, researchers reject the null statement when the value of the statistical test lies outside the common area and in the tail or critical region. If the value of the test falls in the critical region, then researchers say there is a significant relationship, significant difference, or significant association between the two variables. Figure 11.3 illustrates the rejection regions.

The researcher establishes the critical values and regions, which depend on the direction of the statement and the amount of accuracy the researcher is willing to sacrifice. Relationship testing uses a two-tailed test or a one-tailed test where the one-tailed test is either a left-tailed test or a right-tailed test. Two-tailed tests examine the difference between two variables, whereas a one-tailed test signifies a statement of direction, as if one group's ages are higher than the other group's or one variable is less than another variable.

Regardless of the results from the statistical tests, there is a chance that the researcher will be wrong; that is, the researcher may draw the wrong conclusion.

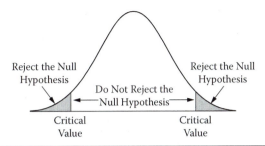

Figure 11.3 The rejection regions for hypothesis testing.

For example, the results may tell the researcher to conclude a significant relationship between two variables exists; however, this might be incorrect. The presence of sampling and nonsampling errors may produce statistics that lead researchers to state the wrong conclusion. If we reject a true null or do not reject a false null then we have committed Type I and Type II errors, respectively. Table 11.1 illustrates these errors. A Type I error, called alpha, occurs when the researcher concludes that a significant relationship exists when, in fact, no relationship is present; the researcher rejects a true null statement. The opposite is true for a Type II error, where a researcher maintains that no relationship is present between the two variables but in reality, a significant relationship exists.

Researchers can easily control the Type I error because they can modify the alpha, which defines the critical regions. For instance, the critical regions in Example B of Figure 11.1 contain 5% of the data, 2.5% in each tail. Overall, a researcher has a 5% chance of rejecting a true null statement. In other words, if the researcher says a significant relationship exists when one does not, the researcher has committed a Type I error. This will occur 5% of the time when researchers use a 5% alpha level. To reduce the probability of committing a Type I error, the size of the tail is decreased, which increases the critical value. Figure 11.4 illustrates this phenomenon.

Table 11.1   Errors in Hypothesis Testing

Null	Hypothesis Test: Null Not Rejected	Hypothesis Test: Null Rejected
True null	☺ No error	☹ Type I error (alpha)
False null	☹ Type II Error (beta)	☺ No error

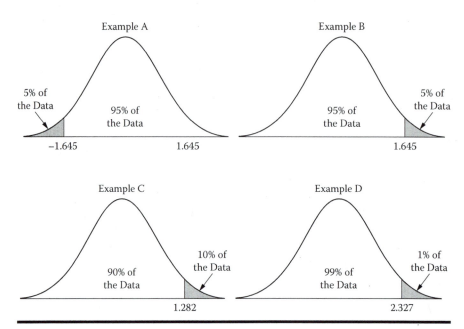

Figure 11.4   Illustrations of different alpha levels and critical values.

In each of the examples in Figure 11.4, a one-tailed distribution is displayed. Examples A and B present a critical region with an alpha of 5%, whereas Examples C and D present critical regions of 10% and 1%, respectively. The critical value for Example C is 1.282, which is smaller than the others because its alpha is larger. Researchers using an alpha level of 10% have a better chance of finding a significant relationship than those researchers using a smaller alpha; however, the probability of committing a Type I error (rejecting a true null hypothesis) is larger with an alpha of 10%. In social science research, using an alpha of 5% or less is the best practice, considering the presence of many nonsampling errors.

Each statistical test yields two results: a test statistic and a p-value. Researchers compare the value of the test statistic to the critical value that establishes the critical regions, and compare the p-value to the alpha value. The p-value is essentially the probability of committing a Type I error; therefore, the smaller the p-value, the better the probability of not committing a Type I error. Furthermore, if the p-value is smaller than the alpha, then the test statistic will be larger than the critical value in absolute terms and vice versa. Researchers analyze these values concurrently. Below is the recommended set of criteria to follow when conducting any of the four tests discussed in this chapter.

1. Reject the null and conclude the relationship between the two variables is significant when:
   - The test statistic is larger than the critical value, in absolute terms
   - The p-value is smaller than the alpha value

2. Do not reject the null and conclude there is no relationship between the two variables when:
    - The test statistic is smaller than the critical value, in absolute terms
    - The p-value is larger than the alpha value

Overall, testing relationships is similar to being tried in a court of law. The person on trial is either not guilty (i.e., innocent) or guilty. The null statement is that the person is not guilty, that there is no relationship between the person on trial and the crime, whereas the alternative statement is that the person on trial is guilty as charged. In order for the court or jury to reject the null (innocence) and convict the person on trial, a preponderance of evidence (the data) must exist such that the conclusion—a finding of guilt—is beyond a reasonable doubt. In other words, the evidence is so overwhelming that the relationship between the person on trial and the crime is significant. However, there is a chance that finding is wrong. For example, the judge or jury may commit a Type I error, saying the person is guilty, when in fact the person is innocent or they may commit a Type II error by setting a guilty person free—accepting a false null hypothesis. The propensity of error results from the lack of evidence.

Researchers rely on samples, rather than populations, to test relationships, and the inability to know everything about the entire population creates error. These errors, coupled with the fact that many of the measures used in social science research are based on perceptions and opinions, should lead researchers in our field to use a relatively conservative (i.e., small) alpha level to reduce the probability of claiming a significant relationship when one does not exist. For this text, and as good practice, we assume an alpha level of 5% (0.05) when testing relationships. Now we turn our attention to four different bivariate analyses that test the relationship between two variables: cross-tabulations, difference of means, analysis of variance, and correlation.

11.3   Cross Tabulations

A cross tabulation or contingency table is a two-way frequency table where two nominal or ordinal variables are crossed with each other to examine a relationship. A cross-tabulation presents the frequency of each paired attribute, placing the attributes of the independent variable in the columns and the attributes of the dependent variable in the rows. For example, Table 11.2 presents a cross-tabulation table for the political philosophies of faculty and students. Which variable is the dependent variable and which is the independent variable? What level of data are the variables? Political philosophy is the dependent variable, and the type of person—faculty or student—is the independent variable. Both variables are nominal, and each attribute of the variables is crossed to describe how many conservative or liberal faculty and students are present.

Table 11.2   Political Philosophy of Faculty and Students

Political Philosophy	Students	Faculty	Total
Conservative	1259	70	1329
Liberal	1391	220	1611
Total	2650	290	2940

Table 11.3   Political Philosophy of Faculty and Students

Political Philosophy	Students		Faculty		Total	
	n	%	n	%	n	%
Conservative	1259	47.5	70	24.1	1329	45.2
Liberal	1391	52.5	220	75.9	1611	54.8
Total	2650	100.0	290	100.0	2940	100.0

However, comparisons between the two groups are difficult because there are more students than faculty in the sample. Therefore, column percentages are calculated and included in the table as displayed in Table 11.3.

The percentages are calculated for the independent variable rather than the dependent variable, allowing the researcher to compare the attributes of the independent variable. The results show almost twice as many students than faculty consider themselves politically conservative.

The difference between the groups (23.5%) is large enough for many to claim a causality; however, such a conclusion is not possible until a statistical test—a test of the relationship between the two variables—is conducted and the other criteria (time order, eliminate alternatives and spurious relationships, and randomization) are met. Many researchers falsely conclude significance without properly testing relationships; therefore, in any research paper, we reserve the word "significant," in any form, for null statements that are rejected. In other words, the word significant should not be included when referring to descriptive statistics in the text of a research paper unless some test of significance has been completed.

The chi-square (χ^2) is the test statistic used to describe the relationship between two nominal or ordinal level variables. The chi-square distribution is different from the normal distribution in that there are no negative critical values, but the approach to testing the relationship is the same. The null statement says that there is no relationship between the variables—the variables are independent, or that their proportions are the same. The alternative statement makes the claim that a relationship exists, that the variables are dependent, or that their proportions are different.

The chi-square test compares what is happening between the attributes of the variables (the observed frequencies) to what should be happening (the expected frequencies), given the row, column, and grand totals. The more similar the observed frequencies are to the expected frequencies, the less likely a relationship exists between the variables. However, a larger difference between the values suggests that the variables or groups are different.

The process for calculating the chi-square involves determining the expected frequencies. Next, expected frequencies are subtracted from the observed frequencies, squared, and divided by the expected frequencies. Finally, all of these values are summed to compute the chi-square. The chi-square formula is as follows:

$$\chi^2 = \sum \frac{\left(f_o - f_e\right)^2}{f_e} \tag{11.1}$$

Where

f_o is the observed frequency
f_e is the expected frequency
$f_e = \dfrac{\text{row total*column total}}{\text{grand total}}$

To calculate the expected frequency of the political philosophies of the students and faculty, we multiply the row total by its respective column total, and then we divide this product by the grand total. For example, to find the expected frequency for conservative students, the row total, 1329, is multiplied by the column total, 2650, and then divided by the grand total, 2940, yielding 1198. Parts B and C of Table 11.4 illustrate this process and show the results for each crossed attribute, respectively.

The observed frequency for conservative students (1259) is similar to its expected frequency (1198), whereas the expected frequency for conservative faculty (131) is almost twice that of the observed frequency (70). We will revisit these differences after calculating the chi-square and the p-value. Next, each expected frequency is subtracted from its corresponding observed frequency, and the difference is squared and divided by its respective expected frequency (Part D of Table 11.4). Finally, all of these values (shown in Part E of Table 11.4) are summed to obtain the chi-square as illustrated at the bottom of Table 11.4.

We calculate a chi-square value of 57.6, which has a p-value of 0.000. (The Excel functions for calculating the p-value and critical value are provided at the end of this section.) The critical value is 3.841. This value, for an alpha of 0.05, separates the do not reject region from the rejection region. The chi-square test statistic of 57.6 is larger than the critical value, and the p-value is smaller than the alpha level. What can we say about the relationship between the two variables? The relationship between political philosophy and the type of person is significant. Therefore, political philosophies between faculty and students at this university are significantly

Table 11.4   Chi-Square Calculation

A. Observed Frequencies

Political Philosophy	Students	Faculty	Total
Conservative	1259	70	1329
Liberal	1391	220	1611
Total	2650	290	2940

B. Calculation of Expected Frequencies

Political Philosophy	Students	Faculty
Conservative	(1329*2650)/2940	(1329*290)/2940
Liberal	(1611*2650)/2940	(1611*290)/2940

C. Expected Frequencies

Political Philosophy	Students	Faculty	Total
Conservative	1198	131	1329
Liberal	1452	159	1611
Total	2650	290	2940

D. Calculation of $(f_o - f_e)^2/f_e$

Political Philosophy	Students	Faculty
Conservative	$(1259 - 1198)^2/1198$	$(70 - 131)^2/131$
Liberal	$(1391 - 1452)^2/1452$	$(220 - 159)^2/159$

E. $(f_o - f_e)^2/f$

Political Philosophy	Students	Faculty
Conservative	3.1	28.5
Liberal	2.6	23.5

Chi-square (sum of $(f_o - f_e)^2/f_e$)	57.6
p-value	0.000000000000031
Chi-square critical value	3.841

different. Moreover, looking at the differences between the expected and observed frequencies we find additional information about this significant relationship. If the faculty and students were similar, we would expect to see the numbers and percentages presented in Table 11.5, there each group would have the same percentage. That is, we would expect, given the row, column, and grand totals, that 45% of students and faculty would be conservative and the other 55% liberal.

This is not the case, however. Comparing the expected frequencies in Part C of Table 11.4 to those of the observed frequencies in Part A, we see there are 61

Table 11.5 Expected Frequencies and Percentages

Political Philosophy	Students		Faculty		Total	
	n	*%*	*n*	*%*	*n*	*%*
Conservative	1198	45.2	131	45.2	1329	45.2
Liberal	1452	54.8	159	54.8	1611	54.8
Total	2650.0	100.0	290.0	100.0	2940.0	100.0

fewer conservative faculty (70–131), 61 fewer liberal students (1391–1452), 61 more liberal faculty (220–159), and 61 more conservative students (1259–1198) than we would expect. The difference of 61 has a larger effect on the faculty numbers (and percentages) because the faculty sample size is smaller than the student sample size. Part E of Table 11.4 reveals the magnitude of the differences between the observed and expected frequencies. Here, we see that the faculty proportions are much different from the students' proportions, which is why we are able to conclude that there is a significant difference between the political philosophies of the faculty and students, specifically, their proportions are significantly different. There are significantly more politically liberal faculty than we would expect.

Let us look at one more example. Researchers want to know if transit problems experienced by public transit riders are dependent on place of residence. To examine this relationship, they asked 1329 residents in different locations who rely on public transportation about the frequency of transit problems. Which variable is the dependent variable and which one is the independent variable? What level of data are each variable? Frequency of transit problems is the dependent variable and is measured using an ordinal scale, and place of residence is a nominal level independent variable. Table 11.6 provides the results.

The chi-square calculation, presented in Table 11.7, reveals a chi-square of 5.54 and a p-value of 0.232. Although differences exist among attributes, there is no relationship between transit problems and area of residence because the p-value is larger than the alpha. Therefore, no one person in any particular area experiences more (or fewer) transit problems than others do; their proportions are similar.

Table 11.6 Transit Problems by Residential Area

Transit Problems	Residence			
	Urban	Suburban	Rural	Total
Never	571	353	122	1046
Sometimes	123	60	17	200
Often	49	22	12	83
Total	743	435	151	1329

Table 11.7   Chi-Square Calculation for Transit Problems

A. Observed Frequencies

Transit Problems	Residence			
	Urban	Suburban	Rural	Total
Never	571	353	122	1046
Sometimes	123	60	17	200
Often	49	22	12	83
Total	743	435	151	1329

B. Expected Frequencies

Transit Problems	Residence			
	Urban	Suburban	Rural	Total
Never	585	342	119	1046
Sometimes	112	65	23	200
Often	46	27	9	83
Total	743	435	151	1329

C. $(f_o - f_e)^2 / f_e$

Transit Problems	Residence		
	Urban	Suburban	Rural
Never	0.3	0.3	0.1
Sometimes	1.1	0.5	1.4
Often	0.1	1.0	0.7

Chi-square	5.584
p-value	0.232
Chi-square critical value	9.488

Overall, researchers find the chi-square test useful to describe relationships between two variables, which are nominal or ordinal level. Specifically, we can compare the proportions of the crossed attributes to determine where differences exist; but the chi-square does not provide information about the direction of a relationship. This is not a problem when direction is absent, as it is in nominal data. However, researchers are unable to draw statistical inferences about the associations between the two ordinal variables when the ordinal variables use direction (i.e., increasing frequency, quality, or favorable opinion). There are additional tests available to evaluate the associations between two ordinal level variables; however, these are beyond the scope of this text.

Microsoft Excel offers a variety of statistical functions, including the calculation of p-value and critical value for chi-square. In order to calculate the p-value of the chi-square, we calculate the expected frequencies first. All functions begin the same way: in an empty cell, select Insert from the menu bar, and then pick Function from the list of options. The function list can also be obtained by selecting the f_x on the formula bar illustrated in Figure 11.5.

Statistical is selected from the category dropdown box as shown in Example A in Figure 11.6. In doing so, a list of available statistical functions emerge in alphabetical order (Example B of Figure 11.6). CHITEST is the function necessary to calculate the p-value. Once selected, another dialog box appears, displayed in Figure 11.7, requesting the observed and expected frequency ranges. Once the ranges are entered, the p-value appears toward the bottom of the box and will show up in the spreadsheet when OK is selected.

CHIINV is the function in the list of statistical options that calculates the critical value. Upon its selection, the alpha value (probability) of choice (remember we are using 0.05) and the degrees of freedom are entered in the box that appears as shown in Figure 11.8. By clicking OK the critical value appears in the spreadsheet.

We calculate the degrees of freedom (df) by multiplying the number of columns less one by the number of rows less one or using the following formula: $[(c-1)*(r-1)]$. The column and row headings and totals are not included in this calculation; only the cells representing the frequencies. In this example, the df is one because the table is a 2 × 2 table, faculty and students crossed with conservative and liberal. If the table were a 3 × 4, then the degrees of freedom would be 6.

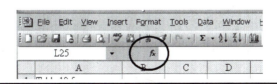

Figure 11.5   The function option on formula bar in Excel.

Example A   Example B

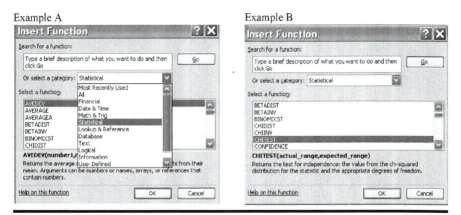

Figure 11.6   Statistical function options available in Excel.

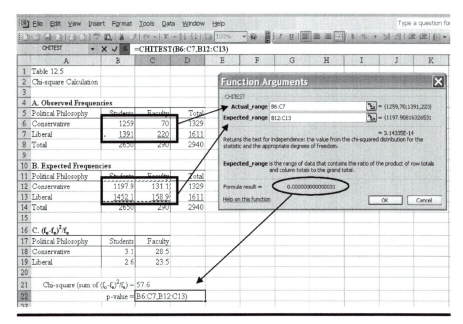

Figure 11.7   CHITEST function arguments.

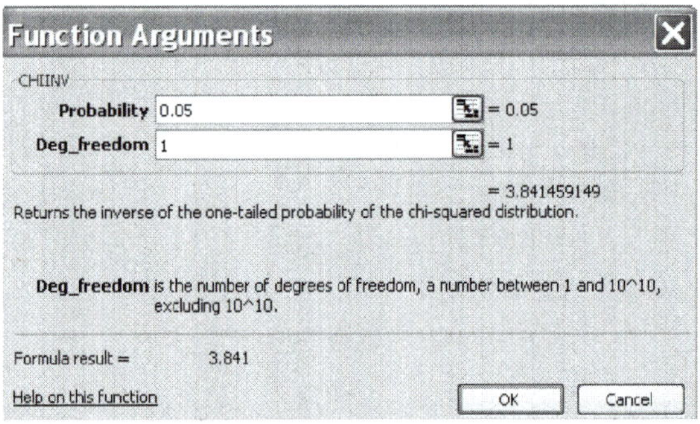

Figure 11.8   CHIINV function arguments.

11.4   Difference of Means

A difference of means test is used to study the difference—improvements or otherwise—between two groups. For example, for a researcher to claim that average math scores increased by five points or that, on average, males score higher than females on the SAT, is only ancillary to the significance of the improvement or difference. In addition to the average, the standard deviation and sample size are necessary to compare groups, and a difference of means test and its t-statistic provide researchers with the ability to evaluate the significance these relationships. The t-statistic is appropriate when the data are randomly selected and have a normal distribution, when the dependent variable is ratio level data, and when the independent variable consists of two categories or groups. Examples include comparing the before test to the after test, males to females, doctors to nurses, the treatment group to the control group, and so forth.

The two groups studied by researchers come from dependent samples or from independent samples. Dependent samples represent the same people; they are involved in the before and after, for instance, the pretest and posttest. The independent sample consists of two different groups of people, such as the treatment and control groups, males and females, urban and nonurban residents.

The null statement for the difference of means test is that there is no difference between the two groups, whereas the alternative statement says that there is a difference between the two groups or that a direction exists. For example, we could state that students perform better on the posttest than the pretest, that the incomes of males are higher than females, or that nonurban residents drive farther to work than urban residents. Each one of these alludes to a direction of the difference.

The difference of means analysis produces a t-statistic that is used to determine statistical significance. Although the interpretation of the t-statistic is the same, two different formulas exist, one for dependent samples (Formula 11.2) and the other for independent samples (Formula 11.3).

$$t = \frac{\bar{d}}{s_d / \sqrt{n}} \tag{11.2}$$

Where:

t is the t-statistic result for the difference of means
$\bar{d}$ is the average difference between the two groups
s_d is the standard deviation of the differences between the two groups
n is the sample size

$$t = \frac{\bar{x}_1 - \bar{x}_2}{\sqrt{\dfrac{s_1^2}{n_1} + \dfrac{s_2^2}{n_2}}} \tag{11.3}$$

Where:

t is the t-statistic result for the difference of means
$\bar{x}_1$ is the mean of group 1
$\bar{x}_2$ is the mean of group 2
s_1^2 is the variance (standard deviation squared) of group 1
s_2^2 is the variance (standard deviation squared) of group 2
n_1 is the sample size of group 1
n_2 is the sample size of group 2

Researchers use the average difference and standard deviation of this difference to determine the t-statistic, for dependent samples. However, when researchers study independent samples, they calculate the t-statistic using each group's respective average, standard deviation, and sample size.

We begin with dependent samples using the math program for fourth graders discussed in Chapter 5 as an illustration. School administrators decide to implement a new math program that is being marketed as significantly improving the math skills of fourth graders. To study the program's efficacy, school officials devise a study using a pretest–posttest design for one fourth grade class. Prior to implementing the program, the teacher of that class administers a pretest. Scores averaged 65 (out of 100) with a standard deviation of 6.7. At the conclusion of the new program, the teacher tests the students again and the average scores increase to 70 with a standard deviation of 12.0.

A five-point increase is ostensibly an improvement in math scores. Figure 11.9 suggest something similar, showing the improvement (the difference between the pretest and posttest). Seventy percent of the students improved their cores by at least one point.

Is this enough evidence to suggest a significant improvement? No, this is not enough evidence. Remember, they need to include the standard deviations, as well as the sample size; therefore, they need to conduct a statistical test before claiming significance.

Using the Formula 11.2, the difference between the pretest and posttest for each student are calculated, as presented in Table 11.8.

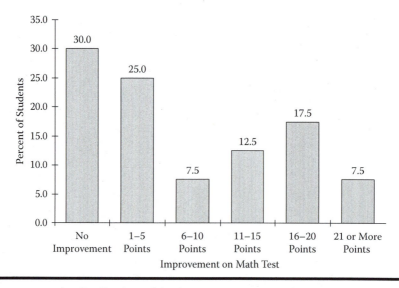

Figure 11.9 The distribution of the improvement on math scores.

Table 11.8 Math Test Results Before and After Implementation of New Math Program

Student ID	Pretest	Posttest	Difference (Pretest/Posttest)
1	62	66	4
2	55	85	29
3	74	76	2
4	65	66	1
5	73	90	17
6	55	56	1
7	64	74	10
8	69	59	−11
9	66	78	12
10	53	63	10
11	70	69	−1
12	61	77	16
13	65	95	30
14	73	91	19
15	59	68	8
16	75	75	0
17	65	76	11
18	58	45	−12
19	62	81	19
20	59	79	19
21	74	74	1
22	62	65	3
23	81	69	−12
24	69	38	−32
25	77	69	−8
26	58	58	0
27	69	64	−5
28	67	68	1
29	61	73	11
30	52	52	−1
31	61	73	12
32	70	66	−5
33	68	70	2
34	60	61	1
35	67	56	−11
36	58	76	17
37	68	90	22
38	66	59	−7
39	64	70	6
40	58	74	16

Next, the average difference and standard deviation of the difference are calculated, yielding 5 and 12.4, respectively. Lastly, these numbers are substituted into Formula 11.2:

$$t = \frac{5}{12.4 / \sqrt{40}}$$

$t = 2.53$, p-value $= 0.008$

Because the p-value is less than the alpha level of 0.05, and the t-statistic is larger than the critical value of 1.645 (using Example B from Figure 11.4), we can say that there is a significant improvement in test scores. Can we say that the math program is the cause of this improvement? No, there is not enough evidence to claim causality but a statistical association is one of the elements necessary to support cause and effect.

When we analyze the differences between the pretest and posttest (see Figure 11.9), we find that 30% of the students did worse or showed no improvement on the posttest, and an additional 25% improved only as much as the average difference. In other words, less than half (45%) of the fourth graders improved their scores beyond the average. Is this information, coupled with the statistical significance, enough to conclude that the program positively affects math skills? Or, is more information still necessary? What about a better research design? Although a statistical association and time order are present, the presence of the pretest and the lack of a control group threaten the validity of this design. Therefore, a better research design will help the school administrators determine the efficacy of the math program.

The next year, the school officials conduct a posttest-only control group design to examine the effectiveness of the math program. In doing so, they implement the math program in one of the fourth grade classes but not in the other; Class A receives the treatment (they participate in the program) and Class B is used as the control group (they do not participate in the program). After the program concludes, the teachers test and compare the math skills of both groups. Table 11.9 presents these results.

Overall, the test reveals a difference, an improvement in fact. The treatment group's average is three points higher than the control group's average. However, looking at a graphic of these data, as shown in Figure 11.10, the scores seem to be similar, with the exception of the scores below 50 and those in the 70s. That is, the treatment group does not have any scores below 50 and has more students scoring in the 70s.

Can the analyst rely on a three point differences and the graphic to claim that the math program is effective—that the program significantly improves math skills?

Table 11.9   Math Test Results for Control and Treatment Groups

Student ID	Control Group	Treatment Group
1	64	67
2	54	79
3	69	73
4	80	64
5	79	75
6	84	84
7	45	82
8	65	72
9	78	80
10	56	77
11	60	63
12	50	56
13	49	67
14	57	61
15	59	78
16	46	70
17	61	74
18	63	67
19	68	65
20	63	80
21	64	51
22	63	75
23	80	67
24	66	64
25	65	81
26	62	72
27	87	60
28	76	70
29	91	71
30	60	69
31	84	72
32	51	66
33	72	74
34	76	59
35	86	63
36	66	78
37	62	92
38	74	64
39	63	65
40	75	68
Average	66.9	70.3
Standard deviation	11.7	8.3

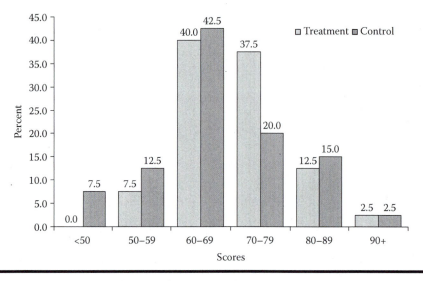

Figure 11.10 **The distribution of test Scores by percentage for the treatment and control groups.**

No, a test of significance must be conducted. Using Formula 11.3, we calculate a t-statistic of 1.538:

$$t = \frac{70.35 - 66.83}{\sqrt{\dfrac{8.32^2}{40} + \dfrac{11.67^2}{40}}}$$

$$= \frac{3.52}{\sqrt{1.73 + 3.41}}$$

$$= \frac{3.40}{2.27}$$

$$= 1.538, \text{ p-value} = 0.064$$

The t-test reveals that there is no significant difference between the two groups—the math program does not significantly improve math skills because the t-statistic is less than 1.645 (using Example B in Figure 11.4), and the p-value is larger than 0.05. However, those people promoting the new program insist that the program is effective. How? They argue that the school officials should use an alpha of 0.10, rather than 0.05. By increasing the alpha to 0.10 (and decreasing the critical value to 1.282, see Example C in Figure 11.4), the relationship goes from no relationship to a significant relationship suggesting an effective program. Just like that, an insignificant finding becomes significant. What should the administrators do?

They might design an even better study, but as consumers of their own research, they must pay attention to the levels of significance, as they play a major role in the arguments for and against policy changes. A higher-level alpha means the researcher increases the probability of committing a Type I error, which could have serious consequences; for example, eliminating useful, existing programs, or instituting new, ineffective ones.

Overall, the difference of means test allows researchers to examine the differences between two groups where ratio level information is collected. Calculating the t-statistic in Microsoft Excel is relatively simple as Excel provides a Data Analysis add-in (discussed in Chapters 7 and 10) of useful statistical tools, including difference of means tests for dependent and independent samples. We begin with the process for calculating the t-statistic for dependent samples.

The t-Test: Paired Two Sample for Means is selected from the list of options in the Data Analysis box. The dependent samples analysis box appears, as illustrated in Figure 11.11. We enter the ranges for the two groups, and the order in which the group's range is entered in Variable 1 or Variable 2 does not matter.

After entering the necessary information, we select OK, and the output shown in Figure 11.12 appears in the spreadsheet. Along with the means and variances, Excel computes the t-statistic, the p-values [$P(T<=t)$], and the critical values for one- and two-tailed tests, the values necessary to evaluate the difference between the pretest and posttest of the dependent samples.

The process for calculating the t-statistic for independent samples is very similar; however, the t-Test: Two Sample Assuming Unequal Variances is selected from the Data Analysis box. The box, shown in Figure 11.13, appears and requests variable ranges.

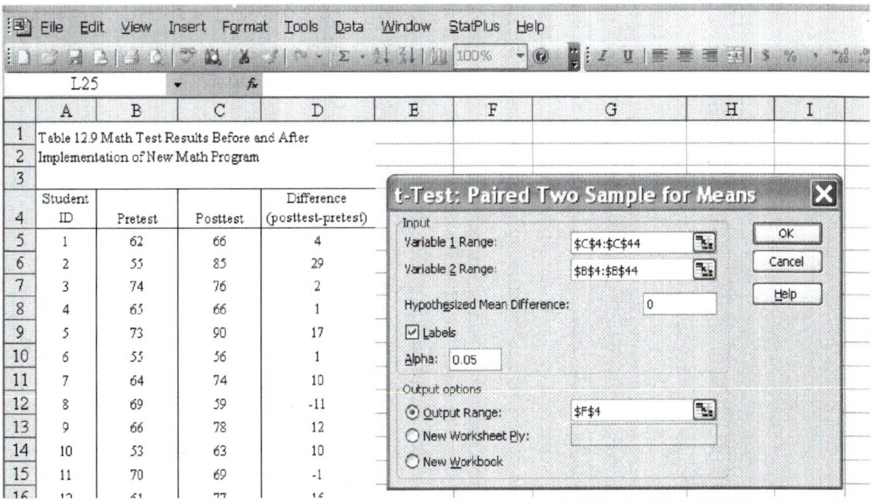

Figure 11.11   The t-test process for dependent samples.

	F	G	H
	File Edit View Insert Format Tools Data Window StatPlus		
	K29 ▼ *fx*		
4	t-Test: Paired Two Sample for Means		
5			
6		*Posttest*	*Pretest*
7	Mean	69.818	64.863
8	Variance	143.507	45.237
9	Observations	40	40
10	Pearson Correlation	0.2180	
11	Hypothesized Mean Difference	0	
12	df	39	
13	t Stat	2.5286	
14	P(T<=t) one-tail	0.0078	
15	t Critical one-tail	1.6849	
16	P(T<=t) two-tail	0.0156	
17	t Critical two-tail	2.0227	

Figure 11.12   The t-test output for dependent samples.

	A	B	C	D	E	F	G	H	I	J
	File Edit View Insert Format Tools Data Window StatPlus Help									
	E5 ▼ *fx*									
4	Student ID	Control Group	Treatment Group							
5	1	64	67							
6	2	54	79							
7	3	69	73							
8	4	80	64							
9	5	79	75							
10	6	84	84							
11	7	45	82							
12	8	65	72							
13	9	78	80							
14	10	56	77							
15	11	60	63							
16	12	50	56							
17	13	49	67							
18	14	57	61							

t-Test: Two-Sample Assuming Unequal ...

Input
Variable 1 Range: $C$4:$C$44
Variable 2 Range: $B$4:$B$44
Hypothesized Mean Difference: 0
☑ Labels
Alpha: 0.05

Output options
⦿ Output Range: $E$5
○ New Worksheet Ply:
○ New Workbook

OK   Cancel   Help

Figure 11.13   The t-test process for independent samples.

Again, the order of variables does not matter. Upon entering the appropriate information and clicking OK, the output presented in Figure 11.14 appears. Excel provides the same information: the t-statistic, the p-values, and the critical values—all the figures necessary to examine the difference between two independent samples.

	E	F	G	H
	🖳 File Edit View Insert Format Tools Data Window StatPlus Help			
	🗋 🖿 🖬 🖳 ⏴ 🖫 ⏴ 🖫 ✂ 🍼 ➦ ▾ Σ ▾ ⏶↓ ⏷↓ ⏰ 100% ▾ ⊚			
	O31 ▾ *fx*			
5	t-Test: Two-Sample Assuming Unequal Variances			
6				
7		*Treatment Group*	*Control Group*	
8	Mean	70.346	66.859	
9	Variance	69.288	136.246	
10	Observations	40	40	
11	Hypothesized Mean Difference	0		
12	df	71		
13	**t Stat**	**1.538**		
14	**P(T<=t) one-tail**	**0.064**		
15	**t Critical one-tail**	**1.667**		
16	P(T<=t) two-tail	0.128		
17	t Critical two-tail	1.994		
18				

Figure 11.14   The t-test output for independent samples.

11.5   Analysis of Variance

An analysis of variance (ANOVA) is similar to a difference of means test, except the means of three or more groups are studied and the test used is an F-test rather than a t-test. A one-way ANOVA is a bivariate analysis of a ratio level dependent variable and a categorical independent variable with three or more groups. An ANOVA is used when the data are normally distributed, the variances are the same, and the samples are random and independent. The null statement says that there is no difference among the groups' means, whereas the alternative hypothesis claims that at least one mean is different. Although the ANOVA determines if any one group (or groups) is significantly different from the others, it does not reveal which one is different.

The school administrators decide to try a better research design that examines three groups—two treatment groups and one control group. The two treatments consist of two different math programs, each with the guarantee of significant improvement in the math skills of fourth graders. In Class A, the original math program is implemented, the newer math program is used in Class B, and Class C serves as the control group where no math program is used. Subsequent to completion of the program, each class takes the math skills test. Table 11.10 presents the distribution of scores by class.

The means are all different; in fact, the control group has the lowest mean, suggesting that perhaps the math programs are effective. However, a statistical test is necessary to determine if significance is present, and the F-test reveals this information. The F-test reveals a statistic of 6.404 and a p-value of 0.002, which is smaller than the

Table 11.10 Distribution (by Percentage) of Scores by Class

Scores	Class A	Class B	Class C
< 50	0.0	2.5	12.5
50–59	7.5	12.5	15.0
60–69	40.0	10.0	37.5
70–79	37.5	52.5	22.5
80–89	12.5	22.5	12.5
90+	2.5	0.0	0.0
Total	100.0	100.0	100.0
Average	70.3	72.8	64.9
Standard deviation	8.3	10.1	11.7

Note: The F-test for the one-way ANOVA is 6.404 with a p-value of 0.002.

alpha of 0.05. What does this suggest? We can claim that at least one mean is significantly different from the others; however, we cannot say which mean (or means) is different from the rest. When the ANOVA results are significant, additional testing is necessary determine if the treatment group means are different from the control group means. Such tests are available in other statistical software programs like SPSS, but not in Excel, and therefore they are beyond the scope of this text.

Microsoft Excel does provide an analysis of variance tools under its Data Analysis option. Selecting Anova: Single Factor from the list options, produces the box shown in Figure 11.15. We enter the ranges for all the different groups and the output presented in Figure 11.16 appears once we select OK. The summary table shows the averages and variances for each group, and the ANOVA table provides the F-statistic, p-value, and critical F value.

11.6   Correlation

Sometimes researchers are interested in the association between two ratio level variables. For example, the police chief wants to understand what happens to the crime rate when the number of officers on patrol changes, and the administrator of the emergency department at the local hospital wants to know if there is a relationship between the number of specialists on duty and the number of patient deaths. To answer these questions, the researchers conduct a correlation analysis where they create a scatter plot and calculate the correlation coefficient.

The correlation analysis measures the linear association between two ratio level variables and the scatter plot graphically depicts this relationship. The correlation analysis is appropriate when the sample is randomly selected and the distributions are normal. The null statement for the correlation analysis says that the independent

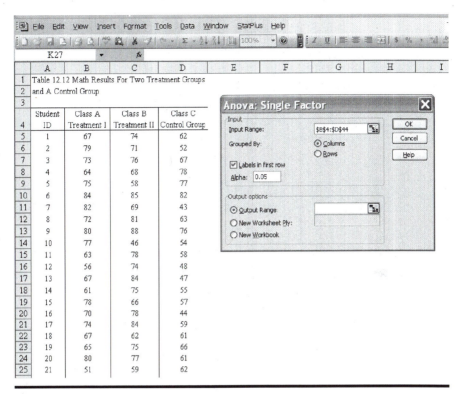

Figure 11.15 The ANOVA process in Excel.

K	L	M	N	O	P	Q
Anova: Single Factor						
SUMMARY						
Groups	Count	Sum	Average	Variance		
Class A Treatment I	40	2813.83	70.35	69.29		
Class B Treatment II	40	2911.14	72.78	102.82		
Class C Control Group	40	2594.37	64.86	136.25		
ANOVA						
Source of Variation	SS	df	MS	F	P-value	F crit
Between Groups	1316.409	2	658.205	6.404	0.002	3.074
Within Groups	12025.672	117	102.784			
Total	13342.081	119				

Figure 11.16 The ANOVA output.

and dependent variables are not related, whereas the alternative statement claims that a significant association exists.

The test statistic for the correlation analysis, denoted as r, is called the Pearson's correlation coefficient and is a number between –1 and +1. The sign indicates the direction of the relationship, and the value of the coefficient represents the strength or magnitude of the relationship. A correlation of –1 suggests that the two variables have a perfectly negative relationship, whereas a coefficient of +1 reveals a perfectly positive association. Therefore, the closer the correlation coefficient is to 1 in an absolute sense, the stronger the relationship. However, the strength of the association diminishes as the correlation coefficient approaches zero.

For example, let us analyze two relationships. The first analysis examines the correlation between per capita taxes collected by states and the percentage of their population with a bachelor's degree. The second analysis evaluates the correlation between median income levels and the percentage of the population with a bachelor's degree. In both cases, education is the independent variable. The correlation coefficients for the relationships are 0.376 and 0.826, respectively. The direction for both is positive, suggesting that as the percentage of the population with a bachelor's degree increases, per capita taxes and median income levels increase. However, the strength of the relationship between education and income is stronger than the relationship between education and taxes.

The scatter plot graphs the paired values of the independent variable, placed on the x-axis, and the dependent variable, located on the y-axis. The graph assists researchers with the interpretation of the correlation statistic. The paired values of the scatter plot for a weaker relationship will be scattered in a nonlinear fashion, as shown in Example A of Figure 11.17. However, the stronger the relationship between the dependent and independent variables, the more concentrated and linear the paired points will be, as illustrated in Example B of Figure 11.17.

The correlation coefficient and scatter plot tell researchers that the relationship between income and education is strong, linear, and positive, whereas the relationship between taxes and education is positive, but not as strong or linear. Overall, the correlation analysis and scatter plot allow researchers to examine the statistical association between two variables, both of which use ratio level data.

Calculating the correlation coefficient and creating scatter plots is easy in Microsoft Excel. The scatter plot is created using the Chart Wizard discussed in Chapter 10. The correlation coefficient is calculated one of two ways. The function CORREL can be chosen from the Statistical Function list of options or Correlation can be selected from the list of choices in the Data Analysis box. When following the directions for the Data Analysis approach, a box will emerge as shown in Figure 11.18.

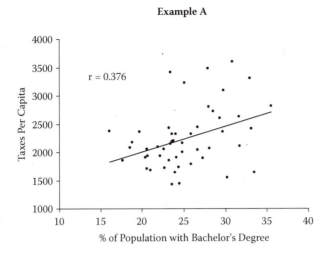

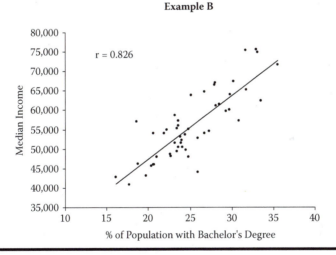

Figure 11.17   Scatter plots for states per capita taxes and education and median income and education.

The input range can include two or more variable ranges; that is, many correlation coefficients can be calculated at once. When we enter the appropriate information and select OK, the output displayed in Figure 11.19 appears in the spreadsheet. We are only interested in two of the three correlations, but because all three variables were selected, coefficients are calculated for all possible combinations.

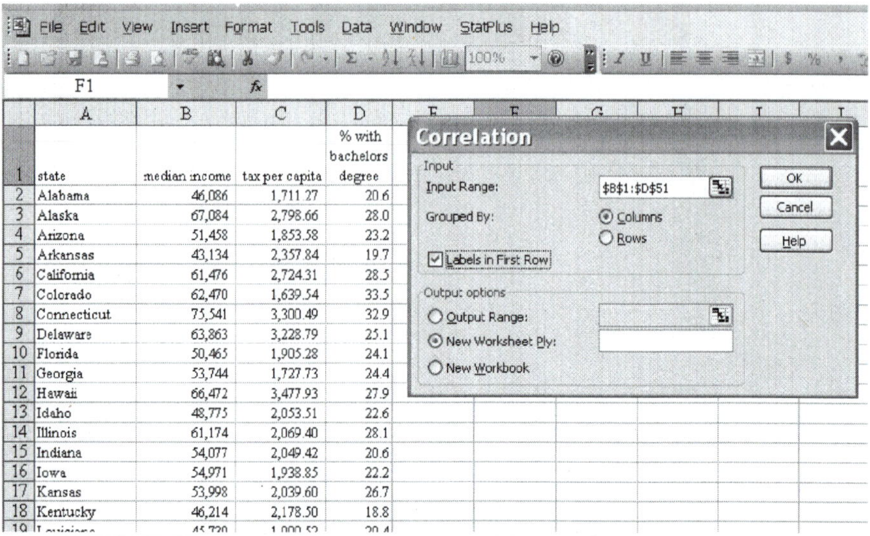

Figure 11.18   The correlation analysis process in Excel.

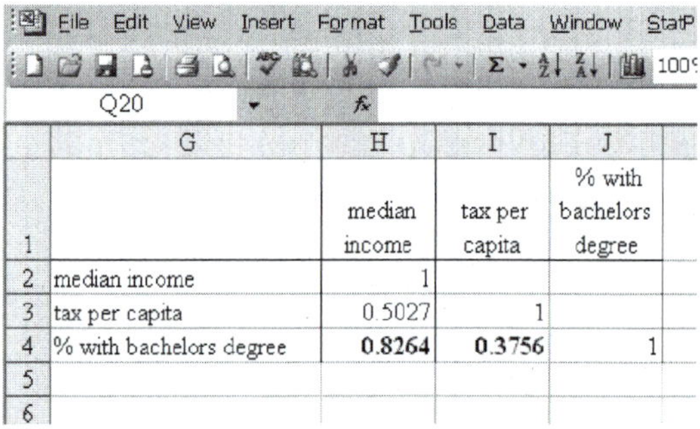

Figure 11.19   The correlation analysis output.

11.7   Summary

The statistical tests presented here are those that are most popular and useful in our field to describe and assist in the explanation of relationships between two variables. Most reports and briefings provided by governments and nonprofits—and even scholarly research prepared by academics—rely mostly on univariate statistics and their graphics, and where bivariate analyses are conducted, contingency tables and difference of means tests are particularly useful. This is why this chapter spends more time on chi-square and t-statistics, rather than on ANOVAs and correlation analysis.

Regardless of the test, all those discussed in this chapter are testing for a significant relationship—dependence (the chi-square), differences (t-statistic or F-statistic), or associations (correlation coefficient)—between two variables or groups. The test used depends on the type of type of data, its distribution, and randomness. The chi-square is used when both variables are categorical—nominal or ordinal, whereas the correlation analysis is appropriate when the ratio level variables are present. The differences of means and analysis of variance examine differences among groups, two groups for the difference of means test and three or more groups for the analysis of variance test.

All of the tests yield a statistical value and a p-value, and researchers use these values to determine the significance of a relationship between the two variables. The quickest way to determine significance is to compare the p-value and alpha level. The generally accepted alpha levels are 0.10, 0.05, and 0.01, where smaller alphas reduce the probability of committing a Type I error. Where p-values are equal to or larger than the selected alpha, the researcher does not reject the null statement and concludes that no relationship exists. On the other hand, when the p-value is less than the alpha level, researchers reject the null statement, and the alternative statement prevails—the researcher claims significance.

Finally, as a producer and consumer of research, there are two important rules to follow when testing hypotheses. First, a statistically significant relationship does not imply causation. Second, researchers should not alter their definition of significance (the alpha level) to accommodate self-interest or the interest of others; choose an alpha and do not change it. Adhering to these tenets improves the efficacy of research.

Key Terms

Alpha level	Difference of means	One-tailed test
Alternative hypothesis	Expected frequency	p-value
Analysis of variance	F-statistic	Rejection region
Association	Hypothesis testing	Scatter plot
Correlation coefficient	Independent samples	Significance level
Chi-square	Independent variable	t-statistic
Critical value	Normal distribution	Two-tailed test
Cross tabulations	Null hypothesis	Type I error
Dependent samples	Observed frequency	Type II error
Dependent variable		

Exercises

1. Is it appropriate for researchers to change their p-value to alter the outcome of the hypothesis test? Explain the role and importance of the p-value in hypothesis testing.
2. Is the test of a relationship enough for the researcher to claim causality? Why or why not? Explain.

3. Find news articles, opinion pieces, or "letters to the editor" that make claims of causality. What is the basis for these claims? Did they or some else conduct a hypothesis test? Have they met all the conditions of causality? What more should they do in their research to help justify the link between cause and effect?

4. Consider the most recent research project conducted by your organization. Did the researcher test for relationships? If so, what did they do? What tests did the researcher use? How did the researcher define significance? What would you have done differently if you were the researcher?

5. Minorities, who make up 30% of the residents in one local community, are charging the police chief and his officers with incompetence. They argue that minorities make up a disproportionate number of crime victims. The police chief asks you to investigate these claims using the information below. What can you tell the police chief? Communicate these findings in a memo.

Type of crime	Race/ethnicity of victim		
	White	Black	Hispanic
Robbery	422	134	52
Felony assault	655	764	689
Assault and battery/ domestic violence	2035	1693	1407

6. The mayor of a large city received a lot of negative press when the residents learned that females make less than males. To investigate these charges, the mayor hires you to analyze a random sample of incomes from both genders. The data are listed below. What can you tell the mayor about income disparity?

Annual Income: Females

20,352	22,841	22,996	26,073	26,163	26,483	28,242	29,170
42,745	42,788	43,600	43,994	44,195	44,881	44,962	45,039
29,629	29,791	29,896	45,108	45,355	45,676	39,042	39,835
35,759	36,852	37,940	38,140	38,237	38,536	38,599	38,809
41,414	41,614	41,886	42,621	55,703	60,306	60,565	50,355
45,823	46,288	47,155	48,442	48,832	48,842	48,927	49,738

Annual Income: Males

58,962	35,911	36,148	39,749	43,720	45,293	45,592	65,032
107,292	20,755	79,979	22,541	24,871	28,650	31,841	82,054
46,956	32,281	73,693	75,300	79,361	57,845	82,783	32,488
48,498	48,721	49,645	51,063	51,262	53,366	56,953	21,961
67,184	67,428	67,736	68,935	69,160	69,776	72,795	73,553
60,043	61,333	61,956	85,849	86,016	89,185	95,377	102,608

Recommended Reading

Berk, K. and Carey, P. (2004). *Data Analysis with Microsoft Excel*. Belmont, CA: Thomson.

Field, A. (2005). *Discovering Statistics Using SPSS*. London: Sage Publications.

Norusis, M. J. (2006). *SPSS 15.0 Guide to Data Analysis*. Upper Saddle River, NJ: Prentice Hall.

Chapter 12

Communicating
Research Results

12.1   Introduction

Researchers communicate their research and findings in a variety of ways in papers, such as academic journal articles, applied technical reports, research briefings, and presentations using slides or poster boards. Although the components of the papers and presentations differ, researchers organize the information in such a manner that conveys to the target audience the purpose and importance of the research in a comprehensible manner.

Researchers must understand the target audience and its familiarity with statistics when penning the report. Many audiences similar to the ones for whom you will write research papers—the general public, nonprofit directors, policy makers, hospital administrators, stakeholders, clients, politicians, news writers, and reporters—only have a general understanding of the simplest statistics, such as frequency distributions, averages, and perhaps the errors associated with sampling. The audience's knowledge beyond these simple statistics is rare, and found only in those individuals who have taken advanced statistics and mathematics courses, and use research in their everyday life. The presence of different audiences is apparent when comparing a newspaper, magazine article, or a research briefing to an empirical research article published in an academic (i.e., scholarly) journal. In technical reports and briefings, the statistics researchers present are simple at best, and often communicated through graphics, whereas the journal articles contain few graphics and more tables that are likely to present bivariate and multivariate findings. Box 12.1 illustrates the simplicity of a research briefing.

BOX 12.1   EXAMPLE OF A RESEARCH BRIEFING[1]

Food: Economics, Nutrition, Health, and Education

Many individuals throughout the United States have limited access to food (i.e. food insecurity) according to the United States Department of Agriculture's Economic Research Service. Research from the Centers for Disease Control and Prevention (CDC) shows that food insecurity contributes to malnutrition, which exacerbates disease, increases disability, and decreases resistance to infection. Compromised food choices can lead to poor nutrition affecting the health status of many individuals. According to the CDC, the effects of insufficient nutrition may go beyond obesity, diabetes, and heart disease to improper brain development and behavioral disorders. Food insecurity, over time, may result in a decreased ability to grow, work, and learn. Economic disparities account for much of the problem. Initiatives such as the Food Assistance Program and Women, Infants, and Children (WIC) seek to alleviate economically rooted nutritional hardship. Lack of education and access to information can also contribute to inadequate nutrition and the health issues surrounding it. Many new initiatives seek to educate the public, in order to quell the negative effects associated with improper nutrition.

Food Security and Health Status

Data from the 2005/2006 Greater Grand Rapids Community Survey show a relationship between food security and health status. Respondents who showed signs of food insecurity due to financial hardship were more likely than others to rate their health as 'fair' or 'poor'. Only 11% of people who had skipped or reduced the size of a meal considered themselves to be in excellent health, whereas 30% of people who did not face food insecurity indicated being in excellent health *(see graph below).*

RESPONDENTS' RATINGS OF THEIR HEALTH BY WHETHER THEY HAD SKIPPED OR CUT THE SIZE OF MEALS IN THE LAST 12 MONTHS

HOW WOULD YOU RATE YOUR HEALTH?

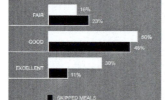

- ■ SKIPPED MEALS
- ▢ DID NOT SKIP MEALS

Food Security in Kent County

The 2005/2006 Greater Grand Rapids Community Survey was designed, in part, to assess the food security of Kent County. Economic stress affects the nutrition-related behaviors of Kent County residents. Six percent of respondents stated that they had skipped meals or cut meal size due to a lack of money for food *(see Indicator 1)*. Of those who had skipped or reduced meals, three-quarters said that they had done so multiple times in the past year. More than a quarter of survey respondents indicated that they worry, at least occasionally, about being able to afford food or clothing *(see Indicator 2)*.

INDICATOR 1:

IN THE LAST 12 MONTHS, DID YOU OR OTHERS IN YOUR HOUSEHOLD EVER CUT THE SIZE OF YOUR MEALS OR SKIP MEALS BECAUSE THERE WASN'T ENOUGH MONEY FOR FOOD? IF "YES", HOW OFTEN DID THIS HAPPEN?

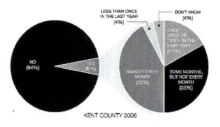

KENT COUNTY 2006

Who is Going Hungry in Kent County?

The food insecurity described above does not affect all groups of people equally. Food security data and demographic information—including sex, weight, marital status, income, race/ethnicity—were analyzed to determine the segments of the Kent County population most at risk of food insecurity. There was no correlation between gender and skipping meals for economic reasons. The average weight of those skipping meals and those not skipping meals was nearly the same. According to survey responses, those who are married are less likely to skip meals. People living below the poverty line are more likely than wealthier individuals to skip meals because of financial hardship. The average (mean) number of people living in a household had no relationship with skipping meals. Homeownership is directly related to food security. In terms of race, 22% of those indicating that they had skipped meals were white, meaning that most food insecurity occurs among minority populations. While many residents of Grand Rapids had skipped or reduced the size of a meal, the rural population was proportionally more likely to do so. One reason for this may be that residents of rural areas may have less access to social services and food programs than city residents. Those skipping meals in rural areas are predominately white, while those in urban settings are in minority groups. One use of the data regarding food insecurity in Kent County could be social services providers' improved ability to target specific populations in trying to remedy and prevent malnutrition.

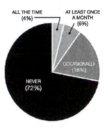

INDICATOR 2:

HOW OFTEN DO YOU WORRY ABOUT RUNNING OUT OF MONEY FOR FOOD OR CLOTHING?

- ALL THE TIME (4%)
- AT LEAST ONCE A MONTH (6%)
- OCCASIONALLY (18%)
- NEVER (72%)

KENT COUNTY 2006

What is Kent County Eating?

The majority of Kent County residents surveyed indicated that they did not eat five servings of fruits and vegetables daily (see Indicator 3). Men were less likely than women to eat five servings of fruits and vegetables. The average weight of those eating fruits and vegetable is less than those who do not, regardless of sex. Racial and ethnic differences exist as well: Asian Americans and Latin Americans are more likely to eat five servings of fruits and vegetables each day than Caucasians, while African Americans are less likely to do so.

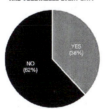

INDICATOR 3:

DO YOU EAT 5 SERVINGS OF FRUITS AND VEGETABLES EVERY DAY?

- YES (38%)
- NO (62%)

KENT COUNTY 2006

Food Security and Children

Survey data point to an emerging relationship between parenting status and food insecurity. Eight percent of respondents who were parents of at least one child under the age of 18 indicated having reduced a meal size or skipped a meal due to economic difficulties. Among those who were not parents, 5.3% had skipped or cut the size of a meal. The data also show that as family size grows, the likelihood of food insecurity increases.

The most dramatic relationship between parenting and food insecurity is among single parents. Nearly 17% of single parents skipped or reduced the size of a meal in the past year. Among single mothers, this percentage increases to 18.4%. These data illustrate the need for programs alleviating food insecurity among single mothers, since nearly one in every five single mothers and her children face the negative effects of this problem.

This chapter focuses on writing technical reports and briefings rather than scholarly articles, because of the functionality the technical report provides the practitioner. Therefore, this chapter presents the major components of the comprehensive, technical research paper, as well as effective communication strategies for describing and explaining the data and results (i.e., creating tables and graphics).

However, before writing the paper or briefing, the administrator develops a communication strategy or plan to communicate the research, its purpose, importance, and findings. The manager informs many people about the research and its findings, particularly when the purpose of the research is to direct policy initiatives. For example, the practitioner writes briefings to the senior management, and prepares testimony for legislative committees, fact sheets, or talking points for the news media, and pamphlets or Web materials for the public. All of these forms are essential to the communication of the research; moreover, these forms emerge from the comprehensive, technical report.

12.2   The Components of a Research Paper

The sections in technical papers differ from those in scholarly journal articles in that journal articles provide comprehensive literature reviews used to establish the theoretical model and include information about the research methods, such as variable construction and definitions, and sampling techniques. In most technical reports, this information is absent or reserved for the appendix, because the target audience generally lacks theoretical and methodological knowledge. This does not imply that a technical report is any less rigorous in its data analysis or that its findings are any less valuable than the analysis and findings in a scholarly article. Many authors of reports are analyzing the data using the same statistical procedures as those writing scholarly articles; however, researchers modify the technical report to fit its target audience. In fact, the majority of technical papers and journal articles rely on simple descriptive statistics, those discussed in this book.

The purpose of a research report is to describe a topic of interest, answer specific questions, or analyze relationships. Regardless of the purpose, the major sections of any research report include an executive summary, an introduction, a section for the findings, and a conclusion.

12.2.1   The Executive Summary

The executive summary provides a one- or two-page stand-alone section that summarizes the research report. The length of the summary is linked to the overall length of the research paper; longer reports tend to have longer executive summaries. The summary includes the purpose and importance of the research as well as key findings. In some instances, where researchers examine questions or relationships or where the researchers state their positions (e.g., agenda, beliefs), the summary provides implications, actions, proposals, or suggestions.

Unfortunately, the executive summary is often the first and only section read by the target audience, making it the most important component of the paper. Therefore, the arguments provided must be persuasive enough to convince the audience that the research has importance and purpose; this provides the justification readers need to continue to read the whole document. Therefore, the executive summary is like a movie trailer (i.e., a preview). If the trailer is good, you are eager to go see the movie; however, if it is dull, uninviting, and unimpressive, you are less likely to want to see it. The same is true with the executive summary. A well-written and interesting summary invites additional attention to the rest of the paper.

BOX 12.2   EXECUTIVE SUMMARY EXAMPLE[2]

EXECUTIVE SUMMARY

Regional growth-management planning makes housing unaffordable and contributes to a business-unfriendly environment that slows economic growth. The high housing prices caused by growth-management planning were an essential element of the housing bubble that has recently shaken our economy: for the most part, this bubble was limited to urban regions with growth-management planning.

In 2006, the price of a median home in the 10 states that have passed laws requiring local governments to do growth-management planning was five times the median family income in those states. At that price, a median family devoting 31% of its income (the maximum allowed for FHA-insured loans) to a mortgage at 6%, with a 10% down payment, could not pay off the mortgage on a median home in less than 59 years. In contrast, a median home in the 22 states that have no growth-management laws or institutions cost only 2.7 times the median family income. This meant a family could pay off a home in just 12.5 years.

Growth-management tools such as urban-growth boundaries, adequate-public-facilities ordinances, and growth limits all drive up the cost of housing by artificially restricting the amount of land available or the number of permits granted for home construction. On average, homebuyers in 2006 had to pay $130,000 more for every home sold in states with mandatory growth-management planning than they would have had to pay if home price-to-income ratios were less than 3. This is, in effect, a planning tax that increases the costs of retail, commercial, and industrial developments as well as housing.

The key to keeping housing affordable is the presence of large amounts of relatively unregulated vacant land that can be developed for housing and other purposes. The availability of such low-cost land encourages cities to keep housing affordable within their boundaries. But when state or other planning institutions allow cities to gain control over the rate of development or rural areas, they lose this incentive, and housing quickly becomes unaffordable. States with growth-management laws should repeal them, and other states should avoid passing them.

Box 12.2 provides an example of an executive summary. The executive summary conveys a position against growth-management and explains why and what should be done. Are you convinced there is purpose and importance in the research report? Are you interested in reading the rest of the report? The summary does well at selling its positions. As a practitioner, the best approach is to remain somewhat neutral in the writing, and this is accomplished by avoiding strong language. The absence of strong language gives the researcher and research more credibility—more reliability and validity.

12.2.2 The Introduction

The function of the introduction is to place the paper in the context of its purpose and significance. The introduction is brief, describes the problem, the importance of the research, and contains an explicit statement of purpose. In addition, the introduction provides an overview of the paper—what the paper sets out to do and how it accomplishes this. The introduction is different from the executive summary in that the introduction does not provide the research findings, although some introductions include findings from other research papers to substantiate the importance of the research. However, the introduction and executive summary are similar because each communicates the significance of the study to the reader.

Box 12.3 provides two different illustrations of introductions. The first example poses three research questions in the second paragraph and answers these,

---

BOX 12.3   EXAMPLES OF INTRODUCTIONS

INTRODUCTION[2]

More than two out of three Americans live in an urbanized area, which the Census Bureau defines as "a densely settled area that has a census population of at least 50,000." Urbanized areas are identified by the name of the most prominent city or cities in the area, such as St. Louis or Minneapolis–St. Paul. But, in fact, most urban areas are made up of dozens, and sometimes hundreds, of municipal units of government, including cities, towns, villages, counties, and special districts of various kinds.

What is the best way to govern these urbanized areas? Should cities and other municipal governments be allowed to compete with one another for residents, businesses, and funding from state and federal governments? Or should planning and certain other regional functions be given to a regional government that oversees each urban area?

Many planners and some economists have argued that regional governments are better suited than local governments to solving problems such as housing. Urban planners say that regional governments can make cities and their suburbs more livable and affordable for both businesses and residents. Planners specifically oppose leap-frog development, in which a developer builds housing or other development on land that is physically separated from existing urbanized land. More recently, planners have tried to discourage all Greenfield development, even if it is physically next to existing urbanized land, preferring instead infill development, or development of vacant parcels within an urban area.

One of the major claims for infill development is that it is less expensive than development on the urban fringe. A 2002 report from the Rutgers University Center for Urban Policy Research titled "The Costs of Sprawl—2000" estimated that low-density suburban development at the urban fringe imposes about $11,000 more in urban-service costs on communities than more compact development.

To avoid such costs, planners favor a form of planning known as growth-management planning, which uses urban-growth or urban-service boundaries; rules requiring adequate financing for urban services before the issuance of building permits; and similar tools to direct growth to certain areas and away from areas designated as preserves or reserves.

Economists have focused on specific urban problems. Harvard economist Edward Glaeser sees regional governments as a solution to housing affordability problems. "Land use regulations seem to drive housing supply and determine which regions are growing," Glaeser observes. "A more regional approach to housing supply might reduce the tendency of many localities to block new construction" (emphasis added).

Despite these claims and speculations, there has been little research showing whether regional governments can actually make urban areas more attractive and more affordable. As UC Berkeley political scientist Margaret Weir observes, the literature on regional governments "does not connect regional processes with regional outcomes, [so] we do not know enough about what makes regions successful."

Another argument for planning is that there are certain problems that are regional, and only a regional government staffed by regional planners can solve those problems. This argument has been strongly promoted by former Albuquerque mayor David Rusk. In fact, most of the supposedly regional problems—including housing, open space, solid waste, infrastructure, and transportation—can easily be handled at the local level. The few problems that are difficult to solve locally are not made any easier by magnifying those problems to a regional scale. As Jane Jacobs wryly observed, a region is "an area safely larger than the last one to whose problems we found no solution."

A close look at the data for America's urbanized areas reveals that regional growth management planning generally does not produce the benefits claimed for it. States and regions with strong regional governments tend to have the least affordable housing and are often growing more slowly than regions with weak regional governments. This suggests that state and local officials should dismantle or avoid regional governments, and in particular regional growth-management planning.

INTRODUCTION[3]

The period from birth through age [five] is a critical time for children to develop the physical, emotional, social, and cognitive skills they will need to be successful in school and the rest of their lives. Children from poor families, on average, enter school behind children from more privileged families. Targeting preschoolers in low-income families, the Head Start program was created in 1965 to promote school readiness to enable each child to develop to his or her fullest potential. Research shows that acquiring specific pre-reading, language, and social skills strongly predict future success in school.

As our knowledge about the importance of high quality early education has advanced dramatically since 1965, so have data on the outcomes for children and families served by Head Start. The knowledge and skill levels of low-income children are far below national averages upon entering the program. When the school readiness of the nation's poor children is assessed, it becomes clear that Head Start is not eliminating the gap in educational skills and knowledge needed for school. Head Start is not fully achieving its stated purpose of "promot[ing] school readiness by enhancing the social and cognitive development of low-income children."1 Head Start children show some progress in cognitive skills and social and emotional development. However, these low-income children continue to perform significantly below their more advantaged peers once they enter school in areas essential to school readiness, such as reading and mathematics.

States and the federal government fund a wide variety of programs that are either intended to enhance children's educational development or that could, with some adjustments, do a better job of preparing children for school. Head Start is one of many federal and state programs that together provide approximately $23 billion in funding for child-care and preschool education (see Appendix A). Because these programs have developed independently, they are not easily coordinated to best serve the children and families who need them. In programs other than Head Start, states have the responsibility and the authority through planning, training, and the regulatory process to have a substantial impact on the type and quality of services provided, and are held accountable for the delivery of high quality programs. However, Head Start funding goes directly from the federal level to local organizations, and thus states do not have the authority to integrate or align Head Start programs with other early childhood programs provided by the states.

The single most important goal of the Head Start reauthorization should be to improve Head Start and other preschool programs to ensure children are prepared to succeed in school. This paper describes the limited educational progress for children in Head Start and the problems resulting from a fragmented approach to early childhood programs and services. The paper also presents evidence from early childhood research and documents state efforts that have successfully addressed these problems. Finally, the paper explains the President's proposal for Head Start reauthorization, which builds on the evidence to strengthen the program and, through coordination, improve preschool programs in general to help ensure that children are prepared to succeed in school.

briefly, by the last paragraph of the introduction. However, the introduction does not explicitly state the purpose of the research, nor provide an overview of the paper; rather, it offers solutions and suggestions that are generally reserved for the conclusion. The second example explicitly states the purpose of the research in the final paragraph and uses the preceding paragraphs to validate the significance of the report.

12.2.3   The Findings

The findings of the paper, armed with charts and tables, exist to provide the evidence necessary to describe or explain the phenomenon of interest. Therefore, the findings are imperative to substantiate the purpose and importance of the research. The findings section is one of the more difficult ones to compose because writing about numbers often results in terse descriptions that are boring to read. This is one reason why so many readers of reports skip this section, and why the methods generally are provided in the appendix to the report.

The information contained in, and the organization of, the findings section depends on the focus of the research and the target audience. If the target audience has a general understanding or less of research methods (i.e., the designs, measurement theory, sampling, and statistics), then the researchers provides an appendix that explains the methods, labeled Technical Notes, Methods, or Research Approach; however, do not call it "methodology," as this is the study of methods.

The most useful way to organize and present the findings is by theme or topic. Each subsection or theme summarizes key findings by describing or explaining the happenings—the what, why, and how often—of the data. Not all of the findings need be discussed; this is why graphics are included. The figures and tables provide the whole picture of the findings, whereas the text of the section supplies the reader with the most interesting findings. In addition, when researchers gather data using questionnaires, they sometimes include the instrument as an appendix, with summary findings provided for each question.

Box 12.4 illustrates a findings section, also called a results section, from a technical paper. Here, the authors organize the results by the following questions:

- Who are the uninsured?
- Why do they report that they are uninsured?
- Who is most affected by the high cost of coverage?
- Have high health insurance costs become more of a problem over time?
- How have the other reasons for uninsurance changed over time?

12.2.4 The Conclusion

The ending of the paper is tailored for the type of research being conducted. For example, policy papers will have a policy implications section, whereas a program evaluation might end with a recommendations or lessons learned component. Regardless of its label, the conclusion summarizes the paper, links the findings to the purpose, and provides generalizations, inferences, and sometimes hyperbole, to support the significance of the research and the importance for continued evaluation.

Box 12.5 shows the conclusion for the growth-management planning research paper highlighted in previous examples. This final section of the paper solidifies the significance of the research and offers actionable recommendations.

12.2.5 Other Components

Other ancillary components exist, too. All papers should have an interesting title, a byline, and a reference or bibliography page when other sources are used. Some papers provide a glossary of terms important to the study. In addition, when papers are lengthy (ten or more pages), a table of contents adds direction and organization. Some researchers include a section after the introduction to communicate historical or background information to place the research in perspective. This is particularly useful in program and policy evaluations or to highlight research conducted by others providing additional support for the research model.

BOX 12.4   ILLUSTRATION OF RESULTS ORGANIZED BY TOPIC[4]

FINDINGS

Who Are the Uninsured?

Consistent with other research, our samples of uninsured adults and children are quite diverse, encompassing all ages, race/ethnicities, educational levels, family types, and incomes (Table 1). However, some members of the population are more likely to be uninsured than others:

- Among nonelderly adults, younger adults between age 19 and 34 are significantly more likely to be uninsured than older adults.
- Among children, older children age 7 to 18 are more likely to be uninsured; however, the uninsurance rate for these children is much less than that of adults age 19 to 34 (not shown in table).
- Compared to their insured counterparts, both uninsured nonelderly adults and uninsured children are more likely to be Hispanic and to be noncitizens. The latter fact likely reflects that many noncitizens are employed in low-wage jobs without health benefits and are ineligible for public coverage in most states.
- The majority of nonelderly adults and nearly all children are in good or better health; however, uninsured adults are more likely to report fair or poor health than their insured counterparts (11 versus 9%).

When we look at the family circumstances of the insured and uninsured, we find large and significant differences for both nonelderly adults and children (Table 2). Most notably:

- While nearly all uninsured adults and children have at least one worker in their family, only 16% of uninsured adults and 24% of uninsured children have a worker with an ESI offer in their family (though many of those offers may not include coverage for dependents).
- Both uninsured adults and children are much more likely to be low-income than their insured counterparts. Among uninsured nonelderly adults, nearly 60% have family incomes below 200% of the federal poverty level (FPL), as do nearly 70% of uninsured children. Although uninsured, most of these low-income children are likely eligible for public coverage via Medicaid or SCHIP.

BOX 12.5   AN EXAMPLE OF A CONCLUSION[2]

CONCLUSION

As it is usually practiced, regional growth-management planning imposes huge costs on homebuyers, renters, and businesses. Yet it provides negligible benefits: it does little to reduce sprawl (if that can even be considered a benefit), and its greatest social effect is to sort urban areas into central cities largely composed of young singles and childless couples and suburbs with high percentages of families with children. The key to affordable housing is the availability of relatively unregulated vacant land for housing and other urban purposes. The effects of denying homebuilders access to such developable land appears to be an almost relentless upward push of housing prices. In 1979, price-to-income ratios in coastal California cities were greater than 4. By 1989, they exceeded 5.0. Thanks to a major recession in the early 1990s, they were still between 5 and 6 by 1999, but today they are mostly greater than 8. Prices may be declining now, but—unless changes are made—states such as Arizona, Florida, and Oregon whose price-to-income ratios were 4 or more in 2006 can expect to have California's price-to-income ratios in a decade or two.

Remedies for unaffordable housing will require actions at the federal, state, and local levels:

- The federal government should revoke requirements that all urban areas must be represented by metropolitan planning organizations. Congress should also repeal the comprehensive, long-range planning requirements found in federal transportation and housing legislation.
- States with growth-management laws should repeal those laws and other states should avoid passing similar ones.
- Other state laws that give cities power to control the rate of development of rural areas, such as the California law creating local agency formation commissions, should also be repealed. Instead, states should insure that plenty of vacant land is available to meet each region's need for housing and other land uses.
- Local governments should resist efforts by MPOs and other regional agencies to impose region-wide planning on their urban areas.
- As far as possible, infrastructure should be paid for by developers or property owners through annual user fees and special service districts rather than through up-front impact fees or general taxation.

Urban planners, of course, may oppose these actions. Instead, they aspire to pass growth-management laws in every state and impose growth-management plans on every urban area. The predictable result will be increasingly unaffordable housing, declining homeownership rates, and a growing disparity between the elite who own their own homes and a significant number of families who will never become homeowners.

12.3   Presenting Tables and Graphics

A picture is worth a thousand words, or so the old adage goes, and the pictures—figures and tables—used in technical reports, research papers, briefings, and presentations, supplement the text. These tables and figures communicate and describe what is happening, and should be self-explanatory, easy to read, and pleasing to the eye.

Generally, tables communicate many descriptive findings (e.g., frequencies, percents, medians, means, and standard deviations) at once, and are organized by characteristics or topics. For example, the U.S. Census Bureau summarizes census information into four different tables based on the following characteristics: demographic, social, economic, and housing. Box 12.6 presents the table for selected social characteristics.

Tables are more conducive than figures when communicating a great deal of information at once (like Box 12.6). One table offers succinctness, whereas many figures impart excessiveness. For example, rather than including 10 figures in the paper (e.g., a different chart for each of the characteristics in Box 12.6), one table is sufficient and achieves brevity. Figures, on the other hand, are beneficial when the researcher wants to highlight parts of the table. For example, Table 12.1 shows the tonnage of municipal solid waste produced and recovered. Creating figures for each column or for each major type of waste is an inefficient use of time and effort; however, to add illustration, the researcher can create a pie chart showing the major categories of waste as depicted in Figure 12.1.

Besides highlighting portions of a frequency table, graphics are useful to illustrate differences; a graphic is superfluous when the attributes are roughly the same frequency or proportion. For example, Figure 12.2 shows the percent of crime committed by day of the week in one local city. Each day has roughly the same proportion of crime, so the differences do not appear on this graphic; therefore, the figure is unnecessary. However, the chart displayed in Figure 12.3 illustrates the difference between the attributes and is therefore useful to the reader.

BOX 12.6 ILLUSTRATION OF A TABLE ORGANIZED BY SOCIAL CHARACTERISTICS[5]

Table DP-2. Profile of Selected Social Characteristics: 2000

Geographic area: United States

[Data based on a sample. For information on confidentiality protection, sampling error, nonsampling error, and definitions, see text]

Subject	Number	Percent	Subject	Number	Percent
SCHOOL ENROLLMENT			**NATIVITY AND PLACE OF BIRTH**		
Population 3 years and over			**Total population**	281,421,906	100.0
enrolled in school	76,632,927	100.0	Native	250,314,017	88.9
Nursery school, preschool	4,957,582	6.5	Born in United States	246,786,466	87.7
Kindergarten	4,157,491	5.4	State of residence	168,729,388	60.0
Elementary school (grades 1-8)	33,653,641	43.9	Different state	78,057,078	27.7
High school (grades 9-12)	16,380,951	21.4	Born outside United States	3,527,551	1.3
College or graduate school	17,483,262	22.8	Foreign born	31,107,889	11.1
			Entered 1990 to March 2000	13,178,276	4.7
EDUCATIONAL ATTAINMENT			Naturalized citizen	12,542,626	4.5
Population 25 years and over	182,211,639	100.0	Not a citizen	18,565,263	6.6
Less than 9th grade	13,755,477	7.5			
9th to 12th grade, no diploma	21,960,148	12.1	**REGION OF BIRTH OF FOREIGN BORN**		
High school graduate (includes equivalency)	52,168,981	28.6	**Total (excluding born at sea)**	31,107,573	100.0
Some college, no degree	38,351,595	21.0	Europe	4,915,557	15.8
Associate degree	11,512,833	6.3	Asia	8,226,254	26.4
Bachelor's degree	28,317,792	15.5	Africa	881,300	2.8
Graduate or professional degree	16,144,813	8.9	Oceania	168,046	0.5
			Latin America	16,086,974	51.7
Percent high school graduate or higher	80.4	(X)	Northern America	829,442	2.7
Percent bachelor's degree or higher	24.4	(X)			
			LANGUAGE SPOKEN AT HOME		
MARITAL STATUS			**Population 5 years and over**	262,375,152	100.0
Population 15 years and over	221,148,671	100.0	English only	215,423,557	82.1
Never married	59,913,370	27.1	Language other than English	46,951,595	17.9
Now married, except separated	120,231,273	54.4	Speak English less than "very well"	21,320,407	8.1
Separated	4,769,220	2.2	Spanish	28,101,052	10.7
Widowed	14,674,500	6.6	Speak English less than "very well"	13,751,256	5.2
Female	11,975,325	5.4	Other Indo-European languages	10,017,989	3.8
Divorced	21,560,308	9.7	Speak English less than "very well"	3,390,301	1.3
Female	12,305,294	5.6	Asian and Pacific Island languages	6,960,065	2.7
			Speak English less than "very well"	3,590,024	1.4
GRANDPARENTS AS CAREGIVERS					
Grandparent living in household with one or			**ANCESTRY (single or multiple)**		
more own grandchildren under 18 years.	5,771,671	100.0	**Total population**	281,421,906	100.0
Grandparent responsible for grandchildren	2,426,730	42.0	*Total ancestries reported*	*287,304,886*	*102.1*
			Arab	1,202,871	0.4
VETERAN STATUS			Czech [1]	1,703,930	0.6
Civilian population 18 years and over	208,130,352	100.0	Danish	1,430,897	0.5
Civilian veterans	26,403,703	12.7	Dutch	4,542,494	1.6
			English	24,515,138	8.7
DISABILITY STATUS OF THE CIVILIAN			French (except Basque) [1]	8,325,509	3.0
NONINSTITUTIONALIZED POPULATION			French Canadian [1]	2,435,098	0.9
Population 5 to 20 years	64,689,357	100.0	German	42,885,162	15.2
With a disability	5,214,334	8.1	Greek	1,153,307	0.4
			Hungarian	1,398,724	0.5
Population 21 to 64 years	159,131,544	100.0	Irish [1]	30,594,130	10.9
With a disability	30,553,796	19.2	Italian	15,723,555	5.6
Percent employed	56.6	(X)	Lithuanian	659,992	0.2
No disability	128,577,748	80.8	Norwegian	4,477,725	1.6
Percent employed	77.2	(X)	Polish	8,977,444	3.2
			Portuguese	1,177,112	0.4
Population 65 years and over	33,346,626	100.0	Russian	2,652,214	0.9
With a disability	13,978,118	41.9	Scotch-Irish	4,319,232	1.5
			Scottish	4,890,581	1.7
RESIDENCE IN 1995			Slovak	797,764	0.3
Population 5 years and over	262,375,152	100.0	Subsaharan African	1,781,877	0.6
Same house in 1995	142,027,478	54.1	Swedish	3,998,310	1.4
Different house in the U.S. in 1995	112,851,828	43.0	Swiss	911,502	0.3
Same county	65,435,013	24.9	Ukrainian	892,922	0.3
Different county	47,416,815	18.1	United States or American	20,625,093	7.3
Same state	25,327,355	9.7	Welsh	1,753,794	0.6
Different state	22,089,460	8.4	West Indian (excluding Hispanic groups)	1,869,504	0.7
Elsewhere in 1995	7,495,846	2.9	Other ancestries	91,609,005	32.6

- Represents zero or rounds to zero. (X) Not applicable.

[1] The data represent a combination of two ancestries shown separately in Summary File 3. Czech includes Czechoslovakian. French includes Alsatian. French Canadian includes Acadian/Cajun. Irish includes Celtic.

Table 12.1   Municipal Solid Waste Materials Produced and Recovered in the United States (in Millions of Tons), 2005

Type of Goods	Weight Generated	Weight Recovered	Recovery as a Percentage of Generation
Durable Goods			
Steel	11.40	3.43	30.09
Aluminum	1.08		
Other metals	1.74	1.26	72.41
Glass	1.83		
Plastics	8.72	0.37	4.24
Rubber and leather	5.68	0.96	16.90
Wood	5.37		
Textiles	3.02	0.28	9.27
Other materials	1.45	1.17	80.69
Total durable goods	40.29	7.47	18.54
Nondurable Goods			
Paper and paperboard	44.90	19.00	42.32
Plastics	6.55		
Rubber and leather	0.99		
Textiles	7.91	1.42	17.95
Other materials	3.36		
Total nondurable goods	63.71	20.42	32.05
Containers and Packaging			
Steel	2.37	1.5	63.29
Aluminum	1.90	0.69	36.32
Glass	10.90	2.76	25.32
Paper and paperboard	39.00	22.9	58.72
Plastics	13.70	1.28	9.34
Wood	8.56	1.31	15.30
Other materials	0.24		
Total containers and packaging	76.67	30.44	39.70
Other Wastes			
Food	29.20	0.69	2.36
Yard trimmings	32.10	19.9	61.99
Miscellaneous inorganic wastes	3.69		
Total other wastes	64.99	20.59	31.68
Total Municipal Solid Waste	245.66	78.92	32.13

Source: United Stales Environmental Protection Agency, Municipal Solid Waste Generation, Recycling, and Disposal in the United States, 2005.

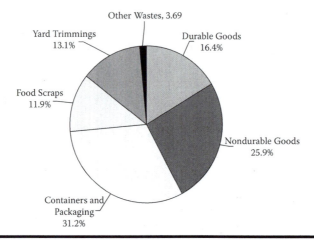

Figure 12.1   Municipal solid waste materials produced in the United States, 2005.

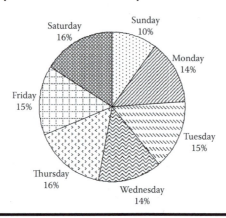

Figure 12.2   Percent of crimes committed by day.

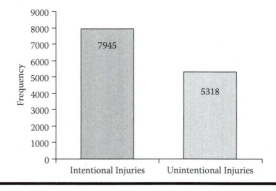

Figure 12.3   Numbers of deaths due to intentional and unintentional injuries in the city, 2006–2007.

When showing change, percentages, or frequencies, particularly over time, the y-axis of line graphs plays an important role. The scale of the y-axis, which the graph-maker formats, can be manipulated to illustrate inconsequential changes when changes are, in fact, large, or substantial changes when the change is trivial. For example, Charts A, B, and C of Figure 12.4 communicate the same information; however, because the y-axis scaling is different, the fluctuations in crime over time look more dramatic in Chart A and relatively unchanged in Chart C.

Why is there such a difference when the information is the same? The scale for Chart A is 10 times smaller than the scale in Chart C. That is, the y-axis for Chart C begins at zero and ends at 40,000 (a difference of 40,000), whereas the y-axis for Chart A starts at 24,000 and ends at 28,000 (a difference of 4,000). Which scale is better? The answer depends on the data, its range, and change from one point to the next. Starting a scale higher or lower than zero is acceptable when the data

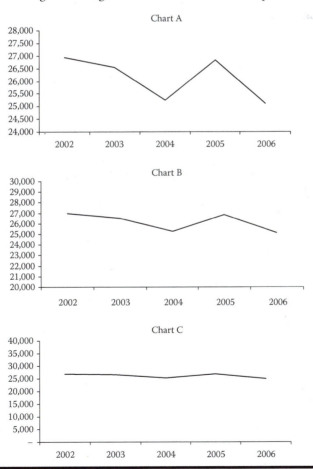

Figure 12.4 Total number of crimes committed per year from 2002–2006.

never reach zero as in Figure 12.4 (there is always some crime); however, the scale should be relative to the amount of change. For example, the change in crime from one particular year to the next is as much as 8%, so Charts A and B better illustrate the changes that are not captured in Chart C.

The opposite is happening in Figure 12.5. Chart A shows what is really happening to the crime rate in another city—that there is little to no difference over time between a 1 to 1.2% change. However, graphing the same data using a line chart with a small-scaled y-axis, as illustrated in Chart B, shows drastic change over time when these changes are in fact inconsequential. Graph makers get away with this shock and awe because consumers of research rarely look at the y-axis, instead the substantial changes in the line captures their attention and influences their decision-making processes.

All tables and graphics should provide enough information to the reader to be self-explanatory and include embedded notes when appropriate; that is, the reader should not have to consult the accompanying text to figure out what the graphic or

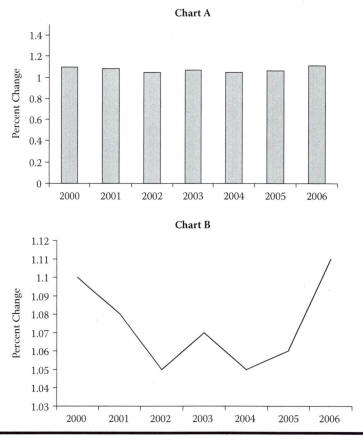

Figure 12.5   Percent change from 2000–2006.

table is depicting. The information in the graphic or table should include answers to the questions of who, what, where, and when—they should say to whom or what the data refer, from where the data are derived, and when the data were collected. Therefore, all figures and tables should have a title, a number, a source when appropriate, and should be clearly mentioned in the text of the report.

Researchers label the figures and tables as exhibits, charts, figures, or tables; for example, "Exhibit 1," "Chart A," or "Table 1." However, the naming and numbering system used should be consistent. That is, do not call one graphic Figure 1, the next Chart 2, followed by Exhibit 3. Each graphic should flow sequentially; for example, Exhibit 1, Exhibit 2, Exhibit 3, and so on. In addition, the graphics and tables are presented in the order in which they are discussed in the research report; for example, Table 2 is discussed after Table 1, but before Table 3.

When researchers provide graphics, the data points and axes must be labeled (when appropriate). Moreover, where secondary sources supply the information, a source citation and date should be made available. Figure 12.3 communicates the necessary information but Figure 12.2 needs to address from where (e.g., city) and when (e.g., 2008) the data are derived.

Graphics and tables should be logical and pleasing to the eye; they should not be disorienting, complex, or loud. For example, Figure 12.6 is extremely loud (and would be worse if printed in color); this figure simply presents too much information in too little space. Separate graphics or a table is more suitable when there is too much information for a single graphic.

Keep in mind that colors will be useless when printed with or copied from black and white machines. Rather than using color, researchers with black and white printers or copiers used weighted shades to reflect differences. Moreover, they omit

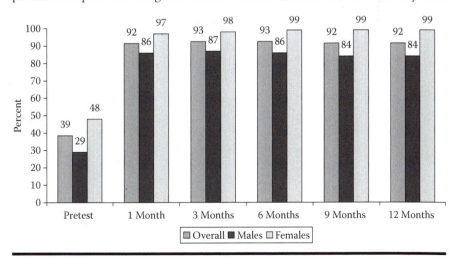

Figure 12.6 Percentages of males and females who retained knowledge after the implementation of a new orientation program.

shading altogether when chart bars or pie wedges are clearly labeled. When creating graphics, the best practice is to be simple and clear.

Finally, tables and graphics are extensions of the text; researchers create and provide them to supplement and complement the prose. Accordingly, we do not need to explain everything that appears in the graphic when writing the text of the report. Consider the following explanation that refers to Figure 12.7:

> Currently, 54% of the population in the United States are married, 27% have never been married, 10% are divorced, 7% are widowed, and 2% are separated.

This explanation is extremely dry and boring, says exactly what the figure says, and lacks crucial information; therefore, we should get rid of the figure or rewrite the explanation altogether. Although the explanation seems to imply the graphic refers to the entire U.S. population, we do not know the actual number of people included in the analysis, we do not know the criteria for being an individual to be included in the population, and we do not know where the information originates. The following sentence adds more detail about the data, but limits the discussion on the individual attributes.

> According to the United States Census Bureau, 27% of the 220 million people eligible for marriage (those who are 15 years of age and older) have never been married. Of those who have been married at one time or another, 75% are currently married.

Here, we know the information is from the 2000 Census and that there are 220 million people classified into the different marital categories. In addition, the explanation offers a different way to look at the graphic. Rather than saying 54% of the eligible population is married, we combine the numbers for married, divorced, widowed, and separated, and analyze currently married as a portion of those categories

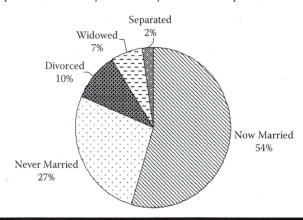

Figure 12.7　Marital status in the United States, 2000.

rather than all categories. This adds variety to the discussion of the analysis. Overall, the purpose of graphics and tables is to demonstrate what is happening with the data. Each is conveyed in an interesting manner that is simple and informative.

12.4   Summary

This chapter presented the different components—executive summary, introduction, findings, and conclusion—of a technical research paper. The executive summary highlights the report in an engaging fashion to capture the interest of the reader. The findings section, and its graphics and tables, play a pivotal role in providing the necessary evidence to validate the purpose and importance of the research. In addition, researchers write the research paper, as a whole, with the target audience in mind. Therefore, the figures and tables should be easy to understand and labeled accordingly and the methodological approach to the research should be provided, but in an appendix. Moreover, because research results are often shared with many audiences, expect to supplement the technical report with briefings, fact sheets, news releases, tri-fold brochures, and other materials not addressed here. The well-crafted reports you produce are investments too valuable to gather dust on a shelf full of reports from other ignored and overlooked research efforts. That would be a waste for everyone.

Key Terms

Conclusion	Graphic	Table
Executive summary	Introduction	Technical notes
Findings		

Exercises

1. Explain why is it important to consider the statistical comprehension levels of those who are most likely to read your report.
2. Compare and contrast an academic paper (from a scholarly journal), a government report, and a nonprofit report. How are the papers organized? What types of graphics are used, if any, and how do they compare? Are the graphics good? Is any one type of report more difficult to understand? Easier to understand? What could each do to improve each report? Explain.
3. Find an article using statistics and graphics in a popular news magazine and evaluate its graphics and analysis. What do they say about the graphics in the text?
4. Evaluate the graphics and tables used by your organization in a recent report or other communication medium. What would you do differently to improve the communication of the findings?

Recommended Reading

Government Accounting Standards Board (2003). Reporting Performance Information: Suggested Criteria for Effective communication. Available at http://www.seagov.org/sea_gasb_project/suggested_criteria_report.pdf.

Miller, J. E. (2004). *The Chicago Guide to Writing about Numbers*. Chicago, IL: University of Chicago Press.

Miller, J. E. (2007). Organizing data in tables and charts: Different criteria for different tasks. *Teaching Statistics, 29*(3), 98–101.

Morgan, S. E., Reichert, T., and Harrison, T. R. (2002). *From Numbers to Words: Reporting Statistical Results for the Social Sciences*. Boston, MA: Allyn and Bacon.

Nelson, D. E. Brownson, R. C., Remington, P. L., and Parvanta, C. (2002). *Communicating Public Health Information Effectively: A Guide for Practitioners*. Washington, DC: American Public Health Association.

Penner, R. G. (2003). Congress and Statistics. The Urban Institute. Available at http://www.urban.org/publications/1000584.html. Accessed November 26, 2007.

Pyrczak, F. and Bruce, R. R. (2000). *Writing Empirical Research Reports: A Guide for Students of Social and Behavioral Sciences,* Third edition. Los Angeles, CA: Pyrczak Publishing.

Tufte, E. (1990). *Envisioning Quantitative Information*. Cheshire, CT: Graphics Press.

Tufte, E. (2001). *The Visual Display of Quantitative Information*. Cheshire, CT: Graphics Press.

Tufte, E. (2003). *The Cognitive Style of PowerPoint*. Cheshire, CT: Graphics Press.

Endnotes

1. Community Research Institute (2006). Food Security. Johnson Center for Philanthropy, Grand Valley State University. Reprinted with permission.
2. O'Toole, Randal. "The Planning tax: The case against regional growth-management planning." Policy Analysis 606. © 2007 The Cato Institute. Reproduced by permission.
3. U.S. Department of Health and Human Services (2003). Strengthening Head Start: What the evidence shows.
4. Graves, J. A. and Long, S. K. (2006). Why do people lack health insurance? Health Policy Online, 14. Washington, DC: The Urban Institute. Reprinted with permission. Available at http://www.urban.org/publications/411317.html.
5. U.S. Census Bureau (2000). Profile of Selected Social Characteristics.

Epilogue

As researchers, we ask two fundamental questions: what do we want to know and how are we going to measure it. We use and conduct research, often unknowingly, to make decisions as well as to explore, describe, and explain what is happing. Regardless of who asks and answers these questions, all researchers need to define and establish valid and reliable measures, select an appropriate design, and develop and execute a rigorous research plan that will accomplish the purpose of the research—to explore, describe, or explain.

Valid and reliable measures are those that truly capture the concepts of interest and do so consistently; this is something easier said than done. In reality, measuring what we really want to know is the most difficult task in the research process. Much of what we do in social science research, particularly in public and nonprofit administration and policy, is an attempt to describe characteristics, beliefs and attitudes, behaviors, and knowledge—some of the more complex concepts to measure. The variables we construct are proxies at best, especially those assessing opinions and beliefs, and sometimes the variables fail to capture the concept. However, we improve the validity and reliability of our measures by testing them before collection of the data and improving last year's measure with this year's knowledge.

The data collection process translates these measures into data. Researchers collect the information in a variety of ways; for example, questionnaires, interviews, observations, or by using someone else's sources. However, the difficulty in creating valid and reliable measures extends to the construction of questionnaires. Each question asked and statement posed must be clear, simple, and ask about one idea or concept.

The problems that arise with questionnaires are numerous and a direct result of human error, from both the researcher and the participant, when human subjects are used. The error from researchers include writing bad questions, providing inappropriate response options, or designing an altogether bad survey (one that is too long, too cluttered, too personal, and so forth). In addition, where interviewers are used to collect information, the interviewer could potentially misinterpret what the respondent said or meant, or could lead the respondent to an answer that does not correctly represent the respondent's opinions, beliefs, or actions. The information collected from human subjects has the potential for being inaccurate because respondents might misinterpret the question and/or response options, or may not have any knowledge of the subject but answers otherwise. Moreover, where personal or sensitive questions are posed, participants may knowingly alter their responses because they are embarrassed about their answers, or, when an interviewer is present, do not want to offend the interviewer.

In addition, the definitions of agreement, frequency, quality, or importance varies among individuals, and the interpretation could be quite different from person to person. What people say can be completely different from how they behave. What people will not say or do not know is unclear when certain response options are not provided. What people perceive is often different from reality. Independently or collectively, these problems threaten the validity and reliability of the questionnaire. However, we improve the quality of the questionnaire, and hence the reliability and validity of the measures and overall research, by testing the data collection tool prior to collecting the information.

Proper measurement alone is not enough, however. Regardless of who collects the data, researchers can be confident in the accuracy of their data, and hence the measures, when the observations (e.g., human subjects, organizations, and the like) are randomly selected via a well-designed sampling process. A probability (random) selection ensures a representative sample. A large sample with a small sampling error maintains reliability and validity that help generalize the findings to other settings, times, and people. When the probability of selection is unknown or absent, we are no longer confident of the accuracy of our measures and cannot generalize. We can only ascertain what is happening within that group.

However, the accuracy of and confidence in the data are diminished when participation is voluntary and when nonresponses are present. We cannot say with certainty that the nonrespondents or overlooked populations are similar to the respondents in opinions, beliefs, and knowledge. We do know, however, that random selection is better than nonrandom selection because more often than not, the generalizations hold true.

The research designs depend on the purpose of the research. If we want to explain why something is happening, then an experiment is conducted. An experiment has the potential to establish time order, eliminate alternative explanations and spurious relationships, analyze statistical associations, and randomly assign research subjects to the different groups. If we want to describe what is happening and generalize these findings to a larger population, then we randomly select participants in a manner that best represents the target population. In descriptive research, at least one of the elements of an experiment is missing, typically a control group. Where randomization is absent in either selection or assignment, the research becomes exploratory in nature, where generalizations or linking cause and effect are limited.

However, the causality discovered in a laboratory setting, one that is controlled, is difficult to replicate in a natural, uncontrolled environment. As a result, generalizations of these findings are limited.

Most of the research we conduct and read about that pertains to public and nonprofit administration is exploratory and descriptive and helps managers predict and prescribe; rarely do practitioners and academics in public and nonprofit administration conduct experiments. When we do conduct these experiments, they are far removed from a laboratory setting. Given the exploratory and descriptive features of our research, the statistical techniques used to evaluate our questions are more simplistic, straightforward, and easy to understand than other research in social science. Further, where statistically significant relationships exist, causality cannot be presumed. This does not suggest that our research is any less valuable; it simply suggests that the statistics fit the research design, the type of measures, and the overall purpose of the research. We rely on the statistics that describe our sample, and even perhaps a larger population, which is more beneficial and effective in the decision-making process.

This book ends as it began, arguing that practitioners understand research, particularly its definition and process, its capabilities, and its role in decision making. The four different examples of research provided in the first chapter—the FDA, the CDC, the San Joaquin Valley, and the United States State Department—illustrate how authoritative, irrefutable, and influential research can be. The subsequent chapters demonstrated that research is far from being irrefutable as it should be but still plays an important and influential role, and communicating the importance of the research falls to the manager. The point here is not to dismiss research or to suggest that we stop conducting research altogether; quite the contrary, in fact.

Research should continue because, without it, anyone can say anything one wants, which is no different from what is claimed with research; but with research we can evaluate the researcher's process, the validity and reliability of the research design and measures, the analysis of the data, and the conclusions. Research provides evidence, but the evidence must be evaluated prior to being influential. Claims without evidence are baseless, and we have no way to investigate how these claims were derived; whereas, claims supported by research can be evaluated for validly and reliability. The claims must fit the research. Overall, research helps us challenge one another, to find alternative ways, even better ways, to measure and analyze concepts and to help the manager plan for tomorrow. Nevertheless, we will always struggle with the proper way to measure concepts in an ever-changing society.

As one student exclaimed at the end of the course, "I have just enough knowledge about research methods to be dangerous." This is true, but dangerous in a good way. The basic concepts are all you need to understand research and to begin to think more constructively about the research you read, conduct, and commission. The basic concepts offered in this book are those that are most useful, practical and, most importantly, appropriate for administrators to use. Now with your newfound knowledge of research, you have an obligation to yourself and to your stakeholders to make sure that the evidence you provide to others or use in your decision making is valid and reliable. Onward!

Bibliography

Abbott, A. (2004). *Methods of Discovery: Heuristics for the Social Sciences*. New York: W. W. Norton.

American Association for Public Opinion Research (2005). Protection of human participants in survey research: A source document for institutional review boards.

Babbie, E. (2001). *The Practice of Social Research*. Ninth edition. Belmont, CA: Wadsworth/ Thomson Learning.

Berk, K. and Carey, P. (2004). *Data Analysis with Microsoft Excel*. Belmont, CA: Thomson Learning.

Best, J. (2001). *Damned Lies and Statistics: Untangling Numbers from the Media, Politicians, and Activists*. Berkeley, CA: University of California Press.

Bolton, M.J. and Stolcis, G.B. (2003). Ties that do not bind: Musings on the specious relevance of academic research. *Public Administration Review*, *63*, 626–630.

Brady, H.E. and Collier, D. (2004). *Rethinking Social Inquiry: Diverse Tools, Shared* Standards. Lanham, MD: Rowman and Littlefield.

Campbell, D. T. and Stanley, J C. (1963). *Experimental and Quasi-Experimental Designs for Research*. Boston, MA: Houghton Mifflin.

Cook, T., D. and Campbell, D.T. (1979). Quasi-Experimentation: Design and Analysis Issues for Field Settings. Boston, MA: Houghton Mifflin.

Council of Graduate Schools (2006). *Graduate Education for the Responsible Conduct of Research*. Washington, D.C.: Council of Graduate Schools.

Council of Graduate Schools (2003). *On the Right Track: A Manual for Research Mentors*. Washington, D.C.: Council of Graduate Schools.

Cronbach, L.J. (1951). Coefficient alpha and the internal structure of tests. *Psychometrika*, *16*: 297–333.

DePaul, Tony (2006, January 17). At T.F. Green, Security Screeners Watch Behavior to Detect Terrorists. Transportation Security Administration.

DeVellis, R.F. (2003). *Scale Development: Theory and Applications*. Second edition. Thousand Oaks, CA: Sage Publications.

DeVellis, R.F. (1991). *Scale Development: Theory and Applications*. Newbury Park, CA: Sage Publications.

Dillman, Don A. (2006). *Mail and Internet Surveys: The Tailored Design Method*. New York: John Wiley.

Dillman, Don A. (1978). *Mail and Telephone Surveys*. New York: John Wiley.

Dodge, J., Ospina, S.M. and Foldy, E.G. (2005). Integrating rigor and relevance in public administration scholarship: The contribution of narrative inquiry. *Public Administration Review*, *65*, 286–300.

Donnelly, Sally B. (2006, May 17). A new tack for airport screening: Behave yourself. Time.com.

Field, Andy (2005). *Discovering Statistics Using SPSS*. London: Sage Publications.

Fink, Arlene (2006). *How to Conduct Surveys: A Step-By-Step Guide*. Thousand Oaks, CA: Sage.

Fowler, Floyd J. (1995). *Improving Survey Questions: Design and Evaluation*. Thousand Oaks, CA: Sage.

Groves, Robert M. (2004). *Survey Errors and Survey Costs*. New York: John Wiley.

Government Accounting Standards Board (2003). Reporting performance information: Suggested criteria for effective communication.

Jacoby, W.G. (1991). *Data Theory and Dimensional Analysis*. Newbury Park, CA: Sage Publications.

Jones, L.F. and Olson, E.C. (2005). *Researching the Polity: A Handbook of Scope and Methods*. Second edition. Cincinnati, OH: Atomic Dog Publishing.

King, G., Koehane, R.O. and Verba, S. (1994). *Designing Social Inquiry: Scientific Inference in Qualitative Research*. Princeton, NJ: Princeton University Press.

Kuhn, T.S. (1962). *Structure of Scientific Revolutions*. Chicago, IL: University of Chicago Press.

Lee-Treweek, G. and Linkogle, S. (2000). *Danger in the Field: Risk and Ethics in Social Research*. London: Routledge.

Maloney, Dennis (1984). *Protection of Human Research Subjects: A Practical Guide to Federal Laws and Regulations*. New York: Plenum Press.

Miller, J.E. (2004). *The Chicago Guide to Writing about Numbers*. Chicago, IL: University of Chicago Press.

Miller, J.E. (2007). Organizing data in tables and charts: Different criteria for different tasks. *Teaching Statistics, 29*(3), 98–101.

Mokken, R.J. (1971). *A Theory and Procedure of Scale Analysis*. Netherlands: Mouton.

Morgan, S.E., Reichert, T. and Harrison, T.R. (2002). *From Numbers to Words: Reporting Statistical Results for the Social Sciences*. Boston, MA: Allyn and Bacon.

Nelson, D.E. Brownson, R.C., Remington, P.L. and Parvanta, C. (2002). *Communicating Public Health Information Effectively: A Guide for Practitioners*. Washington, D.C.: American Public Health Association.

Neuman, W.L. (2004). *Basics of Social Research: Qualitative and Quantitative Approaches*. Boston, MA: Allyn and Bacon.

Norusis, Marija J. (2006). *SPSS 15.0 Guide to Data Analysis*. Upper Saddle River, NJ: Prentice Hall.

Ospina, S.M. and Dodge, J. (2005). It's about time: Catching method up to meaning: The usefulness of narrative inquire in public administration research. *Public Administration Review, 65*, 143–157.

Ospina, S.M. and Dodge, J. (2005). Narrative inquiry and the search for connectedness: Practitioners and academics developing public administration scholarship. *Public Administration Review, 65*, 409–423.

O'Sullivan, E., Rassel, G.R. and Berner, M. (2003). *Research Methods for Public Administrators*. Fourth edition. New York: Addison Wesley Longman.

Penner, R.G. (2003). *Congress and Statistics*. The Urban Institute.

Pyrczak, F. and Bruce, R.R. (2000). *Writing Empirical Research Reports: A Guide for Students of Social and Behavioral Sciences*, Third edition. Los Angeles, CA: Pyrczak Publishing.

Romm, Norma R.A. (2001). *Accountability in Social Research: Issues and Debates*. New York: Kluwer Academic/Plenum.

Ruby, S. (2005, January 27). Holy cow! Study cuts emissions in half. *Bakersfield Californian*.

Sadredin, S. (n.d.). New poll reveals strong feelings, commitments. San Joaquin Valley Air Pollution Control District Commentary on the Air Quality.

Schwarz, N., Knauper, B., Hippler, H.J., Noelle-Neumann, E. and Clark, L. (1991). Rating scales: Numeric values may change the meaning of scale labels. *The Public Opinion Quarterly, 55*, 570–582.

Sieber, Joan E. (1992). *Planning Ethically Responsible Research: A Guide for Students and Internal Review Boards*. Newbury, CA: Sage Publications.

Spector, P.E. (1992). *Summated Rating Scale Construction: An Introduction*. Newbury Park, CA: Sage Publications.

Steneck, N. H. (2003). ORI Introduction to the responsible conduct of research. Washington, D.C.: Department of Health and Human Services, Office of Research Integrity.

Stouffer, S.A., Guttman, L., Suchman, E.A., Lazarsfeld, P.F., Star, S.A. and Clausen, J.A. (1950). Volume IV, *Measurement and Prediction*. New York: John Wiley.

Sudman, S. and Bradburn, N. M. (1974). *Response Effects in Surveys: A Review and Synthesis*. Chicago: Aldine Publishing.

Sudman, S. and Bradburn, N.M. (1982). *Asking Questions: A Practical Guide to Questionnaire Design*. San Francisco: Jossey-Bass.

Sudman, S. and Bradburn, N. M. (1988). *Polls and Surveys: Understanding What They Tell Us*. San Francisco: Jossey-Bass.

Sudman, S., Bradburn, N. M., and Schwarz, N. (1996). *Thinking about Answers: The Application of Cognitive Processes to Survey Methodology*. San Francisco: Jossey-Bass.

Thurstone, L. L. and Chave, E. J. (1929). *Measurement of Attitude: A Psychophysical Method and Some Experiments with a Scale for Measuring Attitude Toward the Church*. Chicago, IL: The University of Chicago Press.

Thurstone, L.L. (1959). *The Measurement of Values*. Chicago, IL: The University of Chicago Press.

Trochim, W.M.K. (2001). *The Research Methods Knowledge Base*. Second edition. Cincinnati, OH: Atomic Dog Publishing.

Tufte, E. (1990). *Envisioning Quantitative Information*. Cheshire, CT: Graphics Press.

Tufte, E. (2001). *The Visual Display of Quantitative Information*. Cheshire, CT: Graphics Press.

Tufte, E. (2003). *The Cognitive Style of PowerPoint*. Cheshire, CT: Graphics Press.

United States Census Bureau (2002). *Measuring America: The Decennial Censuses from 1790 to 2000*.

United States Census Bureau (2006). *Design and Methodology: American Community Survey*.

United States Food and Drug Administration Center for Veterinary Medicine (2006). *Animal Cloning: A Draft Risk Assessment*. Rockville: MD: Department of Health and Human Services.

United States Department of Health and Human Services, *Code of Federal Regulations*, Title 45, Public Welfare Part 46, Protection of Human Subjects.

Yee, D. (2005). Panel says children need an hour of exercise over the course of a day, NCTimes.com.

Yin, R.K. (2004). *The Case Study Anthology*. Thousand Oaks, CA: Sage Publications.

Index